THE
BEAUTIFUL
FIGHT

Also by Gary Thomas

Authentic Faith
The Beautiful Fight
Devotions for a Sacred Marriage
Devotions for Sacred Parenting
The Glorious Pursuit
Not the End but the Road
Sacred Influence
Sacred Marriage
Sacred Parenting
Sacred Pathways
Seeking the Face of God

Surrendering to the
Transforming Presence of
God Every Day of Your Life

THE
BEAUTIFUL
FIGHT

GARY THOMAS

BESTSELLING AUTHOR OF *SACRED MARRIAGE*

ZONDERVAN®

ZONDERVAN.com/
AUTHORTRACKER
follow your favorite authors

The Beautiful Fight
Copyright © 2007 by Gary L. Thomas

Requests for information should be addressed to:

Zondervan, *Grand Rapids, Michigan* 49530

Library of Congress Cataloging-in-Publication Data

Thomas, Gary (Gary Lee)
    The beautiful fight : surrendering to the transforming presence of God every day
of your life / Gary Thomas.
        p.   cm.
    Includes bibliographical references.
    ISBN-13: 978-0-310-27273-1
    ISBN-10: 0-310-27273-4
    1. Christian life. I. Title.
    BV4501.3.T47153   2007
    248.4 – dc22   2007019929

Published in association with Yates & Yates, LLP, Attorneys and Counselors, Suite 1000, Literary Agent, Orange, CA.

Printed in the United States of America

---

07 08 09 10 11 12 13 • 23 22 21 20 19 18 17 16 15 14 13 12 11 10 9 8 7 6 5 4 3 2 1

To Dr. J. I. Packer, in honor of his eightieth birthday

I was greatly honored and blessed to have been a student of the esteemed Dr. Packer. Long before he was my teacher and adviser at Regent College in the mid-1980s, I gained insight from his classic works such as Knowing God *and* Evangelism and the Sovereignty of God. *At Regent, in addition to attending as many of his classes as I could fit into my schedule, I benefited from his guiding me through my master's thesis and enjoyed being part of the faculty/student advisory group that occasionally met in his home.*

To recount all that Dr. Packer taught me would require a book in itself, but a few things stand out: his love for the Puritans (John Owen's work in particular), his faithfulness to the authority of Scripture, and his passion for the gospel — all combined with a refreshing and delightful generosity of spirit. He has a unique gift for building up and encouraging a person while dismantling his or her logic with his superior intellect. He modeled how to disagree and still maintain a godly spirit and how to garner bits of truth from other traditions while taking exception to many of their points. His example opened the door for me to read widely, and the benefits have been invaluable.

Dr. Packer is now entering his ninth decade of life and service. It is with great appreciation and respect that I dedicate this book to him.

Contents

Acknowledgments

I am very grateful to a faithful cadre of readers who helped refine and critique this book. They include Dr. Randy Roberts, Dina Horne, Todd Fetters, Mary Kay Smith, Dr. Rebecca Wilke, Deb Steinkamp, Laurie Prall, Mark Grambo, Jerry Thomas, and Dan Little. I am also very thankful for the day-to-day administration provided by my assistant, Laura Thompson, whose gentle spirit and competency bless my wife and me on a daily basis.

Everyone reading this book has been well served through the editing expertise of John Sloan and Dirk Buursma. I would also like to thank Michael Ranville, Leslie Speyers, and the marketing team at Zondervan for their commitment and labor on behalf of this work, as well as Curtis Yates and the entire Yates and Yates team.

Part 1

Splashes of Glory

The grand point is not to wear the garb, nor use the brogue of religion, but to possess the life of God within, and feel and think as Jesus would have done because of that inner life. Small is the value of external religion unless it is the outcome of a life within.

Charles Spurgeon

⊘

Lord Jesus Christ, I know I am a sinner and unworthy, for today the ornaments of a harlot have shone more brightly than the ornaments of my soul.

Bishop Nonnus

⊘

God wants you to be holy.

Paul, in 1 Thessalonians 4:3 NLT

Chapter 1

Kissing the Leper

Christianity is not merely a philosophical theory or a moral code, but involves a direct sharing in divine life and glory, a transforming union with God "face to face."

Kallistos Ware

The LORD will restore the splendor of Jacob
*   like the splendor of Israel,*
though destroyers have laid them waste
*   and have ruined their vines.*

Nahum 2:2

I have fought the good fight, I have finished the race, I have kept the faith. Now there is in store for me the crown of righteousness, which the Lord, the righteous Judge, will award to me on that day.

Paul, in 2 Timothy 4:7–8

Shortly after the young Francis of Assisi embraced a faith that would help color the face of Christianity for centuries to come, he sensed God telling him, "Francis, all those things that you have loved in the flesh you must now despise, and from those things that you formerly loathed you will drink great sweetness and immeasurable delight."

If a believer heard such words today, he or she would likely write them down in a journal and then forget them. Or perhaps the new Christian might compose a poem or a song, celebrating the sentiment. If the person were an author, he or she might even find a publisher and entomb the lofty notions inside a book.

But not Francis.

Almost immediately, he *applied* the divine admonition in a horrifically beautiful way.

As the young Christian rode his horse out of town, he saw what he once most despised — a leper. It is difficult for most moderns to understand the terror of that once untreatable disease. Leprosy is an insidious malady in which bacteria seek refuge in the nerves and then proceed to destroy them, one by one. Since the bacteria prefer the cooler parts of the body, toes, fingers, eyes, earlobes, and noses are most vulnerable. When your nerves lose all sensitivity, you become your own worst enemy, not realizing the damage you're causing to your own body. You could literally rub your eyes blind.

Eventually, you lose your ability to see, and then you lose your ability to feel, and suddenly, you're living in a senseless world. The only way to know what you're holding in your hands is to find any remaining, stubbornly sensitive part of your body — perhaps a quarter-inch stretch of your lips or an eighth-inch spot on your cheek — and try to guess from the texture and the weight what it is you're carrying.

Even apart from the macabre appearance of a leprosy victim, no one wants to end up alienated from the world, so most people kept an understandably wide berth around lepers. It was one of the most feared diseases of its time. "During my life of sin," Francis wrote, "nothing disgusted me like seeing victims of leprosy."[1]

Exuberant in his newfound faith and with joy flooding his soul — and remembering he was now to love and even treasure those things he formerly loathed — Francis chose not to run from the leper, as he would have done earlier in his life. Instead, he leaped from his horse, knelt in front of the leper, and proceeded to kiss the diseased white hand.

He *kissed* it.

Francis then further astonished the leper by giving him money. But even that wasn't enough. No, Francis was determined to "drink great sweetness" from what he formerly loathed, so he jumped back on his horse and rode to a neighboring leper colony. Francis "begged their pardon for having so often despised them" and, after giving them money, refused to leave until he had kissed each one of them, joyfully receiving the touch of their pale, encrusted lips. Only then did Francis jump back on his horse to go on his way.

In that indelible moment, Francis's faith became incarnate. His belief didn't just inspire him; it transformed him.

Francis's initial conversion was invisible, exhibited only in the changed expression on his face. That's as far as many of us ever go — a superficial change of mind in response to a compelling argument for faith. *This* act was astonishingly explicit — a grotesquely gorgeous parable of a radically changed man. The very instant Francis's lips touched the leper, what could have been merely a religion crumbled under the weight of a new way of life. The horse no longer carried a man; that beast transported a saint, whose example continues to challenge us yet today.

Perpetua's Passion

Nobly born, wealthy, well married, and a young mother, Vibia Perpetua typified the ideal of a successful North African woman at the dawn of the third century. But her Christian faith soon turned her idyllic existence into a battleground of alienation when Emperor Septimus Severus announced a decree forbidding conversion to Christianity — and requiring all citizens to offer sacrifices to him, as if he were a god. Those who refused would be thrown to the beasts at the amphitheater for entertainment.

Perpetua's father, beside himself, tried vainly to convince his daughter not to "throw her life away." He pleaded with her not to bring shame onto his own head, nor to abandon her child, still nursing at the breast. Was it really such a big deal, he asked, to make such a small ceremonial sacrifice?

Perpetua pointed to a ceramic pitcher. "Father, do you see this pitcher?"

"Yes, of course I see it."

"Can it be called by any name other than what it is?"

"No."

"So I also cannot be called anything else than what I am, which is a Christian."[2]

In her diary, Perpetua tells us, "Enraged by my words, my father came at me as though to tear out my eyes."

She escaped violence — that time. But on March 7, AD 203, Perpetua, accompanied by her servant Felicity, entered the amphitheater to face a gruesome death. The young women were stripped naked, but even this bloodthirsty crowd could not bear such a sight. A medieval sourcebook describes the crowd's horrified reaction: "The people shuddered, seeing one a tender girl, the other her breasts yet dropping from her late childbearing. So they were called back and clothed in loose robes."[3]

Seeking ultimate humiliation, the young women's executioners chose a bull. Unlike a bear, who could kill his prey with one swipe of his paw, a bull's killing took time — death by a dozen gores, so to speak. After yet another mauling that left the young women torn but not dead, the crowd appealed to the emperor: "Enough!"

The order was given, and a gladiator came out. He was supposed to behead the women, but as he walked up to Perpetua, the hardened killer's hands started to tremble. Perhaps it was something in Perpetua's face, something about her eyes — who knows? — but the distracted gladiator's first blow once again injured but did not kill the young twenty-two-year-old.

Now people became sick to their stomachs. Finally, Perpetua showed all of them mercy by clutching the gladiator's hand and guiding his killing blow to her neck.

Generations of believers have seized inspiration from the passionate, strong, and heroic faith of a young woman just past adolescence, who boldly proclaimed to her enraged father, "I cannot be called anything else than what I am, which is a Christian," and who willingly faced a horrific death rather than deny her Lord. In fact, her story so energized the early church that warnings often went out not to treat her diary like Scripture. No less a light than Saint Augustine preached several sermons in Perpetua's honor on March 7, the anniversary of her death.

A Wrecked Word

Witnessing the dynamic witness of a young Francis or Perpetua, I feel embarrassed at how small-minded we can be when discussing the Christian faith with young people today. The apostle Paul exalted life in Christ as the most exciting and compelling life anyone could choose. In a marvelous take on 2 Timothy 4:7 (MSG), Eugene Peterson recounts Paul telling Timothy, "This is the only race worth running."

Today's believers often lose touch with this sense of the glory of being a Christian. We settle for so little — a tame religion, a few rituals, maybe even an occasional miraculous answer to prayer — and so pass our lives without understanding our true identity in Christ, embracing our calling as God's children, or fulfilling our divine purpose.

Is the Christianity taught today large enough to seize our hearts? Does its promise of transformation so compel us that we would give all we have to take hold of it?

Most of us have heard the modern translation of 2 Timothy 4:7 that says, "I have fought the good fight, I have finished the race, I have kept the faith." The Orthodox fathers looked at the passage in a different way. They translate the reading like this: "I have fought the Beautiful Fight." What a mesmerizing twist of a phrase! We can easily think of what is beautiful, and our minds can quickly grasp what constitutes a fight.

But putting the two together? A *beautiful* fight?

Here's the brilliance of it all: in the Christian life of real transformation and sacrificial service, there is drama, passion, struggle, and vision — everything our souls need to feel alive. And yet compare this exaltation of the Christian life with how it often gets presented today. Far too frequently, Christianity becomes a list of prohibitions. I'll never forget talking to one young woman, who said, "Why would I ever want to become a Christian? All they want me to do is dump all the good music from my iPod and wear ugly clothes." Her words tell me that, at least in our preaching, if not in our minds, we have lost our vision for the glorious, transforming presence of Jesus Christ — how he really makes a difference. This transformation goes well beyond a few instances of slightly modified behavior.

Sadly, *holiness* is practically a wrecked word outside the church. As I write these lines, yet another nationally known pastor has seen his scandalous conduct exposed, confirming the suspicions of so many who think that Christians are pitiful creatures of self-hatred who secretly crave what we most vigorously speak against.

Frankly, I don't fault the world for celebrating our hypocrisy. I fault us for defining the faith by what we're *not* supposed to do, setting ourselves up for constant humiliation. If that's what they know us for, if that's what they hear us saying, then we have neither lived nor preached in a way that showcases God's glory.

Let me ask you — what do you most think about when someone mentions the word *holiness*? Does it refer to the words you use or don't use, where you go or don't go on the Internet, how you express or don't express your sexuality? What is a *holy* person? And then ask yourself, can a few prohibitions like this adequately describe the powerful presence of a Francis or a Perpetua?

Without this sense of a powerfully *transforming* faith, we get stuck on lesser battles and smaller aims. We do this primarily by reducing our faith to a set of intellectual beliefs and a list of forbidden practices. Now, doctrine is enormously important, as is morality. But doctrine alone isn't enough. ("Even the demons believe [the doctrine that there is one God] — and shudder" [James 2:19].) And my problem with those who put so much emphasis on moralism is not that they go too far but that they don't go nearly far enough. They mistake the means for the end. Neither Francis nor Perpetua would be likely, in today's world, to spend their time getting drunk, cussing out inconsiderate drivers, or frittering away their time on salacious Internet searches. But you could never define them by these restraints. On the contrary, in their day they became known for what they *were*, not for what they *weren't*.

Here's the challenge of a small-minded faith based only on prohibitions: we still sin. If a successful Christian is defined by what she or he doesn't do, we're all in trouble, because the Bible tells us that "we all stumble in many ways" (James 3:2). Preaching mere moralism is the surest way to tire people out, because in one sense we're all going to fall short of the ideal, and in another sense, spending our lives trying *not* to do something is far less than we were created for. Such a faith will never capture our hearts.

If a young woman won't even empty her iPod for that faith, why would she ever give up her life for it?

Incarnational spirituality — the living, reigning, and ascended Jesus living through us and transforming us into different people — does not exist to uphold a few rules but rather speaks of a process that creates an entirely new person who sees with new eyes, feels with a new heart, hears with renewed ears, and lives with a new passion. It is, I believe, the only life worth living.

By the time you've completed this book, I pray that you will view your eyes as God's servants. You will look at your hands and feet as holy instruments of the mighty Creator. You will offer your ears to be constantly in tune with God's instruction. Your heart will beat with God's passion, and your mind will begin the journey of thinking God's thoughts. Your body will be a living, breathing center of purposeful passion, pointing toward the risen and reigning Christ, who works so powerfully within us.

You've probably heard many sermons and read many books on what you *shouldn't* be and *shouldn't* do. This book seeks to paint a portrait of what you can become. Our creator God is eager to splash his glory on us. The apostle Peter promises us that "[God's] divine power has given us everything we need for life and godliness" so that we "may participate in the divine nature" (2 Peter 1:3, 4).

God didn't create you *not to do something*; if that had been his goal, he never would have formed you, because if you never existed, you never would have sinned. God made each of us in his image, and he wants us to recapture that image, to surrender to his work in our lives, so that we "will be called oaks of righteousness, a planting of the LORD for the display of his splendor" (Isaiah 61:3).

I pray that we will settle for nothing less than the return of this splendor. *The Beautiful Fight* explores how faith in Jesus Christ can be radically different from and better than what we are currently experiencing. Christianity as a spiritual journey is not simply defined by what we believe or how we behave but is marked profoundly by *who we are*. It is a different type of transformation — a transformation of being, not just allegiance; a transformation of experience, not just confession; a transformation of existence, not just adherence. It is a return to splendor — for the glory of God.

Return to Splendor

How can we recapture this splendor today?

The Beautiful Fight invites you to explore the depths of a truly transforming faith, an incarnational spirituality that doesn't dwell merely on a list of prohibitions and forbidden sins but powerfully ushers us into something so precious, so profound, and so stirring that we would gladly give up all we have just to lay hold of it. It is what in our deepest longings we truly want to become.

We want to be like Jesus.

This calling does include a renewed morality, but it goes much deeper. It involves how we see the world, the way we hear God and others, the passions we feel, how we use our hands and feet, the thoughts we think. This is a complete transformation of all of our members.

It's a real struggle to get there, but the destination is so glorious that the fight to attain it is properly called *beautiful*.

The Beautiful Fight.

◌ Looking Back ◌

- We need a more compelling understanding of the Christian life, one that more closely measures up to that described by the apostle Paul, who calls Christianity "the only race worth running."

- "Mere moralists" mistake the means for the end; they have reduced Christianity to a list of prohibitions. "Incarnational spirituality" is a more biblical picture, much broader in its scope, which focuses on what we are to *become*.

- We are invited to become people who are strong "oaks of righteousness" and who reveal God's splendor.

Chapter 2

Aching for Experience

He became what we are that we might become what he is.

Athanasius

We must always behave with good manners, realizing that the Lord is present.

Clement of Alexandria

[God] had given me an experience of his presence in my soul — not merely as an object intellectually perceived by the application of the mind, but as a thing really possessed after the sweetest manner.

Madame Jeanne Guyon

Israel served the LORD throughout the lifetime of Joshua and of the elders who outlived him and who had experienced everything the LORD had done for Israel.

Joshua 24:31

While immersed in Dennis Rainey's pastoral masterpiece *Ministering to Twenty-First Century Families*,[1] I heard a young mother and her son arguing in the aisle of the plane.

"Take the middle seat, honey," she said.

"I don't want the middle seat," the little boy replied.

"It's what we have, honey. There's no other choice."

Realizing this could get ugly, I offered, "You think he'd prefer the window? I'll take the aisle if it will help out."

The boy's face lit up, and the mother thanked me profusely, but as I took the aisle seat, I noticed that the woman kept looking back.

"Do you have another child with you?" I asked.

"Yeah. She's in the back of the plane."

By "back," she meant one row away from the toilets, a cannon shot away from United's "Economy Plus" section. Back there, the seats get shoved together like sticks of gum in a new Wrigley's pack.

"How old is she?"

"Eleven."

I paused. I've traveled "back there" enough to know what it's like, especially right next to the toilets. People line up, waiting to get in, making the back of a plane the only place on this planet more crowded than a Manhattan sidewalk. And then, when the bathroom door swings open — well, it doesn't exactly smell like roses.

And a *middle seat*? All the way to *Seattle*?

After a big sigh, I heard myself saying, "Tell you what; I'll go trade seats with your daughter, and she can come sit up here."

"Are you sure? I've been back there. It's a middle seat and it's pretty awful."

"My wife has traveled alone with our kids plenty of times; I have a lot of empathy for mothers on their own."

When I got to the back, I saw the little girl, nestled between two grown men, one of whom was busily writing graffiti in a notebook, a cigarette box peeking out of his shirt pocket.

After squeezing myself into a space designed for a ninety-pound person with twenty-four-inch legs, I put Rainey's book in the seat pocket in front of me and smiled at the irony. My reading of this book did *nothing* to minister to families. If every church had a campaign in which members read the book, discussed it, prayed about it, and confirmed its truth, *nothing would change* until, like Francis, we found ways to apply it. Something so simple as relinquishing a plane seat — something I'm sure you would gladly have done as well — did far more to "minister to twenty-first-century families" than my reading of that book.

And yet *church* as we define it today is often structured around "discussing" issues, praying about them, and feeling inspired at the thought of them. We need to become like Francis, finding ways to enflesh — live out and apply — the stretching truths of our faith.

Believe me, giving up a good seat isn't in my nature; but I believe that doing so was a small step toward holiness. And when I saw the young girl's smile and the relief on her mother's face, I felt a momentary splash of God's glory. At that moment, I was engaged in the Beautiful Fight, the only race worth running. I realized it's not enough to discuss issues, pray about them, and merely feel inspired by them. No, to actually participate in the Beautiful Fight, we have to find ways to put them into action.

A Dynamic Force

Biblical holiness and personal transformation depend on how Christ becomes really present in his followers' lives and how he makes a real difference there, to such an extent that a man who once loathed lepers would go out of his way to embrace and even kiss one. In such a life, Jesus is a genuine reality, a dynamic force, that goes far beyond mere belief. Jesus prayed for his future disciples "that I myself may be in them" (John 17:26). Paul added, "[Christ] is not weak in dealing with you, but is powerful among you" (2 Corinthians 13:3).

Jesus and Paul spoke of people who are benevolently invaded by and radically available to God. This is what the Orthodox Church talks about when it says that Christianity must go beyond Christocentrism to embrace Christification — that is, becoming like Christ, through Christ. In other words, "Christified."

If we don't think about God, pray to God, listen for God's voice, and consciously serve God, by definition we live an *ungodly* life. We usually think of "ungodly" as being *against* God, but ungodly can also be a life that simply ignores God or — out of busyness, indifference, religiosity, or apathy — simply doesn't tap in to God. In this sense, it is possible to give an *ungodly* sermon that may be theologically accurate. It is possible to lead *ungodly* family devotions that nevertheless focus on spiritual truth. Christianity doesn't address only the ends; it has a lively interest in the *means*. That's why every healthy, growing believer should experience God every day — his presence, his power, his wisdom.

The early church fathers — as well as the entire Eastern wing of the Christian church — took this reality of personal experience with God so strongly that they often spoke of "deification." Such language (most famously, "God became man that man might become God") understandably causes us evangelicals to choke on our confessions. Reading the church fathers carefully, however, assures us that the best of them didn't teach that we actually become God, but that we should become God*like*. The Godlike quality never becomes our own possession; rather, it is a fruit of the "continuing, uniting work of the Holy Spirit."[2]

The great Reformed theologian J. I. Packer warned us more than thirty years ago of the tremendous difference between knowing God and knowing *about* God. We face the great temptation to fall into living the Christian life without Christ — a "Christless Christianity." Haven't we all, at one time or another, awakened with a start after realizing that we had begun practicing some major discipline of our faith — whether Bible study, imitating Christ, prayer, witnessing, fellowship — without truly relying on God's dynamic presence? We begin coasting and relying on our own strength. Packer taught that any truly godly spiritual discipline "is an activity of holy thought, consciously performed in the presence of God, under the eye of God, by the help of God, as a means of communion with God."[3]

If we divorce these spiritual disciplines from true presence, even they cannot still our hunger — indeed, our craving — for real experience of God. We want to experience his power, transforming us into his image.

A Deeper Longing

The great hymnist Frances Ridley Havergal ("Take My Life and Let It Be") grew up in a strong Christian home and seemed, to the outward world, to be a model Christian woman. By her early twenties, she had memorized the whole of the Gospels, all of the Epistles, the book of Revelation, the Psalms, and even the sixty-six chapters of Isaiah. And yet "still she longed for a deeper, richer, fuller Christian experience."[4]

She wrote in one book, "I still wait for the hour when I believe he will reveal himself to me more directly; but it is the quiet waiting of present trust, not the restless waiting of anxiety and despair."[5] Though she clearly had a deep love for Scripture (show me just one other twenty-two-year-old who has memorized virtually all of the New Testament and much of the Old), she longed for a deeper experience of God, dwelling within her: "So I want Jesus to speak to me, to say 'many things' to me, that I may speak for him to others with real power. It is not knowing doctrine, but *being with* him, which will give this."[6]

What was true of Frances is, I believe, true for all of us. Knowing, reading, and studying the Bible are essential activities — but even Bible study, on its own, cannot take the place of directly experiencing, knowing, and being empowered by God. That's why I'm so thankful for our Eastern brothers and sisters, who remind us of the importance of "the action of God on the soul."[7]

I fully understand the danger of talking about deification. "God became man that man might become God" is not a phrase I would use. But I do appreciate the ability of Orthodox teaching to resolve a tension that Protestants often trip over. Though we are likely to confess that *conversion* depends on grace, sometimes we speak as if *discipleship* is built primarily on human effort and natural means; we tend to be deeply suspicious of anything that could conceivably be considered "mystical."* So rather than talking about God's empowering presence, we place the most emphasis on being faithful and obedient to what God already has revealed and are deeply distrustful of anything that seems to allow God direct input.

I remain an evangelical for sound theological reasons. But shame on us if we go so far in the other direction that we reject the notion of God's real presence in our lives. Austin Farrer, a popular Anglican

---

*When I use the words *mystic* or *mystical*, evangelicals can get really nervous, in part because of some Eastern, non-Christian uses of the words. I'm using them in their classical, orthodox sense, connoting direct experience with God. Please don't read any other meanings into these words. We don't question the legitimacy of preaching just because some preach heresy; instead, we question the heresy. Likewise, why throw out all mystical experience just because a false religion may claim such experience?

preacher of the twentieth century, wrote, "If God is anywhere more than elsewhere, it is because he works there more richly and more revealingly. He is more present in men than in beasts, in Christians than in pagans, in saints than in Laodiceans."[8]

If it seems there are places and even people where God works "more richly and more revealingly," isn't it reasonable to wish that it would be so with us? To experience God is to be transformed by him. This takes us beyond mere belief to dynamic reality. Do we not all aspire to become what the early church father Gregory of Nazianzus described as "an [instrument] which the Holy Spirit blows and on which he plays"?[9]

A Compelling Ascent

Though historically the Christian church has taught that the spiritual life ascends through stages,* many believers today have never heard of this truth. In fact, it sounds elitist or even prideful to many — with the result that contemporary, Westernized Christianity focuses far more on conversion than on transformation.

Without a clear vision of what it means to mature and of how to get there, we focus on the "mechanics" of conversion. Why? Because we think we can understand it. Yet what other organization would hope to compensate for a lack of depth by seeking to grow in breadth? That's a prescription for disaster!

In my view, the contemporary church is severely tempted to compensate for its lack of spiritual weight with reliance on cleverness and cultural awareness — as if these two qualities can overcome a lack of God's empowering presence. While I applaud the God-given desire to engage our culture, how much better it would be if *we* were first transformed. Then we could demonstrate to the world true, God-breathed creativity instead of cleverness, and familiarity with the Trinity instead of an obsession with proving how well we can read the latest cultural trend. We cannot compensate for being strangers to God by becoming friends with the culture. On the

---

*Most often it is described as purgative, illuminative, and unitive, though there are many variations.

contrary, we become our culture's truest friend by becoming more aware of the God who not only engages our culture but also inspires, critiques, and transforms it.

Perhaps one of the best ways to engage our culture is to do the hard work necessary to cooperate fully with God to develop a compelling life. Bono isn't a compelling figure just because he's a rock star; he's compelling because he's a rock star *who has something to say.*

What defines a compelling life? Someone who is available to God and regularly experiences God's fellowship, presence, and empowerment. There are no substitutes, no shortcuts. *We* are not compelling; on the contrary, we are sinful, often poor imitations of our Lord. But when God lives through us, shines through us, and overcomes our worst inclinations with his merciful transformation — *that's* compelling. People become interested not so much *in* us but in what's so different *about* us. The non-Christian notices the changes as we become more and more like Christ — if indeed we *are* experiencing more and more of Christ.

Divine Delight

Experiential Christianity is much more than a human yearning; it is a divine one. What I want is secondary; what God desires is primary. Just because I *want* to experience God isn't, on its own, enough to make it a noble calling (part of me would also really like the ability to fly). What matters is that *God* wants to manifest his presence through us by his Spirit, which makes experiential faith a Christian obligation.

Just as an earthly parent takes delight in family resemblance, so our God feels enormous delight when we begin to resemble him in a spiritual sense. This is, in fact, our ultimate glorification: "For those God foreknew he also predestined to be conformed to the likeness of his Son" (Romans 8:29). The clear teaching of Scripture is that such a manifestation calls us to at least some human cooperation.[10]

Paul warns the Thessalonians, "Do not put out the Spirit's fire" (1 Thessalonians 5:19). Many have applied this warning exclusively to the use of the charismatic gifts, but to reduce the Holy Spirit to his gifts alone does not do justice to the forceful reality championed by Paul. Paul here teaches us that it is possible to reduce the role of the Holy Spirit in our lives, to somehow put out his fire in such a way that God becomes less active, less of a force, and even less of a factor in our daily experience. Paul pleads with the early church, "Don't let this happen!"

But has it happened today?

Evangelicalism has spent the last several decades making the apologetic and historical case for Jesus. We have published books, offered seminars, and filled magazines with the historical claims and compelling intellectual arguments for the Christian faith. Thank God for this important work — but sadly, some of us have neglected the experiential case for the Christian faith, a case that may be even more persuasive with younger generations.

No less a mind than C. S. Lewis warned us of this error. In the conclusion of a talk he once gave, the famed apologist for the Christian faith confessed this:

> I have found that nothing is more dangerous to one's own faith than the work of an apologist. No doctrine of the Faith seems to me so spectral, so unreal, as one that I have just successfully defended in a public debate. For a moment, you see, it has seemed to rest on oneself: as a result, when you go away from that debate, it seems no stronger than that weak pillar. That is why we apologists take our lives in our hands *and can be saved only by falling back continually from the web of our own arguments . . . into the Reality — from Christian apologetics into Christ himself.*[11]

I am in no way arguing for anti-intellectualism; our faith is based on the authority of an intellectually accurate understanding of Scripture. What I *am* trying to challenge is the sense of "either/or" that often fuels the debate. Why must we choose between good theology and experiential living? They are not competitors but allies. When Francis of Assisi sent his followers to evangelize the Saracens, he reminded them that there are *two* ways to witness: teaching the Word of God and "comporting themselves as Christians without arguing or quarrelling with anyone."[12]

Jesus himself chastised the Pharisees with a scathing "Are you not in error because you do not know the Scriptures or the power of God?" (Mark 12:24). Jesus is telling us that we can fall into two kinds of error: *doctrinal error*, based on ignorance or misunderstanding, and *experiential error*, based on the denial of God's powerful reality in a believer's life. Have we become so obsessed with the former that we've neglected the latter?

So what will draw new disciples in a world that, at best, says "Ho hum" to the historical claims of Jesus' deity and, at worst, views our evangelism with hostility? Isn't it true that most evangelism today runs up against the wall of "Well, that's just *your* opinion"? In a world busy dropping the truth of absolutes and eager to wear the clothes of intellectual and moral relativism, what will take us beyond opinion to making a compelling case for faith? *Beginning to live compelling lives that can be explained only by the truth of what we believe.*

Charles Spurgeon wrote about this issue many years ago: "We cannot force truth on men, but we can make our teaching clear and decided, *and make our lives consistent with our words.* Truth and holiness are the surest antidotes to error and unrighteousness."[13]

Rodney Stark, a sociologist, reminds us that "typically people do not *seek* a faith; they *encounter* one through their ties to other people who already accept this faith."[14] If we don't stress experience as well as reason, people will never encounter the reality of our faith, because they simply cannot read our minds.

Marvelous, Miraculous Manifestations

In fact, what really drew people to the Christian faith in the first century was the way of life modeled by its adherents — the reality of the presence of God in Christian lives. People saw how these Christ-followers lived differently — how they treated others differently — and their changed lives provided compelling evidence for the supremacy of Jesus' claims. Church historian Dr. Aaron Milavec puts it this way:

> In truth, potential members assessed the movement not so much on the basis of claims made on behalf of Jesus who was

absent, but on the basis of their experience of the way of life of members who were very much present to them. It is no surprise, therefore, that the entire system of the *Didache* [an early first-century document used to explain the Christian life to new believers] displays little taste for negotiating, defining, and defending the exalted titles and functions of Jesus. Rather, the *Didache* is taken up with the business of passing on the Way of Life revealed to its authors by the Father through his servant Jesus. Converts came forward ready to assimilate that Way of Life as it was formulated and lived out by the tried and tested members of the movement.[15]

This emphasis continued on into the third century, particularly during a terrible epidemic around AD 260 that wiped out vast swaths of the population. People saw Christians acting differently. Dionysius, the bishop of Alexandria at that time, explains:

Most of our brother Christians showed unbounded love and loyalty, never sparing themselves and thinking only of one another. Heedless of danger, they took charge of the sick, attending to their every need and ministering to them in Christ, and with them departed this life serenely happy; for they were infected by others with the disease, drawing on themselves the sickness of their neighbors and cheerfully accepting their pains. Many, in nursing and curing others, transferred their death to themselves and died in their stead.... The best of our brothers lost their lives in this manner.[16]

Contrast this with the way those who were not Christ-followers responded:

The heathen behaved in the very opposite way. At the first onset of the disease, they pushed the sufferers away and fled from their dearest, throwing them into the roads before they were dead and treating unburied corpses as dirt, hoping thereby to avert the spread and contagion of the fatal disease.[17]

Our faith will always rest securely on absolute truth, orthodox belief, and the compelling, rational case for Christianity. But before many in our culture will accept these absolutes, they need to see how such dogmas work their way into our experience. And faith working its way into our experience is a must. The early church moved forward on the backs of the "nursing martyrs" and others like them.

When Jesus rose from the dead and ascended back into heaven and then sent his Holy Spirit to indwell believers, Christianity became a dynamic, supernatural faith of God's touching the world through us. It is *not* merely a list of beliefs. While rooted in history, it is a living kingdom that spreads even as we speak. This Christianity has a pulse; Paul tells the Corinthians, "To each one the manifestation of the Spirit is given for the common good" (1 Corinthians 12:7).

Pause a moment and think hard about that phrase — *manifestation of the Spirit*.

Please, let's not reduce such powerful language to a relatively narrow discussion about spiritual gifts. In a far greater sense, this means we are called to be temples of the Holy Spirit. The really startling idea here is that we, finite humans with earthly bodies, are given a manifestation of God's Holy Spirit. This is no mere belief. This is a divinely benevolent invasion! Paul tells us in 1 Corinthians 4:20, "The kingdom of God is not a matter of talk but of power."

When Christianity combines the brilliance of its intellectual basis with a commitment to practice its compelling truth, it takes hold in a culture. Sociologist Rodney Stark explains: "I believe it was the religion's particular doctrines that permitted Christianity to be among the most sweeping and successful revitalization movements in history. *And it was the way these doctrines took on actual flesh, the way they directed organizational actions and individual behavior*, that led to the rise of Christianity."[18]

Oh, how we need to catch a glimpse of this sacred truth today and recapture this "way" — the way of incarnational spirituality.

Breaking into Blessedness

I'm pleased to report that God finally answered Frances Ridley Havergal's prayers for a more genuine spiritual experience. The great hymn writer had written as far back as 1858 of her desire for a deeper, empowering presence of God: "I want Jesus to speak to me, to say 'many things' to me, that I may speak for him to others with real power. It is not knowing doctrine, but *being with* him, which will give this" (cited earlier in this chapter).

God made Frances wait — as he makes most of his saints wait — but Frances recorded this on an Advent Sunday, December 2, 1873: "I first saw clearly the blessedness of true consecration. I saw it as a flash of electric light, and what you see, you can never *un*see."[19]

The intimacy with God, the growth in personal holiness, the power for ministry — everything Frances longed for — she received. She was truly transformed and later asked the church, "Why should we pare down the promises of God to the level of what we have hitherto experienced of what God is 'able to do,' or even of what we have thought he might be able to do for us? Why not receive God's promises, nothing doubting, just as they stand?"[20]

Out of this experience, following a joyous time of very fruitful ministry, Frances wrote one of the most beloved worship songs of the past two hundred years: "Take My Life and Let It Be."

Are you tired of trying to keep connected with God through mere morality? Are you tired of knowing an awful lot *about* God but precious little *of* God? Are you exhausted from trying to make the Christian life work in your own strength? If so, then enter the experiential side of Christianity, where God becomes not just the goal of our lives but the engine that takes us *to* the goal. I pray that "you may be filled to the measure of all the fullness of God" (Ephesians 3:19).

The next step in this process is to recapture a crucial doctrine — the ascension of Christ — that is commonly ignored or marginalized. This foundational understanding of our faith deserves a chapter all its own.

⚘ **Looking Back** ⚘

- Biblical holiness must always involve the personal experience of God's presence.

- "Ungodly" doesn't only mean being against God; it can also describe those who live without God's power and presence.

- Our experience with God must incorporate the way *he* acts on our souls. Christian discipleship must not be limited to human energy and earthly means.

- One of the best ways to reach our culture is by living compelling lives.

- God desires for us to live in experience even more than we do. Just as an earthly parent takes delight in family resemblance, so our God takes great delight in us as we begin to resemble him in a spiritual sense.

- Jesus warns us that we can err in two ways: by lacking biblical understanding and by failing to live in God's power.

Chapter 3

Still in Flesh

Jesus' ascension into heaven is the completing step that makes all the benefits of his life among us available now. In fact, the doctrine of the ascension, so seldom discussed in the church, actually provides the gateway through which we may understand how we participate in the triune life of God through the work of Jesus Christ.

Gerrit Scott Dawson

We must behold [Jesus Christ] as the pivotal and cardinal reality, round which all life and history have moved.

H. R. Mackintosh

In his ascension in the flesh, Jesus holds now for us in heaven the hope of a glorified humanity against the ravages of mortality we endure in the world.

Gerrit Scott Dawson

The Lord Jesus Christ ... will transform our lowly bodies so that they will be like his glorious body.

Paul, in Philippians 3:20–21

Question of the day: Does Jesus, as we speak, still have elbows?

Knees?

Fingernails?

These aren't silly questions; they run to the very heart and foundation of biblical Christianity. They also point to a key theological doctrine called "the ascension."

It's difficult for us to ascertain the exact state of Jesus' glorified body, but we know that after the resurrection, Jesus went to great pains to demonstrate that his body was both real and physical: "Put your finger here; see my hands. Reach out your hand and put it into my side" (John 20:27). Even after the ascension, Stephen saw Jesus "standing" (Acts 7:56). Scripture tells us that Jesus "sat down" (Hebrews 1:3), and the last book of the Bible describes Jesus as "walking" among golden lampstands (Revelation 2:1).

Other biblical language describes Jesus as sitting on a throne and paints pictures of heavenly feasts, both of which require some type of body. Paul uses the idea of Jesus' body to describe our future bodies, telling us that Jesus "will transform our lowly bodies so that they will be like his glorious body" (Philippians 3:21).* Some may suggest that this is nothing more than metaphorical language, and while I have no desire to debate the issue, I will insist that the fact that Jesus still lives in a body adds a certain dignity to our own bodies. It also has major implications for spiritual formation: we are called to become more and more like Jesus is now.

The Westminster Confession (8.4) affirms, "On the third day [Jesus] arose from the dead, *with the same body* in which he suffered, with which also he *ascended* into heaven, and there *sits* at the right hand of his Father, making intercession, and shall return to judge men and angels, at the end of the world."

It is our human nature to gravitate toward certain events recorded in the Gospels and their corresponding theological truths: Christ's birth (the incarnation), his death (atonement), and his resurrection (justification), for instance. But when did you last hear a sermon on Christ's *ascension*? When did you last hear this orthodox belief unpacked — that after his resurrection, Jesus rose into the heavens *in the same body* in which he lived his life on earth?

There's a reason — a *good* reason — that the Bible records the ascension. It's not a superfluous event, as if after Jesus died and rose from the dead, we can rush through the rest and say, "And, oh

---

*Admittedly, Paul insists that our resurrected bodies will differ markedly from our current ones: "There are also heavenly bodies and there are earthly bodies; but the splendor of the heavenly bodies is one kind, and the splendor of the earthly bodies is another.... So will it be with the resurrection of the dead" (1 Corinthians 15:40, 42). I'm not interested in speculating on the difference here; let's leave that to the theologians. For our purposes, it's enough that Paul speaks of the splendor of *both*. Jesus now inhabits *some* kind of body that bears *some* kind of resemblance to our own, though it has far more glory and splendor.

yeah, he went back up into heaven." God's inclusion of this historical fact in the written record of Scripture is both purposeful and significant. We might preach one hundred sermons on Jesus' death and resurrection for every one preached on his ascension, but this serves only to reveal our cultural blinders. Christmas and Easter are ingrained in American culture and stand out on the calendar of the contemporary church. But we lose something when the ascension becomes a forgotten appendage to the incarnation, crucifixion, and resurrection.

So what do we lose? Here's the answer of Presbyterian pastor Gerrit Scott Dawson: "The ascended Jesus is the reigning Jesus. Of all the meanings of the ascension, this one is preeminent: Jesus has gone up to the right hand of God the Father, exalted above every name and power. He reigns."[1]

The popular phrase "What would Jesus do?" is stuck on the incarnation. The ascension opens up an entirely new and more appropriate question: "What is Jesus doing *right now*?"

Celebrating Christmas gives us faith; it affirms that our beliefs have roots in the historical fact of the incarnation. Celebrating Easter gives us assurance; it affirms that Christ wiped away our sins by his great sacrifice and triumphed over death. Celebrating the ascension gives us *hope* and points us toward *transformation*; it affirms that we can become more and more like Jesus is *right now*.

Without the ascension, we might look around and forget that Christ is the ruling Lord of this fallen, broken world. This essential doctrine reminds us that, just as we can get discouraged in our sin and momentarily forget the pardon Jesus won for us on Calvary, so we can get discouraged by our lack of progress and effectiveness and forget about Christ's present reign — not just that he *will* reign when he comes again or that he *did* reign over death, but that he *is reigning right now*.

Dawson writes brilliantly about this: "While the boots of the soldiers of the most powerful army in the world resounded in the streets of occupied Jerusalem, an uneducated fisherman from the north of Palestine declared, 'God has made this Jesus, whom you crucified, both Lord and Christ' (Acts 2:36)."[2] The church must recapture this sacred truth so that all of us can have the hope and courage to embrace the presently reigning Jesus, who is manifesting himself through believers by the Holy Spirit.

We serve the ascended *and reigning* Christ. The world may mock our King. We may disdain his rule by our own sinful rebellion — but the fact is, *he reigns.* And we can participate in the spread of his kingdom, in the Beautiful Fight, not simply by imitating how he lived while on earth but by surrendering to his dynamic, life-transforming presence within us, by letting him change the way we see, think, feel, hear, speak, and serve. It's the life of Christ in us, continuing *his* work, exercising *his* reign, manifesting *his* presence.

Without Christ, we have no power to change. Elton Trueblood says it well: "A Christianity which ceases to be Christ-centered may have some other valuable features, but it is usually lacking in power."[3] Christ isn't buried in history; he is risen *and* ascended. He reigns, acts, speaks, guides, and is building his church. The ascension can help to keep us from smothering the supernatural and the mysterious elements of our faith, recapturing the dynamic reality of Christ manifesting himself through us.

Whose Presence?

Julie De Rossi was just forty-four years old when her life was cut short in a horrific crash with a drunk driver. Through the miracle of modern medicine, at least thirty-five lives have benefited from Julie's body, among them National Football League quarterback Carson Palmer. Palmer suffered a potentially career-ending knee injury in January 2006, but doctors used one of Julie's tendons to reconstruct his left knee. Dorothy Hyde, Julie's mother, said her family feels "a special connection when we watch Carson Palmer. My grandson, Burke, has become a big fan."[4]

Palmer talks about the wonder of literally having a piece of someone else inside his own body: "It's an amazing thing. It's something that blew my mind to think that you could use a part of somebody else's body to repair a living body. It's just crazy. I don't think

I'll ever be able to figure any of that stuff out or understand it. It's something that just blows your mind."

Palmer appreciates the opportunity to represent Julie's family on the football field and through his life, to be a living reminder of a much-loved mother and daughter.

"It's like my grandson said," Hyde notes. "No one would have heard of Julie if not for Carson."

No one would have heard of Julie if not for Carson.

While it is a stretch to suggest no one would have heard of Jesus if not for us, the fact is, there are individuals who might not *think* of Jesus if not for us. As a piece of Julie resides in Carson's body, so through the Holy Spirit, a "piece" of God resides in us. Like Palmer, our goal should be to represent the One who has given himself for us and to us. The ascension reminds me that since Christ stills reigns — in fact, reigns *through* me — my goal should be to proclaim his current rule. At best, I'm a signpost, a messenger, for what Christ is doing even now on this earth.

Sadly, like the biblical Esau (see Genesis 25:29–34), we sometimes feel pridefully tempted to sell this amazing birthright of Christ's presence for our own presence. We focus on *our* work, *our* influence, and *our* ministry. *One of the biggest threats to incarnational living is pride.* Instead of manifesting Christ's presence, we want to showcase our own presence; instead of dispensing Christ's wisdom, we want to spotlight our own insight; instead of speaking Christ's truth, we want to spout our own opinions; instead of adopting Christ's agenda, we want to accomplish our own five- or ten-year plans; instead of building Christ's kingdom, we want to spread our own "ministry."

But consider the glorious alternative. When I adopt the ascension as a key theological truth, with its corresponding teaching of the currently reigning Jesus, then I have two distinct choices: build something based on my own intelligence, energy, opinions, and perspective (which, when I die, will die with me); or join a glorious kingdom that has preceded me and will outlive me. The latter alternative must destroy my pride. If Jesus reigns, then by definition, I cannot reign. I must be a subordinate. If Jesus is active today, right now, then I must first and foremost *surrender* to his influence on a minute-by-minute basis.

According to Paul, Jesus remains active: "For he must reign until he has put all his enemies under his feet" (1 Corinthians 15:25). As Gerrit Dawson observes, "The Son may be 'seated' at the Father's right hand, but he is far from sedentary. Rather, he is actively engaged in strengthening his people and subduing the enemy. Though Jesus parts from our sight in the ascension, he does not withdraw from the exercise of his authority or his continuing labor for our renewal."[5]

How does this affect everyday, practical Christian living? In my own life, it means that before I preach, I often meditate on Jesus or imagine him speaking to this very audience. I not only want Christ's words; I want his tone, his joy, his love of life, his fondness for stories, his favor toward children, who are deeply, deeply loved — but most of all, his passion for giving glory to God. My most common prayer is this: "May the risen and ascended Christ manifest himself in me as I submit myself to be his servant today."

When I'm meeting with someone one-on-one, I strive to pray, "Father, help me to love this person with the love of Christ." When I pray for my children, I try to fall into the intercession of the Holy Spirit (see Romans 8:26), letting the true Comforter, who knows all things, plead his case through me. When I counsel others, I pray that I will model God's attitude and speak the ascended Christ's words. When I'm in our small group Bible study and someone is talking, I try to listen with Christ's ears: "Father, what is really being said by this person, and what do you want to say in response?"

A counselor once asked me to meet with a local pastor. She didn't tell me why she wanted me to meet with him, just that she was praying for God to use this encounter to make some necessary points. During the meeting, I felt almost as though I were watching myself. Words came from I don't know where — well, I *do* know where, but not from me. I remember my wife picking me up after that meeting; I felt dazed, but in a good way. I could sense a tiny bit of what Jesus talked about when he told his disciples, "I know that power has gone out from me" (Luke 8:46). Please don't misunderstand —

I'm not talking about *my* power. I truly felt as though Jesus had used *my* ears and *my* tongue to make *his* points. I would never ask people to accept my words as God's words; personally, I would *never* say, "Thus saith the Lord." But I am striving more and more to let the living, reigning Christ work through me to truly touch others.

I've found that sometimes merely speaking a single thought — "You're so focused on becoming a mother; have you ever wondered if God wants you to focus first on being his *daughter*?" — can open many doors of insight, as long as that one tiny phrase was born in heaven and delivered to earth by the Spirit. By making myself available, I see God doing so much with seemingly so little because his work in my life isn't limited by my own wisdom or understanding.

There is nothing I treasure more in any type of ministry or relational moment than to experience the ascended Christ manifesting himself through me. Nothing is even half as rewarding as that. It doesn't always happen when I want it to; in fact, it doesn't happen nearly as often as I wish it did — but when it does, everyone involved gets a refreshing splash of glory.

And this same experience is given to God's church as a whole through the ascended Christ.

Diminished or Released?

This submissive and dependent view of Christian life and ministry doesn't diminish our role or the importance of our work. On the contrary, it exalts us. "Humble yourselves, therefore, under God's mighty hand, *that he may lift you up in due time*" (1 Peter 5:6, emphasis added). God isn't glorified through weak, indecisive, and defeated subjects; he is glorified through weak but *victorious* subjects.

Gerrit Dawson (whose book *Jesus Ascended* I highly recommend) writes the following:

The greatness of a king has always been known through the generosity of the gifts he bestows on his people. One of the first acts of the enthroned Jesus was to open the treasure trove of his love and bring forth a gem of inestimable value. In his bountiful rule, the King of kings showers a priceless gift from his infinite largesse upon his subjects. He receives the Holy Spirit from the Father and pours him out upon the disciples (Acts 2:33). The Spirit ... becomes the bond between the still-incarnate Son in heaven and his people still sojourning on earth. By this boon, the physically absent King establishes a living tie between himself and his subjects. The head pours his life-giving energies and constant direction throughout his body (i.e., into his people) through his Spirit.[6]

God's glory is recognized not just through *forgiven* people but through *transformed* and *compelling* people — this is one of the ways he makes himself visible to many who would never pick up a Bible.

Paul's "spiritual gifts" emphasis in 1 Corinthians isn't on which particular gift we have but on the fact that *one* God constantly works through *many* people in a multitude of ways: "There are different kinds of gifts, but the same Spirit. There are different kinds of service, but the same Lord. There are different kinds of working, but the same God works all of them in all men" (1 Corinthians 12:4–6).

Paul's first letter to the Corinthians is often used to debate which gifts God still hands out today, which particular gift any individual might get, how you can identify your particular gift, and so forth — but any honest reading says that Paul had one overriding concern: God is very active through his people, manifesting himself in many (and, yes, sometimes miraculous) ways. Paul insists that God discloses himself through his people, that he offers divine evidence of his reality by the way he works through his church. You may not be able to see God, but you can surely see him working as his people actively engage in the Beautiful Fight.

Every maturing Christian should bear this dynamic, ongoing mark of God. Your mark will look different from my mark — but both of our marks should be plainly evident to the world. As the living, reigning Lord works in and through us, we can't help but be actively transformed — day by day, week by week, year by year.

This is the faith that Jesus both lived and taught. He lived it: "The words I say to you are not just my own. Rather, it is the Father, living in me, who is doing his work" (John 14:10). And he taught it:

"I tell you the truth, anyone who has faith in me will do what I have been doing" (14:12).

The ascended Christ *still reigns*. Do others see that truth in you and me today?

Our Highest Hope

It may be that we neglect incarnational spirituality because it is not an easy life; the Beautiful Fight is filled with what appears to be constant failure. If we hoped only in what we actually saw, our hope would soon tire out, and we'd give up the entire enterprise as an excruciating exercise in futility. For every time someone has experienced a "splash of glory" through me, they have had to wade through ten sessions of putting up with my own inflated sense of importance and my own tendencies toward misunderstandings, arrogant opinions, and glaring blind spots.

But do you know what keeps me in the fight? Do you know what challenges me to keep going, even though my reality isn't nearly at the level I wish it was? The answer is embedded within the reality of Christ's ascension. Listen to John Calvin's words of encouragement as he thunders home this timeless truth:

> Thus, since [Jesus] has gone up there, and is in heaven for us, let us note that we need not fear to be in this world. It is true that we are subject to so much misery that our condition is pitiable, but at that we need neither be astonished nor confine our attention to ourselves. Thus, we look to our Head, who is already in heaven, and say, "Although I am weak, there is Jesus Christ, who is powerful enough to make me stand upright. Although I am feeble, there is Jesus Christ, who is my strength. Although I am full of miseries, Jesus Christ is in immortal glory and what he has will some time be given to me and I shall partake of all his benefits." ... This is how we must look at his ascension, applying the benefit to ourselves.[7]

Because Jesus reigns now, we have hope. Even though my eyes are weak and greedy and judgmental and lustful, there stands

Christ, with eyes filled with burning purity, holy passion, and self-less love. Even though I sometimes speak with a hurtful tongue or blurt out unkind comments, there is Christ, with his healing tongue in perfect control. And here is where it gets *really* good: Jesus is not simply watching me, asking me to imitate him; on the contrary, he has released, is releasing, and will release his Holy Spirit to help me see and talk just as he does. *He will live through me.*

Some may ask, is it possible to be so truly transformed? Yes, indeed — especially when we see the ascended one now reigning. Not only is such a life possible; such a life already *is*. Perhaps Gerrit Dawson's thoughts sum this up best:

> Out of the most profound hope, the Christian church looks upon the worst setbacks and sufferings and declares, in the very teeth of death and loss, "What of it? Christ reigns in heaven, and so, at the deepest level, all is well. What of my circumstance? I am in Christ, and he has triumphed. In him, by the Holy Spirit, I am kept in heaven." The ascension provides the very ground for our peace in every circumstance.[8]

In this world, we will not experience the full measure of Christ's glorified state. Nor will we see unending victory. But when we look at our weaknesses and our defeats through the lens of Christ's ascension, our trials and sins take on a much different hue.

And since the Bible teaches us that Jesus ascended in a body and will return in a body (see Acts 1:9–11) and that Jesus now reigns in a body (see the first page of this chapter), it's fair to infer that real children are sitting in a real lap (providing hope for those who have lost young loved ones). Shamed and hurting men receive an affirming, masculine hug. Women formerly abused, neglected, or forsaken have their cheeks touched with a selfless, nurturing, 100 percent pure hand.

What is happening there — and it *is* happening there, even as you read these words — can also, in a less perfect way, happen here through us, Christ's representatives. With such a possibility before us, how dare we simply play at church?

Let us discard the pride, the preening, the bloated arrogance of our opinions. Let us shun the small lives of desperate people who try to make themselves large through frenetic activity and modern gimmicks. Let us quiet our hearts long enough to experience the restful, amazingly powerful, and compellingly pure passion of Jesus, changing what we see, tuning us in to what must really be heard, and helping us to feel what God himself feels. This is real human experience, exalted by divine impact; it is our birthright through the ascension — a sacred truth we need to hold dear.

We simply cannot limit our Christian experience to the incarnation and Jesus' death and resurrection. To be sure, those are precious truths that make our salvation possible. But let us press on to embrace the power, hope, and glory of the ascension, the reality of a living, in-the-flesh Jesus. He is the embodiment of all that we can be when we surrender to his reign.

⊗ Looking Back ⊗

- The doctrine of the ascension has major implications for spiritual formation, beginning with the reminder that Jesus still reigns and that we are called to become more and more like he is *now*.

- The ascension also reminds us that the Christian life is about surrendering to the work Jesus is currently doing; it's opening ourselves up to Christ's presence, wisdom, and power rather than trying to make an impression by relying on our own gifts and abilities.

- The gift of the Holy Spirit points toward the truth that God wants to manifest himself through us.

- The ascension gives us hope, because what we want to be, Jesus already is.

Chapter 4

Full-Bodied Faith

Christ, having been made ours, makes us sharers with him in the gifts with which he has been endowed.

John Calvin

My son, pay attention to what I say;
    listen closely to my words.
Do not let them out of your sight,
    keep them within your heart;
for they are life to those who find them
    and health to a man's whole body.

Proverbs 4:20–22

Therefore do not let sin reign in your mortal body so that you obey its evil desires. Do not offer the parts of your body to sin, as instruments of wickedness, but rather offer yourselves to God, as those who have been brought from death to life; and offer the parts of your body to him as instruments of righteousness.

Paul, in Romans 6:12–13

LIVE NUDES.

The neon sign threatened to wreck the romantic tone of our weekend getaway. My wife and I were walking through downtown Seattle on our way to the famous Pike Street Market, where salmon spin through the air as brash salesmen heave the fish to the wrappers and where the first Starbucks (*Hallelujah!*) was born.

And then we had to pass this — this *place*.

As an English major, I hate it when people murder the language. Turning the adjective *nude* into a noun is wrong on a lot of levels, spiritually even more than grammatically. Now they're not even nude *women*. They're just *nudes* — a startlingly honest admission of the disdain inherent in the flesh-selling business. They don't traffic in people; they just traffic in nudes.

And *live* nudes? As opposed to what? *Dead* ones?

Atrocious grammar aside, something in that sign must be working. The owners promise potential patrons, "Hey, if you walk through these doors, you can see living, naked human bodies."

Ah, the body. Worshiped, desired, paraded, disdained, covered up, exposed, revealed, shaped, degraded — it's the world we live in, isn't it? I can't see without eyes, hug without arms, hear without ears, or pray without a mind. This physical reality, this *stuff*, this sack of flesh and bones and blood and water, allows me at present to be everything I am. At various times in various cultures, the body has been celebrated and disdained, in some seasons worshiped and in others blamed for all things evil.

What does it mean for a believer to live within a body? And how does the presence of God change the way I live in this body? Is it limited to issues of morality? Or could it go deeper than that?

Renewed Flesh

Jesus came to this earth in the flesh, and he left it in the flesh. Any spirituality that ignores the body ignores Christ.

Rooted in this world — in some cosmically mysterious way, a part of the world *he* created — Jesus' birth, resurrection, and ascension *in a body* calls us to live in this world as he did. In fact, becoming alive to Jesus makes us newly alive and even acutely sensitive to the world. We are invited to see with new eyes, hear with new ears, and feel with new hearts. It's as though Jesus tunes us into the world's real frequency; the static stops, and true understanding begins.

Relatively few of us, however, see the world as Francis of Assisi or Perpetua did, or more important, as Jesus would have us see and experience it. We can quickly become spiritual lepers, deadened by the distractions that surround us. The apostle Peter promises us that through Christ we "may participate in the divine nature and escape the corruption in the world caused by evil desires" (2 Peter 1:4).

In the Greek text, the grammar has us escaping the corruption of the world *as a precursor* to participating in the divine nature; that is, "we may participate in the divine nature, having escaped the corruption in the world caused by evil desires." Sin has transformational consequences — it squelches God's work within us. In fact, one commentator's definition of this "corruption" is "the disintegrating power of evil."[1] That's a remarkable image.

Sin does indeed blind our eyes, anesthetize our spiritual senses, and lead us into many destructive illusions. As sin begins to creep into more and more parts of our lives, we grow increasingly deadened to God, as well as to the world he created. We stop seeing women as "people," for example, and instead start seeing them as "live nudes." As the disintegrating power of evil takes over, our lives become smaller, more self-absorbed, more trivial, and less like Christ's.

But as we are made alive in Christ and gain release from this corrupting influence, becoming participators in the divine nature through the uniting work of the Holy Spirit, a marvelous transformation takes place. Formerly wasted and even pathetic lives can become *compelling*.

The gospel of Mark captures an extraordinary moment in the life of Jesus: "People were overwhelmed with amazement.... 'He even makes the deaf hear and the mute speak'" (Mark 7:37). What God did through Jesus, physically reclaiming eyesight and hearing and the ability to walk, he now through the Holy Spirit wants to do to us spiritually, namely, sensitize our bodies and tune them in to the true realities of life, helping us to escape "the disintegrating power of evil" as it works its way through our members.

Nobody, of course, is going to be "overwhelmed with amazement" merely because we stop doing certain offensive things (though the "escaping" is still an important part of yielding to God's transformation). I may not walk into a place that advertises "live nudes," but do I look at women through the eyes of God? Do I listen to them and hear them as God hears them? Do I think about them as God thinks about them? And do I speak of them as God would have me speak of them? Have I surrendered the members of my body to become servants of the risen and ascended Christ, instruments of his purpose, sanctified through his continuing presence?

A man who refrains from lust but who looks at women with condescension and disrespect is not a godly man. His corruption may be of a different color from the corruption of the one who undresses women in his mind, but he certainly can't live a compelling life. Why not? Because he hasn't learned what it is to truly *love*.

When we start blessing others with heavenly splashes of glory — when our eyes begin seeing with compassion and our mouths begin speaking words of encouragement; when our hands reach out to heal instead of hurt and our feet take us to places where there is need; when our minds plumb the mysteries of heaven and our hearts open up toward all — then God's splendor breaks forth in a powerful way that may at times lead to overwhelming amazement.

God Oases

As far back as the book of Isaiah, God prophesied this transformational process. Listen to this glorious picture from Isaiah 32:2:

> Each man will be like a shelter from the wind
>   and a refuge from the storm,
> like streams of water in the desert
>   and the shadow of a great rock in a thirsty land.

Let's pause for just a moment. Notice the power of these lives. A holy man or woman is a spiritual force, a "God oasis," in a world that needs spiritually strong people. When the winds of turmoil hit, such people become shelters; their faith provides a covering for all. By their words and actions, by the ways they listen and use their eyes to love instead of lust, to honor instead of hate, to build up instead of tear down, holy women and men are like streams of water in the desert, affirming what God values most. When the heat of temptation threatens to tear this world apart, godly men and women become like the shadow of a great rock. These God oases carry Christ to the hurting, to the ignorant, to those in need. They *will* be sought out — and they *will* have something to say.

Now contrast the power of these lives with those they are called to influence. What difference do they make? What happens when people find their way to these God oases?

> Then the eyes of those who see will no longer be closed,
>> and the ears of those who hear will listen.
> The mind of the rash will know and understand,
>> and the stammering tongue will be fluent and clear.
>
> Isaiah 32:3–4

Isaiah mesmerizes the people of God with a picture of a new seeing, a new hearing, a new feeling, and a new understanding — bodies completely transformed into the service of the King.

This message of transformation gets artfully woven throughout the tapestry of Scripture. Consider Ezekiel's record of the Lord's words to the Israelites (and to us today): "I [the LORD] will cleanse you from all your impurities and from all your idols. I will give you a new heart and put a new spirit in you; I will remove from you your heart of stone and give you a heart of flesh" (Ezekiel 36:25–26).

Jesus came in the flesh to demonstrate how glorious and powerful a fleshly person can be. He spoke words no one had ever heard before. His hands brought healing never before seen. His heart beat for those so often maligned and ignored, and his seemingly untrained mind demonstrated insight no schooled Pharisee could match.

He came as a visible representation of the divine image (see Hebrews 1:3), of what God in a body looks like. Only the corruption of the world kept many from seeing him in his veiled glory. The spiritual lepers of his day remained so blinded by their religious and nonreligious idols that they missed the God-man, even as he taught, performed miracles, and intellectually trumped them with a wisdom that ached for recognition.

Jesus patiently explained all this to his disciples:

> "Though seeing, they do not see;
>> though hearing, they do not hear or understand.

In them is fulfilled the prophecy of Isaiah:

> "'You will be ever hearing but never understanding;
>   you will be ever seeing but never perceiving.
> For this people's heart has become calloused;
>   they hardly hear with their ears,
>   and they have closed their eyes.
> Otherwise they might see with their eyes,
>   hear with their ears,
>   understand with their hearts
> and turn, and I would heal them.'
>
> But blessed are your eyes because they see, and your ears because they hear."

Matthew 13:13–16

It was in this context that Jesus called the Pharisees "blind guides" (Matthew 23:16).

After Jesus died and bodily ascended into heaven, he poured out his Spirit at Pentecost (see Acts 2) — and the bodies of his disciples became participators in the divine nature. They began seeing as they had never seen before; they could feel what they had never felt before. Their minds reached levels of wisdom never before reached.

This great Pentecost was marked, quite significantly, with the releasing of new *tongues*. The tongue is a rather pedestrian part of our body, a decidedly unglamorous piece of flesh, but suddenly, empowered by Christ, that simple tongue could now do something it had never been able to do before — speak in a language the speaker had never learned. It was a relatively "safe" part of the body for God to choose. Who would worship a tongue? How silly to define a faith by such utterances! But these awakened tongues pointed far beyond hidden or unknown languages. They revealed the unfolding of a new existence for God's children, including the reality of how God's presence would transform every part of our bodies and then enlist each part in his kingdom work.

A Profound Transformation

We simply must realize the full-bodied transformation that the early apostles preached. In fact, when the Jewish religious leaders in Rome ultimately rejected the apostle Paul's preaching of Christ (Acts 28:24–25), Paul used the very same passage to scold them that Jesus used (Isaiah 6:9–10):

> "The Holy Spirit spoke the truth to your forefathers when he said through Isaiah the prophet:
>
> "'Go to this people and say,
> "You will be ever hearing but never understanding;
>   you will be ever seeing but never perceiving."
> For this people's heart has become calloused;
>   they hardly hear with their ears,
>   and they have closed their eyes.
> Otherwise they might see with their eyes,
>   hear with their ears,
>   understand with their hearts
> and turn, and I would heal them.'"
>
> Acts 28:25–27

Isaiah and Ezekiel prophesied it; Jesus fulfilled it; and Paul preached it. This historic but new faith, this old/new truth, *must* change the way we see, hear, feel, and think.

The challenge continues today. The hallmark of Christianity, now as ever, is the transformation into a new and far more compelling person: "Therefore, I urge you, brothers, in view of God's mercy, to offer *your bodies* as living sacrifices, holy and pleasing to God — this is your spiritual act of worship" (Romans 12:1, emphasis added).

The "spiritual act of worship" is not just singing songs. It is a total offering of who we are. Renowned New Testament scholar C. E. B. Cranfield wrote, "The Christian, already God's by right of creation and by right of redemption, has yet again to become God's by virtue of his own free surrender of himself. And this self-surrender has, of course, to be continually repeated."[2]

How do I worship God? By continually surrendering the members of my body to become his servants and his instruments of peace. It's a worship that goes far beyond singing choruses or trying to obey a few moral laws; it speaks of a profound transformation. To live under the idols of our age — whether pride, greed, narcissism, or lust — is ultimately to live under a perpetual illusion. Worse, we become unaware of how blind, how deaf, and how shockingly insensitive we have become.

The surprising message of the incarnation — and later of Christ's ascension — is this: "Don't try to escape the world, but rather go deeper *into* the world. See it as you have never seen it. See it with God's eyes. Hear it with God's ears. Feel it with God's heart. Think about it with God's mind."

Jesus asks us the same question he asked his disciples: "Do you have eyes but fail to see, and ears but fail to hear?" (Mark 8:18).

Are you ready for some fresh splashes of God's glory in your life? Will you let go of what you've been and embrace what Christ is calling you to become? Are you willing to escape the corruption of evil desires, "the disintegrating power of evil," so that you can more fully experience God's transforming presence?

You may be asking, "But what does all this talk of transformation mean *practically*?" The next section is designed to answer this very question. We're going to explore a biblical view of transformation that takes us far beyond mere morality to embrace the incarnation and ascension of Christ as he lives through us in *very* practical ways.

∞ **Looking Back** ∞

- Any true Christian spirituality must address a "full-bodied faith," seen in the way God's presence transforms our members.

- Habitual sin blinds our eyes, deadens our spiritual hearing, and desensitizes us to God's work in the world.

- By allowing God to transform us, we can become "oases of God" in a hurting world.

- Our "spiritual act of worship" is demonstrated by continually surrendering the members of our bodies to become God's servants and his instruments of peace.

Part 2

New Spirit, New Bodies

Give of your hands to serve and your hearts to love.
Mother Teresa of Calcutta

It is all-important that we know the glory of Jesus. The more the soul is filled with that glory, and worships [Jesus] in it, the more it will see with what confidence it can count upon him to do a divine and supernatural work in us, and to lead us to an actual living fellowship with God as our Father.
Andrew Murray

Just as you used to offer the parts of your body in slavery to impurity and to ever-increasing wickedness, so now offer them in slavery to righteousness leading to holiness.
Paul, in Romans 6:19

Chapter 5

Eyes That See

His worst trouble is blindness, for he cannot see all this. Then the whole love of God Almighty ... gives him eyes to see himself.

Julian of Norwich

Disregard the study of God, and you sentence yourself to stumble and blunder through life blindfolded, as it were, with no sense of direction and no understanding of what surrounds you. This way you can waste your life and lose your soul.

J. I. Packer

"I have come to judge the world. I have come to give sight to the blind and to show those who think they see that they are blind."

Jesus, in John 9:39 NLT

It was one of those days that looked to be individually and particularly painted by God. Though South Bend, Indiana, had descended into the throes of November, the weather hovered in the low sixties. "Touchdown Jesus" — the gigantic artwork of Christ emblazoned on Notre Dame's library, overlooking the football stadium — loomed large to my right, while the Navy Midshipmen bounced up and down to my left. Rick Callahan, a friend of mine and pastor at the nearby River Valley Community Church, sat next to me. Notre Dame Stadium really doesn't have a bad seat, but we were doubly blessed, sitting near the forty-yard line.

My mind wandered back to a testimony I heard once while leading a Sacred Marriage conference in Arizona. Pastor Randy and Janet Murphy offered a moving account of God's grace and healing in their marriage, and in the midst of their story, they recounted the words of a counselor who reminded them that, apart from Christ's work, we all deserve hell. Not off in the future, but *right now*, at this very moment, we've all qualified for eternal judgment.

"So if it's true that we all deserve hell," Randy's counselor had said, "then isn't it also true that anything less than that is a pretty good day?"

I remember sitting in Notre Dame Stadium — with the sun politely keeping me warm but hospitably not making me hot, with the energy of the students providing more than enough enthusiasm for everyone within ten miles of the stadium, with the beauty of Notre Dame's campus satisfying my soul, with the drama of the football game below me — and thinking, I deserve hell, and I get to experience a day like *this*?

When we look at life through God's eyes, we become lost in wonder and convinced of God's astounding generosity, his marvelous mercy, and his gigantic grace. Sin causes us to look at life through the lens of entitlement — that we deserve salvation without repentance, wealth without work, accolades without self-denial, health without personal discipline, pleasure without sacrifice. Biblical truth reminds us that, in reality, we deserve hell. Because of Adam's and our own sin, we deserve "painful toil" all the days of our lives, eating food only by the "sweat of [our] brow" (Genesis 3:17, 19), and an eternity separated from the God against whom we have arrogantly rebelled.

Every small laugh, each tiny expression of joy, a simple meal — any momentary reprieve from the ongoing agony of hell — truly is an undeserved gift. When we add the assurance that the completed work of Christ guards our eternity, our lives should radiate not merely joy (though there should be an abundance of that) but wonder and astonishment at how good God truly is.

And yet why do so many believers live without this joy? Why do so many walk without this sense of wonder and live in heaviness of heart instead of lightness of spirit?

Perhaps it's because we don't view our reality through God's eyes.

Our spiritual lens has become clouded, and as a result we can't respond with God's heart. Jesus said, "The eye is the lamp of the body. If your eyes are good, your whole body will be full of light. But if your eyes are bad, your whole body will be full of darkness" (Matthew 6:22–23). Clearly, Jesus isn't referring here to our corneas. He doesn't have in mind glaucoma or astigmatism. He's saying, "If your spiritual eyes are dim, then your whole body will be bathed in spiritual darkness." It makes sense, doesn't it? If we don't see ourselves as God sees us, or if we don't see others as God sees others, reality becomes a stranger and perception grows dim. We'll tend to discount his mercy, dismiss his goodness, overlook his kindness, and maybe even question his love and care.

The apostle Paul realized that we need to have our eyes opened spiritually: "I pray also that the eyes of your heart may be enlightened in order that you may know the hope to which he has called you, the riches of his glorious inheritance in the saints, and his incomparably great power for us who believe" (Ephesians 1:18–19).

So what does it mean to see with the eyes of God?

God Is Not Easily Impressed

As our plane ascended out of San Antonio, it passed an enclave of mansions. These homes had to contain at least seven to ten thousand square feet of space, with immaculate lawns and gardens, large pools, and huge garages. But from two thousand feet in the air, it's amazing how small these homes looked. Another few thousand feet, and they became mere playhouses.

And then it hit me: not a home on this planet looks big to heaven; no house looks huge to God. The things that swell our chests with pride look mighty puny from another perspective.

We can't impress God.

And so I prayed, "Lord, help me to see this world with your eyes. Otherwise I might value what you despise and despise what you value."

It dawned on me that I was praying the prayer of St. Francis's conversion, the prayer that led him ultimately to reject his wealth and kiss the lepers. Most of us, however, don't win our spiritual sight in a moment; it comes or goes in fractional increments. By aligning ourselves with supernatural vision, we can keep ourselves from slipping away.

That's what the psalmist experienced when he testified that his "feet had almost slipped" (Psalm 73:2). He began envying the arrogant — perhaps, like me, he had passed some of those ten-thousand-square-foot mansions and wondered what it would be like to cool off in such a picture-perfect pool. He took notice that the inhabitants of those dwellings had no particular belief in God, and he said what many of us have probably wondered from time to time: "Surely in vain have I kept my heart pure; in vain have I washed my hands in innocence" (verse 13).

But then the psalmist changed his point of reference. He couldn't hop on an airplane, but he did something even more effective: "I entered the sanctuary of God; then I understood their final destiny" (verse 17). When he entered God's house, the psalmist's eyes were opened and he understood the riches that surrounded him: "Whom have I in heaven but you? And earth has nothing I desire besides you" (verse 25).

Regaining God's perspective — refocusing our spiritual eyesight — is one of the greatest blessings of the believer. It changes *everything*. If we don't consciously take a step back and adjust our vision, we'll live under a perpetual cloud of illusion. This is a conscious, meditative turning, a determined effort to set our sights on what really matters.

Will you pause for just a moment and consider where your eyesight may be growing dim? Are you blinded to God's daily blessings because you're too focused on financial concerns, health issues, or frustrated relationships? Have you stopped seeing people as important and instead stare persistently at possessions, power, and pleasure? Are your eyes so preoccupied by your comfort that they have grown too tired to look at your life and your circumstances from God's perspective?

Jesus said, "For judgment I have come into this world, so that the blind will see and those who see will become blind" (John 9:39). When people met Jesus, that's exactly what happened — some who claimed to see revealed their blindness, while others who really were blind received true sight. Clear perception and discernment are gifts that come from being united with Christ.

Sometimes, in answer to prayer, God does change our situation. He heals us, restores us, provides for us, and protects us. But just as often, instead of changing the situation, he chooses to change our perception: "You're looking at this entirely the wrong way." He'll allow the frustration to remain so that he can cure us of our spiritual nearsightedness.

Have you ever offered your eyes to God? Have you ever asked him to pour his wisdom into your perception, his perspective into each gaze? Have you ever stepped back and prayed, "God, how does this look to *you?*"

If you do, you'll never look at others the same way again.

True Saints

I remember walking through Chicago's O'Hare Airport and falling into what is probably the closest I'll ever come to a true mystical moment. People were everywhere, talking on their cell phones, getting something to eat, typing on their laptops, waiting in line to board. I saw these people as faceless obstacles, making my trip to the next gate complicated and time-consuming.

But then, almost as if a shadow passed over me, it was as though I could see them as God sees them — real individuals with real concerns — *and God's heart was beating for every single one of them.* I "saw" a glimpse of how involved God is in every life, even when those lives ignore him.

At that moment, the "F" terminal of the Chicago airport suddenly morphed into a sanctuary, a holy place of possibility. I didn't see job titles, expensive jewelry, business success, or power. I just saw people — some alienated from God, others knowing him but not relating to him much, still others actively open to hearing his voice. What I saw were just *people*, without all the trappings — and what defined them beyond anything else was how they relate (or don't relate) to God.

This experience faded by the time I reached the Starbucks just outside the security area, but it shook me up for a good hour. God really *does* care; God really *is* involved, even when we don't acknowledge him.

This perspective, I believe, is the mark of a true saint. Saints are not just people who had a particular experience at a particular moment (as I did), but people who live with God's eyesight. They can look past someone's beauty, fame, power — or lack thereof — and see that person as important to our heavenly Father. True Christian eyesight is about seeing others with the eyes of God — noticing the unnoticed, not being distracted by what the world considers important, caring about those we once would have gladly looked past. Saints have the spiritual ability to care for both victim *and* persecutor; they feel genuinely concerned about each individual, like our God, "not wanting anyone to perish" (2 Peter 3:9).

Without God's eyes, people become invisible to me. The guy shining my shoes at the airport, the woman cleaning up my hotel room, the cashier at the grocery store, the police officer directing traffic in the rain — my human heart has little room for the barely seen. Not God's! His heart overflows with concern for their welfare, and he wants to pass on to us this same concern and compassion.

The experience of compassion is such a beautiful thing in the New Testament. Consider how many times we're told that Jesus demonstrated this attitude. Here's a small sampling:

- "When [Jesus] saw the crowds, he had compassion on them" (Matthew 9:36).
- "When Jesus landed and saw a large crowd, he had compassion on them" (Matthew 14:14).
- "Jesus called his disciples to him and said, 'I have compassion for these people'" (Matthew 15:32).
- "Filled with compassion, Jesus reached out his hand and touched the man" (Mark 1:41).

It's not enough to see someone and refrain from hating him. It's not sufficient to abstain from lust, prejudice, or disdain. The mere moralist says, "Do not lust." Fair enough. I *shouldn't* lust. But is "not doing something" a sufficient goal for God's children? Absolutely not! That's the legalist's trap. The gospel of transformation calls me to progress from not lusting to having eyes that honor, respect, and generate compassion. God wants to transform my eyes from being selfish possessors and consumers to being his servants of selfless love.

Mirror, Mirror, on the Wall

A businessman in a service industry grew weary of being yelled at. He tired of getting sprayed with angry spittle from dissatisfied customers who expected five-star service at Motel 6 prices. One day, he became oddly detached during yet another customer tirade; he felt as though he were watching a movie. In fact, he couldn't help but think that the angry woman's antics made her look like a monkey.

That observation gave him a brilliant idea. He posted a giant mirror behind the front desk — and the customer tirades all but ceased. When people saw how rude and hateful they looked while yelling and screaming, they stopped yelling and screaming.

What is true physically is also true spiritually. Prayer provides a mirror for our attitudes. Through it, we begin to see our motives from a different perspective.

This renewed eyesight — the gift of seeing people and situations from heaven's vantage point — needs to begin at home. In the Sacred Marriage seminars I give, I mention that for married believers, God is our spiritual Father-*in-law*. When I realized I was married to *God's* daughter, everything changed about the way I viewed marriage. It was no longer about just me and one other person; it was very much a relationship with a passionately interested third partner.

Most of us fail to grasp just how fully God loves the person to whom we are married. As the father of three children, I fervently pray that each one will marry a spouse who will love them generously, respect them, and enjoy them. I realize that each of my children has certain quirks or limitations that may test a future spouse's patience, but I pray that their spouses will be kind in these areas rather than use them to belittle my children. I hope with all my heart that each will find a partner who will encourage them with a gracious spirit. I pray they won't marry someone who will demean them and thus magnify their weaknesses, casting a climate of shame. I know my kids aren't perfect — but I want them to have spouses who will love them despite their imperfections.

In the same way, God is fully aware of our spouses' limitations — and he is just as eager for us to be kind and generous with these faults as we are for our kids' future spouses to be kind to them. By looking at my spouse through God's eyes, I invite God into my marriage.

I often see a light go on in attendees' eyes as we talk about this. Many will say that this was one of the most helpful analogies they've ever heard — even though, for a Christian, this should be Marriage 101, a basic, fundamental truth. Their surprise tells me that we tend to have a hard time effectively connecting our faith to our reality. We tend not to look at our spouses through the eyes of God.

When I look at my wife through the eyes of a loving father, I find the motivation to care for her and be gentle, tender, and nurturing with her. When I view her through my own human, sinful, husband's eyes, my sight may be distorted by expectations, disappointments, and various frustrations over the way her quirks and limitations adversely affect my comfort, happiness, and security.

Christian marriage is a journey of maintaining God-sight and cultivating God's heart for my spouse, for my kids, for our family. If it's true that I deserve hell at this very moment (and it is), then I'm going to be grateful for the good times we share and patient with the difficulties of domestic life. When I think of the grace God has shown to me — how much he has forgiven me, how mercifully he has treated me, how generously he has blessed me — how could I even think about abandoning or discarding one of his children because they don't please me at any given moment?

God-sight thus begins with humility — I deserve hell, but God has chosen to spare me — and then gets seasoned by gratitude, shaped by awe, and maintained by reverence. Because of what God has done for me, I cannot ever look at others in quite the same way I once did.

Foresight

God-sight does not stop at avoiding negative thinking however. It goes far beyond to include seeing the blessings God has in store for his people. If we see only with human eyes, we will quickly lose hope in the face of our sin and the tragedies of this fallen world.

Remember Paul's prayer — that the eyes of our hearts may be enlightened so that we may know the hope to which God has called us, including "his incomparably great power for us who believe" (Ephesians 1:19)? God-sight gives us fresh hope and beautiful glimpses of what is possible through God.

Moses' parents "hid him for three months after he was born, because they saw he was no ordinary child, and they were not afraid of the king's edict" (Hebrews 11:23). Moses' parents *saw* God's call on this baby's life; they opened up their minds to a brighter future than that of an indentured slave. As parents, we are invited to do the same.

You may consider yourself poor or disadvantaged intellectually, but it's unlikely that your child was born into an environment marked by centuries of slavery. Will you see with the eyes of Moses' parents, who believed that God could create and then guide a powerful life — even one born in squalor?

Human eyes can be blinded by fear, pessimism, shame, or despair. God-empowered eyes can look past all of that and see "no ordinary" future. When was the last time you consciously quieted your heart long enough to look at your children's future through God's eyes? Are you holding them back because of your spiritual blindness, or are you launching them into the adventure of God's empowering presence?

Or what about a coworker or fellow church member who seems mired in destructive living? If we look at people only through human eyes, we see little hope (and usually a lot of cynicism). But when we see God standing behind someone and see God *in* someone, hope becomes more than wishful thinking; it morphs into a wise choice based on the historical reality of God's changing people from the inside out.

God-sight gives me the ability to see hope for people when they see none for themselves. God-sight allows me to see a purpose for those trapped in triviality. God-sight helps me to confidently proclaim the availability of God's power to those who define themselves only as helpless victims or addicts. When we cooperate with God as he works to transform us into Christ's image, we can become God's eyes for those too blind to see clearly for themselves.

God's Eyes: God's Woman

A friend of mine learned to look through God's eyes in the midst of an extremely intense temptation. He had traveled to another city to conduct a business seminar. After the sessions, an attractive young woman knocked on his hotel room door. The woman worked for the company that had hired my friend, and when he opened the door, she pushed through and walked right into the room.

"You can't be in here," he protested.

"Why not?" she asked teasingly. "Are you scared?"

Then she acted as if she were going to remove her shirt. My friend kept the room door open and said, "Listen, you really need to leave."

The woman started talking and acting seductively. She made it very clear that she was available for any sexual favor of his choosing. When he insisted that she leave, she finally did something I'll not recount because I don't want to put the image in anyone's mind; but it was over-the-top provocative.

Immediately afterward, my friend wisely told two business associates exactly what had happened. He explained everything in detail, lest there ever be any doubt as to what had occurred.

My friend is godly, but he's human. He admits he slept very little that night as lingering visions of the encounter plagued him. He couldn't get this woman's words or the related images out of his mind. He tossed and turned, thankful he hadn't fallen but exhausted from being so provoked.

Two months later, he returned to that city, working with the same company he had worked with on his previous visit — when the provocative young woman pulled him aside.

"We have to talk," she said.

My friend's heart started racing as he feared the worst. Would she make a false accusation? Would she try to spin what had happened, making him sound like the bad guy? Her first words put him at ease.

"I can't thank you enough for being the first man who has ever cared about me more than about my breasts."

My friend learned that this woman had been abused earlier in life. She had been promiscuous ever since her early teen years, and because of her physical appearance, *no* man had ever been willing to walk away from her advances. And so she kept reliving the moments of her deepest hurt.

"I'm going back to church," she told him. "I need to get my life back together. When I finally met a man like you who was more interested in me than in my body, it showed me how messed up I had become."

Because of the way she dressed, acted, and talked, this woman was a sex object in the eyes of most men. But one man dared to look at her through God's eyes — seeing a spiritually injured soul acting out her hurt. By treating her appropriately, he helped open her eyes, brought her out of denial, and put her back on the pathway to God.

A man or woman blinded by the idol of lust sees another person as an object of conquest, a prize to be won, a selfish pleasure to be enjoyed. A believer who looks at a hurting soul with the eyes of tender mercy and compassionate grace is able to rise above his or her worst inclinations and offer an incalculable gift — genuine reality, true perception, absolute truth.

How can you look with God's eyes at a man or woman and still dehumanize him or her? You can't.

How can you dangerously rush through a neighborhood or parking lot, driving recklessly, putting God's children at risk, when you're looking at the world through God's eyes? You can't.

How could you sell someone drugs, steal someone's money, destroy someone's marriage or family, or demolish someone's reputation when you look at the potential victim through the eyes of a heavenly Father who is passionate about their welfare? You can't.

Most sin is born out of spiritual blindness — shown in a vast, ugly forgetfulness of God.

Transformed Sight

The first sin sprang, in part, from the allure of sight: "When the woman *saw* that the fruit of the tree was good for food and *pleasing to the eye,* ... she took some and ate it" (Genesis 3:6, emphasis added). Eve allowed her physical eyesight to foment rebellion against God's commands.

The rest of Scripture chronicles a search for "the oracle of one whose eye sees clearly" (Numbers 24:3). God's sight is the only sight that matters. The Israelites are warned to "listen carefully to the voice of the LORD your God and do what is right *in his eyes*" (Exodus 15:26, emphasis added). God warns Moses to tell the Israelites to "not prostitute yourselves by going after the lusts of your own hearts and eyes" (Numbers 15:39). Why? Because our lusts blind us: "A bribe blinds the eyes of the wise" (Deuteronomy 16:19). We end up as pitiful creatures: "Like the blind we grope along the wall, feeling our way like men without eyes" (Isaiah 59:10).

So what can we do, as believers, to receive transformed sight?

1. Ask God to Give You Light

God-sight is a God-gift. We depend on God for his mercy to give us what we lack: "Open my eyes that I may see wonderful things in your law" (Psalm 119:18). Begin praying with the psalmist, "Look on me and answer, O LORD my God. Give light to my eyes, or I will sleep in death" (Psalm 13:3).

This is a simple verse to memorize and a prayer worth praying every day. You might want to personalize it a bit, perhaps like this: "God, help me to see. Give light to my eyes. Overcome my blindness, lest I fall asleep to your ways."

As part of your daily worship and as an act of self-offering, plead with God to graciously give light to your eyes.

2. Make a Covenant with Your Eyes

Job said, "I made a covenant with my eyes not to look lustfully at a girl" (Job 31:1). The psalmist likewise made a strong commitment: "I will set before my eyes no vile thing" (Psalm 101:3). If our eyes belong to God, if we want to see with *his* eyes, then we need to accept the truth that God will turn away from some things — and so should we. Christianity gives us many, many things; but it also takes away some things. What we are willing to allow ourselves to look at is one of those things.

Remember, however, that we're talking about God-empowered living in the light of Christ's ascension. I'm not suggesting you go back to relying on your own willpower. The psalmist makes this aim a prayer: "Turn my eyes away from worthless things" (Psalm 119:37). When talking to a man who visited strip clubs, I encouraged him to ask God to help him see the young women as the objects of God's affection, as well as to see the harm the women are doing to their souls by working in such a profession. "Look at the strip club as God looks at it," I said, "and then see if it's really so inviting." He was rightly concerned about what visiting the strip club was doing to *him*; yet I also wanted him to see what supporting a strip club was doing to the *young women* being exploited.

Earlier in my life, I worked with a bully. I began praying that God would help me see the insecurity behind his bravado. My temptation is always to look at what someone is doing to me. God-sight is about being less self-obsessed and learning to see the situation as God sees it, in its totality. Yes, God loves me and doesn't want me to be tyrannized — but he also loves the bully and wants him to repent.

In an attitude of humble reliance, pray the prayer of Saint Francis: "Lord, all those things that I have loved after the flesh, make me now despise, and from those things that I formerly loathed, let me drink great sweetness and immeasurable delight."

The brilliance of this prayer is that it goes beyond a mere avoidance of evil to embrace the *positive, transformative* call of compassionate seeing. Make a covenant with God, offering your eyes to be his servants, to notice the discouraged, to have compassion on the poor and hungry, to see what God wants you to see through his eyes. What you once saw as beautiful you may now see as hideous; what you once loathed may now be awe-inspiringly gorgeous.

3. Train Your Eyes

The psalmist says that Scripture can help us train our eyes: "The commands of the LORD are radiant, giving light to the eyes" (Psalm 19:8). Disobedience threatens to lead us into further spiritual darkness. Through increased familiarity with *all* of Scripture, we can train our minds to think more like Christ; by choosing obedience, we can train our wills to submit to God's will so that we can see more clearly.

While we depend totally on God's empowerment, training also involves a conscious act of the will. Solomon tells us, "Let your eyes look straight ahead, fix your gaze directly before you" (Proverbs 4:25). This is clearly a call to discipline ourselves, to accept and submit to God's power within us, to direct where we allow our eyes to roam. The person "who will dwell on the heights" is one who "shuts his eyes against *contemplating* evil" (Isaiah 33:15–16, emphasis added), whereas "a fool's eyes wander to the ends of the earth" (Proverbs 17:24).

To say there is no human effort here is to deny many scriptural exhortations, for example, "Let us fix our eyes on Jesus, the author and perfecter of our faith" (Hebrews 12:2), and, "Whatever is true, whatever is noble, whatever is right, whatever is pure, whatever is lovely, whatever is admirable — if anything is excellent or praiseworthy — think about such things" (Philippians 4:8).

Spiritual blindness may be caused in part by disobedience, but it can also result from *undisciplined laziness*. So Paul exhorts the Corinthians, "We fix our eyes not on what is seen, but on what is unseen. For what is seen is temporary, but what is unseen is eternal" (2 Corinthians 4:18). Passivity in this regard does not honor God; on the contrary, it dishonors his work by keeping us mired in a murky, spiritual twilight.

4. Worship with Your Eyes

Ultimately, only one object is worthy of our clearest vision, namely, the glory of God: "My eyes are fixed on you, O Sovereign LORD" (Psalm 141:8). Our worship must be not only with our tongues but also with our eyes as we consciously fix our sight on the majesty and glory of God. This is the deepest search in every human heart — "The eyes of all look to [the LORD]" (Psalm 145:15) — as well as the fulfillment of history — "In that day men will look to their Maker and turn their eyes to the Holy One of Israel" (Isaiah 17:7).

Worship is a conscious decision: "Lift your eyes and look to the heavens" (Isaiah 40:26). As we do this, we embark on a wonderful cycle of transformation. The more clearly we see, the more faithfully we will obey. The more we obey, the more clearly we will see, and — over time — the more deeply we will mirror the spirit and life and character of Christ.

It all begins with the eyes.

Father God, please transform my eyes from being selfish consumers of personal pleasure, and sanctify them to be your servants of glory. Let them settle on what is pure and true and good, and make them want to turn from whatever is vile. Help me to see with your concern, and awaken me to your perception. I offer my eyes to you as your servants; take them, use them, transform them, for your glory. In Jesus' name. Amen.

❧ Looking Back ❧

- When we remember that we deserve hell, with all of its torments, we are able to "see" God's kindness even in the midst of our present disappointments.

- Through a conscious, meditative turning and a determined effort, we need to consistently reset our eyes to gain *God's* perspective.

- Sometimes God answers our prayers by changing our *perception* instead of our circumstances.

- The gospel of transformation calls us to progress from not lusting to having eyes that honor, respect, and generate compassion. God wants to transform our eyes from being selfish possessors and consumers to being his servants of selfless love.

- Christian family life is a journey of maintaining God-sight and cultivating God's heart for our spouses, our kids, and our families.

- God-sight gives us foresight — the ability to see a better future for those who, apart from God, have no reason to hope.

- Most sin is born out of spiritual blindness — a vast, ugly forgetfulness of God — in which we stop seeing others as God sees them.

- We can cooperate with God to develop God-sight by asking him to give us light, making a covenant with our eyes, beginning to train our eyes, and learning to worship with our eyes.

Chapter 6

Mouths That Speak

*If we are so impoverished that we have nothing to reveal but small talk,
then we need to struggle for more richness of soul.*

Frank Laubach

*O LORD, open my lips,
    and my mouth will declare your praise.*

David, in Psalm 51:15

R. Somerset Ward, England's most famous spiritual director of the twentieth century, saw more than his share of celebrated sculpture throughout his lifetime, but one statue in particular stood out above them all "as a great reality ... a statue erected to the memory of Phillip Brooks, Bishop of Massachusetts, and it stands in the central square of Boston." The statue shows Brooks delivering a sermon. "With supreme art," the sculptor captured an attitude of sudden inspiration, as if in that very instant Brooks "will lean forward over the pulpit with a new power in his voice, which will compel the attention of his congregation, and carry conviction to their hearts."[1]

But even more compelling for our purposes is the spiritual drama that the sculptor captures by placing another figure behind the celebrated preacher. This artist apparently understood true Christian spirituality as well as he understood the art of crafting stone:

> And there behind the preacher in the shadow of the canopy
> stands a majestic figure of Christ, whose outstretched finger
> has rested for one moment on the shoulder of the bishop. It is
> a fine statue because it pictures an eternal truth. For wherever
> God uses human agents, he gives them his power, pours into
> them his life and illuminates them with his light. If men only

realized what it meant to be used as God's instrument, what supreme joy came from the least touch of his hand, there would be no lack of volunteers for his service.[2]

How we have ignored the spiritual drama that can be found by speaking God's words! By denying — or at least de-emphasizing — the power of transformative experience, how many zealous young teachers have we kept from the pulpit? It is exhausting and debilitating trying to make a favorable impression every Sunday; but it is exhilarating and energizing to be an instrument in the hands of such a supreme wordsmith as our Lord and Savior. And this is as true for those whose "pulpit" is a table at Starbucks, the boardroom, the commuting car, or a child's bedroom as it is for those who earn a living by speaking in church.

In a world bursting with communication, transformed speech proclaims God's empowering life.

Power in the Words

Perhaps because I never grew up around cursing, I never understood it. When I heard it spewed in public, I felt turned off by the ugly atmosphere it set. I saw nothing inviting about it. Frankly, I think someone who embeds a swearword in every sentence betrays a serious lack of education, imagination, and syntax. Nor am I one who thinks he needs to demonstrate his "liberation" by occasionally throwing in a swearword now and then, just to prove I'm no legalist. What's the point?

Yet refraining from profanity still belongs to the tired issues of mere moralism. When we talk to young people about their speech, 90 percent or more of our message is likely to focus on what they *shouldn't* say. How very sad, because it turns a dramatic truth — God can and will use your tongue to shape the world — into an exasperating prohibition: "This is the list of forbidden words. Memorize them, but never use them."

We like to focus on taming the tongue, but the Bible calls this a futile enterprise: "No man can tame the tongue" (James 3:8). What we desire is a *transformed* tongue.

The story of Balak, Balaam, and Balaam's donkey contains enough conundrums and fantastical elements to keep a commentator busy for months. But one truth emanating from this account is beyond dispute: words have great power.

Balak the king wants Balaam the seer to curse the Israelites, lest they "lick up everything around us, as an ox licks up the grass of the field" (Numbers 22:4). Inherent in this worldview is the strong belief that words do more than describe; they act. They change things. They have power that Jesus himself endorsed when he said, "I tell you the truth, if you have faith as small as a mustard seed, you can say to this mountain, 'Move from here to there' and it will move. Nothing will be impossible for you" (Matthew 17:20–21). Lest anyone still think Jesus discounted the power of speech, listen to this: "For by your words you will be acquitted, and by your words you will be condemned" (Matthew 12:37).

This is the power that Balak both craved and feared. He begged and bribed Balaam to curse Israel, because "I know that those you bless are blessed, and those you curse are cursed" (Numbers 22:6).

The biblical worldview takes words very seriously. When God called Jeremiah, he sanctified his mouth: "Then the LORD reached out his hand and *touched my mouth* and said to me, 'Now, I have put my words in your mouth'" (Jeremiah 1:9, emphasis added). By touching Jeremiah's mouth, God said, "Today I appoint you over nations and kingdoms to uproot and tear down, to destroy and overthrow, to build and to plant" (1:10). God never told Jeremiah to take up a sword or a backhoe; instead, his prophet-servant would accomplish all of this tearing down, destroying, overthrowing, building, and planting by *faithfully speaking God's words.*

When Isaiah saw God, his initial shame resided, interestingly enough, in his tongue: "'Woe to me!' I cried. 'I am ruined! For *I am a man of unclean lips, and I live among a people of unclean lips*, and my eyes have seen the King, the LORD Almighty'" (Isaiah 6:5, emphasis added). And what did God do about Isaiah's unclean lips? "Then one of the seraphs flew to me with a live coal in his hand, which he had taken with tongs from the altar. With it *he touched my mouth* and said,

'See, this has touched your lips; your guilt is taken away and your sin atoned for'" (6:6–7, emphasis added).

When God called Ezekiel, he said, "Son of man, stand up on your feet and *I will speak to you*" (Ezekiel 2:1, emphasis added). He told Ezekiel that his ministry would essentially be a ministry of words: "And whether they listen or fail to listen — for they are a rebellious house — they will know that a prophet has been among them" (2:5). God is adamant and forceful with Ezekiel: "You must speak my words to them" (2:7). He then prepares Ezekiel by asking him to open his mouth and "eat what is before you, eat this scroll; then go and speak to the house of Israel" (3:1). So Ezekiel opened his mouth, and the Lord "gave [him] the scroll to eat" (3:2).

Is it a coincidence that God calls the three major prophets — Isaiah, Jeremiah, and Ezekiel — by sanctifying their mouths? I don't think so. From a biblical perspective, words reveal the state of our hearts. That's what Jesus was getting at in Matthew 12:37 (quoted above) and in Matthew 15:1–20: *the mouth reveals what the heart conceals.*

It goes beyond this, however, especially with the prophets. There is a holy commissioning behind the power and force of what we say. Words can build up nations or destroy them. Churchill energized England with his fiery oratory, inspiring a beleaguered country to dig a little deeper and "never give up." At the same time, words fueled the hateful Nazi propaganda machine, leading Germany toward a horrific fate of self-destruction. Words can build up or destroy nations, families, churches, careers, or businesses.

Armed with this power, this potential, this force, we are invited by God to submit our tongues to speak the purifying, encouraging, convicting, challenging, soothing, and sometimes confrontational words of Christ. If we do not allow our tongues to be transformed, we risk unleashing great havoc on this earth: "A tiny spark can set a great forest on fire. And the tongue is a flame of fire. It is full of wickedness that can ruin your whole life. It can turn the entire course of your life into a blazing flame of destruction, for it is set on fire by hell itself" (James 3:5–6 NLT).

If we allow our tongues to become God's servants, there is no end to the good God can do through us. There is no limit to the encouragement he can unleash, the number of people he can turn from their sins, and the communities he can build.

The Wonderful Power of Words

God said, "Let there be light," and it was so (Genesis 1:3). God created with words. In fact, Jesus himself is described as "the Word": "In the beginning was the Word, and the Word was with God, and the Word was God" (John 1:1).

In a similar way, God can give his words to us to create, transform, and season. My wife and I will be forever grateful for a young woman in our life. Some years ago, she started a dance school that was rooted in Christian discipleship. Both of our daughters are avid dancers, so Lisa and I have often expressed our thankfulness for Maluhia's faithfulness and vision. She's exactly the type of young woman you want your daughters to hang around.

During one of my morning chai tea runs at Starbucks, I saw Maluhia talking to one of her students. I said, "Hi." When I returned to my office, I couldn't rest until I prayed for Maluhia. And then I felt compelled to write her a prayerful letter. It went like this:

Maluhia,

I'm so very grateful for the way God is using you in the lives of so many girls (and now a growing number of boys). You're a terrific example of someone who has embraced her gifts and who is using those gifts as a platform to help others fall ever deeper in love with Jesus. My wife and I thank God for you.

When I saw you at Starbucks this morning, it was a little reminder to me to pray for you. So when I came home and did just that, I kept getting this inkling that I'm rather hesitant to share, as I realize I could be totally and completely off base. But if I'm wrong, it won't be the first time, and you can throw this letter away.

The nature of someone who is having an impact is that they become a spiritual target. We serve an awesome God, but we also have a real spiritual enemy. And where I believe he may be planning to slowly pull back your influence is through your marriage. I'm not saying he's doing that now; I'm saying I think this may be his desire.

The way you love your husband, respect him, honor him, and live with him will be seen by so many future wives. The way you talk about him, the way they see you treat him, could have profound influence. So it only makes sense that this could be an area of attack.

Every marriage has seasons — the on-the-mountaintop seasons, the difficult seasons, and even just the tired seasons — where two people can slowly drift from each other without even knowing it. I obviously don't have any idea what season your marriage is in, but as a brother I encourage you to continue to move toward your husband, to pray to God about your heart for him, and to ask God to renew your love and devotion. You may already feel like you're completely there, in which case I'd just encourage you to ask God to maintain and sustain that relationship to protect it from future attack. I pray that you and Kurt will grow ever closer toward God and toward each other.

To that end, I'm enclosing a little devotional that came out earlier this year. You may find a couple of entries helpful as you walk this life with Kurt. Have a wonderful Christmas holiday!

The peace of Christ,
Gary Thomas

I always send such letters with more than a little trepidation; what right do I have to speak such personal words into someone's life? But so often — as in this case — the result was overwhelmingly positive. Maluhia told me that God used the letter to spawn several more conversations about her marriage. A month or so later, I listened at the end of a recital as Maluhia gave a glowing tribute to her husband. Even more, I watched the faces of the girls as they listened to Maluhia speak, and I knew that God truly had spoken.

God is speaking. And he will speak. And many times, he speaks even through us: "The words of the wicked are like a murderous ambush, but the words of the godly save lives" (Proverbs 12:6 NLT).

I can't begin to count the number of emails, letters, and personal comments I've received in response to the three marriage books I've written.[3] Public ministry can be a wonderful thing, but there's a certain joy in private, quiet ministry that public ministry never approaches. Speaking the right word at the right time becomes a truly holy moment, inducing awe and wonder.

Will you allow the ascended Christ to use your tongue to encourage, instruct, and occasionally confront others?

Moses' Mouth Remade

Moses demonstrates what happens when an ordinary person allows an extraordinary God to change the way he speaks, thinks, sees, and feels.

When God first tells Moses he's sending him back to the Egyptians to free the Israelites, Moses protests, "O Lord, I have never been eloquent, neither in the past nor since you have spoken to your servant. I am slow of speech and tongue" (Exodus 4:10). On another occasion, Moses complains, "Why would Pharaoh listen to me, since I speak with faltering lips?" (6:12). Moses goes on to repeat virtually the same objection: "Since I speak with faltering lips, why would Pharaoh listen to me?" (6:30). When something gets repeated *three times* like this, it's significant. Clearly, Moses views himself as a pathetically incompetent speaker.

God responds to Moses' original protest with what is essentially the thesis of the book you now hold in your hands: "The LORD said to him, 'Who gave man his mouth? Who makes him deaf or mute? Who gives him sight or makes him blind? Is it not I, the LORD? Now go; I will help you speak and will teach you what to say'" (4:11–12).

God gave Moses such an effective "mouth" that when the early church remembered Moses, they thought of him as strongest exactly where he had considered himself weakest. Stephen, an early biblical martyr, calls Moses "powerful in speech" (Acts 7:22).

What happened? How does a man who speaks with "faltering lips" — in his own mind, pathetically incompetent in speech — go down through the ages as "powerful in speech"? It happens when an ordinary individual becomes an active instrument of an extraordinary God.

Even Moses' rod serves as an example. The first time God talks to Moses, he asks what he has in his hand. Moses replies, "A staff" (Exodus 4:2). To his human mind, this simple stick was nothing special — just "a staff." Moses might even have been thinking, *Wait a minute — I'm supposedly talking to* God, *and he doesn't know what this is?*

God didn't ask Moses what was in his hand to gain information.* God asked Moses what was in his hand to set up the revolution he was about to work in Moses' life. After God has Moses do a snake-transforming miracle with the staff, this ordinary stick, infused with God's activity, becomes an extraordinary instrument — so much so that when Moses sets out, the biblical writer records that "he took the staff of God in his hand" (Exodus 4:20).

An ordinary rod becomes *the staff of God*. A poor speaker becomes *God's effective spokesman*. That's what Christian spirituality is all about: our Creator and Lord taking ordinary people and making them potent instruments of God.

Your weaknesses mean nothing in the light of God's equipping call. In fact, your weaknesses can all the better bring even more glory to God by making it patently clear that you are God's instrument, for nothing else will explain your personal transformation — if indeed you are transformed.

Later, Moses would meet with God for forty days on the top of Mount Sinai. When he finally came down, his face glowed with such radiance that Aaron and the Israelites were afraid to go near him (Exodus 34:29 – 31). Our change may not be nearly so dramatic, but it should be no less certain. Every time Moses entered into God's presence, he came out with a radiant face. If we are serious about spending time in God's presence, we will be changed as well. It is impossible to spend time in the forceful, dynamic, and powerful presence of God and to emerge the same person you were before. People have spoken of the transforming impact of meeting certain personalities such as Billy Graham, Mother Teresa of Calcutta, and Nelson Mandela, but as noble as these people were and are, they

---

*A situation similar to the one in John 6, where Jesus asks Philip, "Where shall we buy bread for these people to eat?" John immediately adds, "He asked this only to test him, for he already had in mind what he was going to do" (verses 5 – 6).

couldn't hold a candle to the sun of God's fiery impact. How can we *truly* see him and then not change?

Don't be misled by the fact that it was Moses whose mouth God transformed. Yes, he is a central figure in the faith, but Jesus promised ordinary people that God would speak through them as well: "Just say whatever is given you at the time, for it is not you speaking, but the Holy Spirit" (Mark 13:11). Paul taught the same thing: "We are therefore Christ's ambassadors, as though God were making his appeal through us" (2 Corinthians 5:20). This response is vastly more than asking, "What would Jesus say?" It is letting Jesus say his words through us.

Trained Tongues

While the tongue can't be tamed, it can be trained. God's empowering presence works in cooperation with our minds to produce a godly transformation in the way we speak. God's Word is quite explicit about the content and purpose of God-honoring speech. The apostle Paul tells us to "encourage one another and build each other up" (1 Thessalonians 5:11). Notice that it is possible to avoid all manner of evil — gossiping, name-calling, lying, and so forth — while still being in a state of disobedience to this verse. This passage doesn't tell us to refrain from saying hurtful things; it compels us to proclaim truthful, redemptive words designed to build others up.

Paul, ever the skillful pastor, knows that simply speaking positive truths won't cut it in a church filled with people who stumble in many ways. So he lays out particular uses of the tongue a few verses later (verse 14):

- Warn those who are idle.
- Encourage the timid.
- Help the weak.
- Be patient with everyone.

It would be wrong to encourage an idle person; instead, we're told to "warn" them. Believers living in a state of disobedience need to be gently and patiently confronted. We must love them enough to speak a word that may make them angry but also calls them to repentance: "The tongue that brings healing is a tree of life" (Proverbs 15:4). Silence, in such situations, is cowardly and a curse.

On the other hand, it would be wrong to confront a timid person. Such people don't need a word of rebuke; they need a word of encouragement: "Reckless words pierce like a sword, but the tongue of the wise brings healing" (Proverbs 12:18).

"The weak" need practical guidance and instruction to help them move from their point of weakness to a place of victorious transformation: "The Sovereign LORD has given me an instructed tongue, to know the word that sustains the weary" (Isaiah 50:4).

And all of our words must be seasoned with grace-filled patience. How much havoc we unleash when our expectations for our spouses, our children, our coworkers, or our fellow drivers amount to perfection! People will regularly disappoint us. If our hearts aren't ready for this, we'll speak only with angry exasperation, our negative words tearing down people for their humanness, instead of using our tongues to cultivate redemptive transformation.

Did you notice the one thing absolutely forbidden in this passage? It's apathetic *silence*. I once watched a man's career implode, in part because his subordinates refused to speak up and challenge his worsening tendencies. Yes, that man bears the responsibility for his own lack of growth; but his staff members admit that their refusal to use words to lovingly challenge him (or in some cases to *keep* challenging him) allowed a bad situation to grow worse until ultimately it blew up.

How many children have fallen over the edge because their parents saw the beginning of a problem but out of fear refused to speak up? Perhaps they noticed that their daughter and her boyfriend were getting a little too "touchy," or that their son's moods seemed fueled by the unhealthy consumption of who knows what — but they also knew the scene it would create to say something. So they stayed silent.

How many marriages have crumbled under the weight of sin because a spouse was afraid to "rock the boat"? How many friends have continued a downward slide because their brothers and sisters in Christ were more concerned about appearing "supportive" than in calling them to live for the glory of God?

Whether you curse is only about 5 percent of what it means to cultivate a transformed, God-honoring tongue. When and how and whether you speak accounts for about 95 percent of your obedience. Surely this is the point behind God's challenge to Ezekiel:

> "When I say to a wicked man, 'You will surely die,' and you do not warn him or speak out to dissuade him from his evil ways in order to save his life, that wicked man will die for his sin, and I will hold you accountable for his blood. But if you do warn the wicked man and he does not turn from his wicked-ness or from his evil ways, he will die for his sin; but you will have saved yourself."
>
> Ezekiel 3:18–19

Clearly, God desires to commandeer our tongues for his service: "The tongue has the power of life and death" (Proverbs 18:21). Will you use this power? Will you begin the journey to have a mouth that speaks the very words of God?

Because words have power, you reset a room's climate every time you speak. Does your negativity pull everyone down? Is your tongue so busy trying to win approval that you refrain from speak-ing the hard word? Are you so eager to spout your opinions that you can't hear the needs of others?

Is your tongue being transformed?

By prayerfully studying Scripture and offering our tongues to God for his use, we can train our mouths to become God's servants. In this way, we can allow his empowering presence to rebuke, en-courage, instruct, and train — all in their proper time and season.

Speaking with God Instead of for God

Life changes when we live it in cooperation with God instead of just working for God. One Sunday before I preached, I came across a marvelous passage by R. Somerset Ward that creatively explains the human/divine dynamic when God speaks through us. Ward uses the image of fishermen pulling in nets bursting with fish to describe this reality:

> [A man] turns to his companion and says, "The fishermen have caught a lot of fish today." To his eyes the only important element in the scene he sees is the fisherman. Yet, in reality, the fisherman is only one, and by far the most insignificant, of all the factors that have brought the fish into the boat. The wind, the tide, the warm currents in the sea, all of them mighty and irresistible forces, have had most to do with the result. The fisherman has only cooperated with them. But although his share was so small, it was most necessary. And this may serve as a picture of the work of intercession.[4]

This was a great encouragement to me just before I preached. I realized that, while people would recognize me as preaching, I am "only one, and by far the most insignificant, of all the factors that [bring] the fish into the boat." Yet there is nobility in the task, for though my share is "so small, it [is] most necessary." But it is only a small share.

God has written his Word and opened it up to me. He has directed my thoughts as I prayerfully considered my task. He has been preparing the hearts of the people before whom I'm about to preach. And his Holy Spirit will convict people's hearts of the truth and remind them of that truth — long after I've left the picture.

Let's say you're meeting a friend for coffee at Starbucks. Let's also imagine you have a very difficult conversation that you know needs to take place. It will help you more than you could know to realize how small (though necessary) a part of the process you really are — when indeed you are relying on God. God has given you the words, cultivated the friendship, prepared your coffee-mate's heart, and will be setting the spiritual climate. You're simply "casting" a few words, that's all.

Here's the delightful spiritual irony: true biblical humility breeds confidence. Many people consider humility a sign of insecurity, but when we accept the Bible's reality that God is already acting, already moving, and already directing the affairs of his world, we can rest in his capability, confident that he has made allowances for our own weaknesses, sin, limitations, and lack of gifting.

What is true of intercession is true of all verbal ministry. R. Somerset Ward made this observation:

> It is the unseen, unknown part of intercession which makes our part both possible and important. It is the wind of the Holy Spirit blowing through us, it is the tide of God's providence, it is the current of the divine desire which really accomplish the work of intercession; and yet the human agent is essential for the accomplishment of the activity.[5]

I faced one of my most difficult preaching assignments when I stood up in front of a church less than ten minutes after the congregation learned that their senior pastor of almost thirty years had been asked to resign by the staff, elders, and deacons. Shock, sadness, and an understandable outpouring of conflicted emotions rippled through the unsettled congregation — and then I was asked to bring a word of healing. Understanding this cooperative reality helped me tremendously. I pointed out that none of this came as a surprise to God. He saw it all coming, even twenty-five years ago. And he had been preparing the church for just this time. He had raised up the necessary individuals, equipped the remaining pastors, and established the members in such a way that they must not be afraid. Since God felt no surprise, they should not imagine that he had been caught unprepared or that he had left them ill equipped and uncared for.

Cooperative reality means we have so very much to offer because we're not limited to our own talents. Ward writes, "Intercession is the expression of God's love and desire which he has designed to share with man, and in which he uses man."[6]

Here's the joy of the God-empowered life: we can cease expending energy trying to be impressive and instead rest in being *used*. The reality of being used, by definition, points people back to the One who is using us. Such a ministry glorifies God by relying on God and by demonstrating the reality of God. It recognizes the providence of God, the activity of God, the grace and generosity of God, and the wisdom of God. And there is no greater thrill — absolutely none — than being used to glorify God.

❧

Lord, let my tongue be a blessing. Empower me so that I will speak redemptively as you guide me. May my tongue bring comfort where people need comfort; may I patiently instruct those trapped in ignorance; may I gently but forcefully challenge the rebellious; may I patiently minister to the downhearted. Use my tongue to keep re-creating your world and to glorify your name. In Jesus' name. Amen.

❧ Looking Back ❧

- Transformed speech proclaims God's empowering life.

- While the church often focuses on what words Christians shouldn't say, we tend to downplay our call to speak healing, encouraging, and instructive words. "Holy speech" has as much to say about using *positive* speech as it does about avoiding negative speech.

- Christian spirituality is about our Creator and Lord taking ordinary people and making them potent instruments of God, in part through the words we speak.

- We are told to "warn those who are idle, encourage the timid, help the weak, be patient with everyone" (1 Thessalonians 5:14), meaning there are different ways we should speak to different individuals at different times, depending on the state of their heart and God's direction.

- Remaining silent can be a destructive course of action.

- We reset a room's climate every time we speak.

- When we speak, we are but a small part of a large process overseen by God; holiness calls us to offer up our tongues to be used as God's instruments.

Chapter 7

Ears That Hear

*When man listens, God speaks.... We are not out to tell God. We are
out to let God tell us.... The lesson the world most needs is the art of
listening to God.*

Frank Buchman

*God has spoken, and God speaks: by himself as well as through his
heralds, prophets, and preachers. There is no doubt about this basic fact.
The problem is that people, even God's own people, do not listen.*

Klaus Bockmuehl

*Invite God to interrupt you. If your heavenly Father wanted to, could
he interrupt you at any time during your day to ask you to do something
with him? I used to view interruptions in life as a nuisance and a
hindrance. Now I see them as opportunities.*

Marilyn Hontz

*"The sheep listen to his voice. He calls his own sheep by name and leads
them out.... His sheep follow him because they know his voice. But
they will never follow a stranger; in fact, they will run away from him
because they do not recognize a stranger's voice."*

Jesus, in John 10:3–5

"Tolle, lege!"
"Tolle, lege!"
A young child's singsong voice calling out, *"Tolle, lege!"* ("Take
and read!") first pierced the ears and then shook the heart of one who
would become one of Christianity's most famous teachers. Something told the young and proud Augustine that these words sprang
from a divinely ordained source. He certainly knew of no child's

game that used the words "take and read," so he accepted them at face value, opened the New Testament, and soon surrendered to the power of God's truth. Thus began a long journey of faith that would leave an indelible mark on what was then a relatively new faith.

Perhaps it is not surprising, given the genesis of his faith, that throughout his life Augustine remained sensitive to the God who speaks. In *The Confessions*, Augustine writes the following:

> You [God] are Truth, and you are everywhere present where all seek counsel of you. You reply to all at once.... The answer you give is clear, but not all hear clearly. All ask you whatever they wish to ask, but the answer they receive is not always what they want to hear. The man who serves you best is the one who is less intent on hearing from you what he wills to hear than on shaping his will according to what he hears from you.[1]

The young man who once had an insatiable desire for renown and a woman's flesh evolved into a strong bishop who sought most dearly God's divine guidance: "Whisper words of truth in my heart, for you alone speak truth."[2]

Though the practice of listening to God remains controversial to some, earnest believers have understood that the benefits and blessings of this biblical practice far outweigh the occasional problems that result when people mistake their own voice for God's. Frank Buchman, whose ministry touched private individuals and influential world leaders during the early part of the twentieth century, argued, "Divine guidance must become the normal experience.... Definite, accurate, adequate information can come from the mind of God to the minds of men. This is normal prayer."[3]

Does God Still Speak?

Some teach that God speaks only indirectly today through preaching and the motivating of people to apply the Bible's "timeless principles." To be sure, Scripture is the only infallible record we have of God's true message and revelation to humankind. Yet this same Bible bursts with stories of God communicating to individual women and men.

Every Old Testament patriarch, as well as the writers of the psalms, not only heard from God but begged him to keep speaking. The book of Acts overflows with accounts of God speaking to individuals — to Peter, Stephen, Philip, Ananias, Paul, Cornelius, and many others. Jesus himself set the example of humble listening: "I have much to say in judgment of you. But he who sent me is reliable, and what I have heard from him I tell the world.... I do nothing on my own but speak just what the Father has taught me" (John 8:26, 28).

I love how my spiritual mentor, Dr. Klaus Bockmuehl, summarizes Christ's stance:

> The common denominator in these passages is a God-inspired, fundamental, and comprehensive suspension of judgment: I will not judge, decide, speak, or do anything on my own, but I will first listen to God. This reservation represents the end of human autonomy or self-governance and establishes, in practice, the primacy and reality of God's kingship in the earthly life of Jesus.[4]

Some earnest believers have taken "listening to God" to an unhealthy extreme, making mundane tasks (for example, which road to take on the way home, whether to order chicken or beef) take on a cosmic importance. On the other hand, I've known some staunch believers who insist that we hear God only through sermons or through Scripture; in their understanding, God doesn't speak to individuals today. Instead of trying to listen for and understand God's voice, we're simply supposed to use our own reasoning and understanding to apply the general principles given in Scripture. In my mind, such believers risk falling into a practical atheism. Dr. Bockmuehl would agree with me:

> Jesus' words, "as I hear, I judge" [John 5:30 NKJV], signal the end of the rule of religious principles that we often assume and then apply independent of God. To do so is a religious version of human self-rule, a kind of practical deism that assumes that once the starting pistol sets the universe spinning, God has no

further input and human designs are called for to fill in from there. Jesus, over against this, uses the present tense to indicate his ongoing, constant teachableness and availability for divine directives.[5]

The thesis of this book stresses the need to *experience* God. Earlier we asked the question, how real is your God? Does your faith have a pulse? Do you enjoy a dynamic relationship, or are you limiting yourself to simply trying to follow "timeless biblical principles"? Whether God speaks today will have a major impact on this view of Christian spirituality. In part, this is how God makes himself real to us and how he has a significant role in our lives.

Scripture goes out of its way to contrast our *living, speaking* God with dead idols (see Psalm 115:2–8). Bockmuehl observes, "Only the pagan idols are mute, and Christians have been liberated from their service. So we have no reason, unless we mean to defy the teaching of Jesus, to turn the Holy Spirit into another mute idol."[6] The writer of Hebrews warns us, "See to it that you do not refuse him who speaks" (Hebrews 12:25).

In 1 John, the beloved disciple tells an early church that "[God's] anointing teaches [present tense] you about all things" and reminds them emphatically that "that anointing is real, not counterfeit" (1 John 2:27). The Word is essential, but we also need the ongoing "anointing" of God's Holy Spirit, his presence, which animates the Word. Renowned scholar John Stott puts it this way:

> The Word is an objective safeguard, while the anointing of the Spirit is a subjective experience; but both the apostolic teaching and the Heavenly Teacher are necessary for continuance in the truth. And both are to be personally and inwardly grasped. This is the biblical balance too seldom preserved by men. Some honor the Word and neglect the Spirit who alone can interpret it; others honor the Spirit but neglect the Word out of which he teaches. The only safeguard against lies is to have abiding within us both the Word that we *heard from the beginning* and the *anointing* that we *received* from him.[7]

The fact is, if you are a believer, you have heard God's voice. Jesus teaches us that those who come to God do so in response to the Father's voice (John 6:45). Why would God speak to us to call us to faith but then fail to speak to us to call us to maturity? Why, indeed, would Jesus proclaim to Pilate, "Everyone on the side of truth listens to me" (John 18:37), if he planned to silence himself in just a few days and never speak again?

Deaf to God's Guidance

Whether God speaks is perhaps not the most pressing issue. Assuming he does, an equally important concern is this: How well do we listen? And can we improve in this practice? See if anything catches you off guard as you take a fresh look at one of Jesus' famous illustrations:

> No one lights a lamp and hides it in a jar or puts it under a bed. Instead, he puts it on a stand, so that those who come in can see the light. For there is nothing hidden that will not be disclosed, and nothing concealed that will not be known or brought out into the open. Therefore consider carefully *how you listen*. Whoever has will be given more; whoever does not have, even what he thinks he has will be taken from him.
>
> Luke 8:16–18, emphasis added

I remember reading this passage and being struck by the seemingly out-of-place "consider carefully *how you listen*." For whatever reason, it wasn't the instruction I expected — Jesus is talking about what we *see* — what is hidden, what is disclosed — but then makes his main point about what we *hear*. When you talk about having and getting more, you don't normally think of *listening* — but this is exactly what Jesus is saying. If our *hearing* goes bad, he seems to be saying, even what we think we know will be taken away. But if we learn to listen — to really listen, to truly hear — we will receive spiritual wealth and understanding beyond imagination.

Let's look a bit more carefully, because there's a rich vein of gold here. The Greek imperative translated "consider carefully" is *blepete*; it means "to watch" or "to take care," "to give the matter due attention." "How you listen" translates *pos akouete*, which addresses the way in which we hear. Put together, these words mean that we should be thoughtful regarding how we hear; it should be no haphazard process. There should be a considered effort to tune in to spiritual truth — an effort that should address not just whether we hear from God's Word but how, in what manner, in what state, and in what frame of mind.

If we fail to listen, or listen in the wrong way, we become spiritually deaf. Eventually, we'll lose even what we have. But if we take heed, we'll be blessed with new insight and new understanding. The transformative process will take hold in our lives, and God will increase our understanding.

This illustration comes on the heels of the parable of the soils (Luke 8:1–15), a story the disciples asked Jesus to explain; as a result, we don't have to do any work to figure it out. Here's where Jesus says our hearing can be stopped:

- Some hear, but the devil comes and "takes away the word from their hearts."
- Some receive the word with joy when they initially hear it, but they have no roots, so when testing comes, they "fall away."
- Some hear but are distracted by life's worries, riches, and pleasures, and so they "do not mature."
- Some hear with a "noble and good heart"; they retain the word and persevere in its truth. This response is what produces a rich crop.

How well do we listen to the word of God? While in context the parable of the soils seems to address how we receive the truth of the salvation message, it's significant that in Luke 8:16–18, Jesus is specifically and privately talking to his disciples, who already have heard the gospel message. It's to *them* that he says, "Consider carefully how you listen. Whoever has will be given more; whoever does not have, even what he thinks he has will be taken from him." Hearing, then, is an *ongoing* process, something you and I need to take to heart as disciples, not just as pre-Christians.

This is almost completely backward from how we view biblical teaching and communication. So often, walking out of church, people evaluate the preacher. "How was the sermon?" someone will ask.

"Well, a little long, kind of boring, but overall a noble effort."

I face this dilemma all the time as a guest speaker. In fact, just recently a member of a church where I was speaking came up between services and said, "Word has it in the women's restroom that you're really good."

What could I possibly say to *that*?

But you know what? The Bible *never* addresses giving a good sermon; it *only* addresses how we *receive* that sermon — which means that the conversation after church, from a biblical perspective, should go like this:

"How was your hearing today?"

"Pretty good. I was attentive, and I've taken the truth to heart. I want to hold on to it, so I've taken some notes, and I'm going to be praying about it this weekend. I don't want to lose what God has given me."

The sad truth is, most of us would worry more about losing our wallets in church than we would about losing the truth that God laid out for us. And doesn't that put us in the dangerous category Jesus warned about when he spoke of "those who hear, but as they go on their way they are choked by life's ... riches ... and they do not mature"?

Others are choked by life's pleasures. They come out of church, and all they can think about is where they're going to eat lunch — or who is going to eat lunch with them, or what they'll watch while they eat lunch, or whether they'll make it to the first tee before one o'clock, or whether the mall closes at five or six.

Still others forget about what they've heard because they allow worry to consume them: "Will I be laid off tomorrow or not?" "Will that contract come through on Wednesday?" "Am I ready for my final exams?" Worries don't need to be blatantly sinful to stop us from hearing; they just need to be loud.

What does this mean, practically? *Every time the word of God is proclaimed, my priorities get tested.* My future spiritual health will be governed in no small part by my hearing. Careless hearing will stop up my spiritual understanding; over time, it can even take away what little I already have.

It's one thing to avoid listening to gossip, lies, vile talk, and hate speech. Doing so should be a given. It's another thing altogether to have our ears attuned to what is pure, what is holy, what is right, what is just, what is divinely ordained. Have your ears become active, available servants of God?

Spiritual Ears

I'll always remember the evening when my good friends Rob and Jill Takemura got engaged. Rob organized such an elaborate proposal that it made the evening news. (I'm not kidding.) Your wedding proposal doesn't get on television unless you do something extraordinary — but that's what love motivates us to do, isn't it? Something extraordinary.

When you truly love someone, you'll go out of your way to show it. That's why I can empathize with a paralyzed man's friends who were so enamored by the compelling power of Jesus' life that they literally cut through a roof to get their friend in front of the wonder-working Rabbi. The attending "teachers of the law" resented this rock-star treatment. *Why cut through someone's roof just to lay a man at this "teacher's" uneducated feet — when we have to go out of our way to attract an audience? Just who does this carpenter's son think he is? In fact, the mere fact that he's not rebuking the men for this act of vandalism is proof enough that he must be an egomaniac.*

When they saw that Jesus was impressed by the men's faith and then heard him say to the paralytic, "Son, your sins are forgiven," they started grumbling silently in their hearts: "Why does this fellow talk like that? He's blaspheming! Who can forgive sins but God alone?" (Mark 2:5–7).

And Jesus *heard* them. I emphasize *heard* because they weren't actually speaking. Yet this fact didn't stop the God-man from picking up on their internal dialogue: "Immediately Jesus knew in his spirit that this was what they were thinking in their hearts" (2:8), and he rebuked them.

Is it possible to hear what isn't literally being said? Or was this a chapter in Jesus' life that none of his followers will ever experience? Well, Peter certainly "heard" what was unspoken about Ananias and Sapphira, the deceitful couple who pretended to give all their earnings to God while keeping back a share for themselves (see Acts 5:1–11). This type of hearing has even personally served me. I can still remember, decades ago, when I was back in college and dating a young woman. One of the female college pastors who listened to God "saw" me in prayer one morning and then asked, "Tell me, is your relationship with ____ absolutely above reproach?"

This was an act of great courage and love that kept an unhealthy situation from growing even worse. God "arrested" my slide before it was too late. *I* had stopped hearing — but this woman had not! And I thank God for her faithfulness.

Jesus seemed to promise a redemptive type of hearing when he said, "He who belongs to God hears what God says. The reason you do not hear is that you do not belong to God" (John 8:47). And Isaiah urges us to "listen" so that we can encourage God's people:

> The Sovereign LORD has given me an instructed tongue,
>> to know the word that sustains the weary.
> He wakens me morning by morning,
>> wakens my ear to listen like one being taught.
> The Sovereign LORD has opened my ears,
>> and I have not been rebellious;
>> I have not drawn back.
>
> Isaiah 50:4–5

If we listen carefully, God may give us an encouraging word to "sustain the weary." We can listen for others who have stopped listening but who still need God's perspective for their lives. This must be done humbly, without prophetic arrogance — and usually without even tipping our hand that we think it may be a divine nudge. We're simply speaking with an "instructed tongue" in the hope that God's insight may be embraced.

It's all about "tuning in" to God. I remember my first appearance on *Focus on the Family*. I rarely grow nervous about public speaking anymore, but the reality that I was about to tape a program heard by millions seemed more daunting than normal. Complicating matters was the realization that when I speak, I have notes, I know where I'm headed, and I'm working with familiar material. That morning the thought hit me, *What if I get asked an unexpected question and I freeze?*

Since I'm not used to dealing with a bad case of nerves, I'm not particularly experienced at making it go away. So I took refuge in the restroom just outside the studio wing and started pacing in front of the sinks. Finally, God's voice broke through so clearly, so convincingly, so therapeutically: "This is *so* not about you."

As I listened to God's still, small voice — not audible, but unmistakable nevertheless — I realized that my nerves came from my pride. I wanted to make a good impression. I wanted to be entertaining, thought-provoking, the type of guest *Focus* would want to ask back. But God wasn't as concerned about *me* that day as he was about reaching families with the message contained in *Sacred Marriage*. I heard a clear call to focus on those struggling in their homes because of a faulty understanding of Christian marriage — and once I began focusing on the ones God really wanted to reach, the nervousness dissipated like my daughter's beloved soap bubbles. It was just gone.

And God's words, "This is so not about you," remain to this day one of the most precious gifts my heavenly Father has ever given me. Whenever I stumble toward nervousness, I now know that the reason is pride. I'm trying to make an impression instead of focusing on being a servant.

How could Christians even think to live without God's gentle correction, his penetrating conviction, and his soul-building encouragement? What do you think God wants to say to *you* today, in *your* situation? Do you really believe he wants to have no input at all in your life?

The Turned Christian

I get a lot of requests to write endorsements for other books. I usually feel somewhat obligated, figuring that if they're coming to me, they're already scraping the bottom of the barrel — Rick Warren, Bill Hybels, and Philip Yancey must have turned them down already, so if *I* say no, this poor author is just about out of options.

During one recent month I received two books, one on prayer and one written by David Benner called *Desiring God's Will*. Benner's book has the wonderful subtitle *Aligning Our Hearts with the Heart of God*. I could have endorsed the book just for its focus, but it proved to be a rich spiritual read as well. While the other book on prayer was helpful and worthy of publication, I'm at a place where I desire to hear God's voice ten times more than I desire to lay out any particular request or complaint. Of course, asking is important, but I tend to think, *If I don't have it, how badly do I really need it?* And what I truly need is to hear God's perspective far more than I need to tell him mine.

That's why I especially appreciated David Benner's book. For every one book on listening to God, there are probably a thousand on talking to God. I wonder how much better we might do if this ratio were reversed. We need to become completely enamored with hearing God's voice: "Speak, LORD, for your servant is listening" (1 Samuel 3:9).

This starts out as a discipline, but eventually it becomes a part of who we are.

Brother Lawrence, Frank Laubach, and many other practitioners of divine listening attest to the development of "turned" Christians. "Turning" to hear God usually begins as an act of the will, involving hundreds of tiny but significant conscious decisions. Over time, this turning becomes our normal bent. At this point, we become what the ancients called "turned" Christians.

In other words, "spiritual gravity" becomes every bit as strong as natural gravity — only this "gravity" lifts us up rather than pushes us down. When I used to wake up in the morning, I haphazardly flipped through my thoughts until I remembered, *Oh yeah, I suppose*

I could pray. Through a long season of inconsistency, the "oh yeahs" became much more frequent. Now such turning has become almost as natural as breathing — I wake up and look into the face of God.

At times, other thoughts try to intrude. Maybe I could fret about a problem, wallow in negativity, or even indulge a fantasy, but then I simply compare the alternative: *Well, I could waste my time thinking about that, or I could listen to God.*

What once was discipline has now become delight. I don't take credit for this practice any more than I can take credit for laughing; it's simply one of the many delights I enjoy as God's adopted son.

This spiritual gravity then prepares us for the rest of the day. Most of us believe that the constant focus of the mystics lies beyond us; the reality is, when our kids or our bosses are talking to us, they expect our full attention. But we *can* work toward a "turned" relationship, a propensity to listen to God; and when we do, we can be amazed at how easily God's voice can break through — as it did for me in the Focus on the Family restroom. Writer Marilyn Hontz recounts her daughter's delightful description: "Mom, you know how we can be in the same room together but be busy with different things? Well, even though we are busy and not engaged in conversation, our ears immediately perk up if one of us starts to speak."[8]

God can alert us to what's "really" being said, or he can emphasize a thought, drop a Scripture into our consciousness, or counteract an attacking thought. Who wouldn't want this? Marilyn's joy in practicing this discipline of listening is evident: "I have learned that listening is crucial in my spiritual growth, my family life, my other relationships, and my ministry. I cannot function without the Lord's input each day."[9]

Who would want to?

Tests for Truth

One reason listening has fallen out of favor in some circles is that Christians can be so spectacularly wrong when it comes to hearing God. A woman once approached John Wesley, who, it's safe to say, was one of the hardest-working servants of the gospel who ever lived. She said she had a "message from the Lord" and proceeded to chastise Wesley for "laying up treasures on the earth" — a curious message given that Wesley lived a heroically frugal life, promising to die with less than ten pounds to his name (a promise he kept, by the way). This "prophetess" also accused the evangelist of taking his ease (if you pick up his journal, you'll get exhausted just reading about his diligent labor for God's kingdom) and being obsessed with eating and drinking.

I wish I could have seen Wesley as he responded: "I told her, God knew me better; and if he had sent her, he would have sent her with a more proper message."[10]

Accounts like this one — and which one of us *hasn't* been party to a message clearly not from God? — make what I'm saying somewhat controversial. The only truly authoritative revelation is Scripture, and the notion of people "writing down what God told them" and presenting it as his word gives me the creeps. I can think of a hundred things wrong with that.

So am I being inconsistent when I nevertheless suggest that God still speaks?

As a practical matter, I believe we can draw a distinction between authoritative revelation — that is, Scripture — and subjective inspiration, a sense of God's Spirit leading us to apply authoritative revelation in a particular way. There's a vast difference between blatantly disobeying Scripture and not following up on an "impression." Wisdom tells us that impressions *must* be tested. They are suggestions, and as such they are open to human error and manipulation. Having said this, the subjective leading, counsel, direction, comfort, and confrontation of God's living Holy Spirit can still be a dynamic force for good in any believer's life.

For me, hearing God's voice is one of the most precious parts of being a disciple. I crave God's insight into my actions and motives. I desire with all my heart to know his particular will for me — not some general direction based on certain principles, but his particular application for my particular need. And I love it when — this is really getting out there — I'm struggling with an issue and God makes everything clear, sometimes even through a dream.

For me, it comes down to this: Should we allow occasional misuse of a clear biblical teaching to steal away the precious reality of actually hearing from God and being directed by him? I would *never* present a dream or an "inner thought" as direct revelation, writing it down and asking others to accept it at face value. On the other hand, if God truly doesn't speak, you might as well stop reading this book right now and toss it in the garbage can, because if that's the case, then I am totally crazy and you're reading the ravings of a madman. God's words have sustained me in so many ways, I can't even imagine what it would be like to serve a silent God.

The First Test: Scripture

In fact, the traditional stance of the Christian church well supports my position. Through his church, God has left us with many concrete, traditionally understood tests for accurately discerning God's voice. The first test, of course, is Scripture. God will not contradict himself. Anything we think we hear from God that does not align itself with scriptural revelation should automatically be disregarded. The only true and certain revelation is God's written Word. But if we listen as we read, God can help us apply those words in very practical and very specific ways. Our first step, then, to hearing God is to become biblically informed. The Bible shapes our thinking and provides the framework for all of God's communication to humankind.

It's no good being lazy in this regard. If someone truly wants to know God's will, he or she should begin by developing a biblically informed mind. This kind of mind is what trains us to understand wisdom and God's perspective, and there is no substitute.

The Second Test: The Church's Witness

The second test has to do with God's church. I am suspicious of anyone who has a novel interpretation of the Word of God. Creativity has its place, but when it comes to understanding truth, faithfulness is a much higher priority. Frank Buchman observed, "No one can be wholly God-controlled who works alone. It is to a group of willing men and women that God speaks most clearly."[11]

We need to heed the warnings of the Reformers that when anyone can claim divine inspiration, the end of the church is in sight. We listen to God humbly, as daughters and sons of God's church. At moments in our history, some elements of the church have clearly been in error, but there still remains a collective wisdom that calls for our respect. None of us should delight in swimming against the current; we must do so only when we are convinced that Scripture insists on it.

On the other hand, I'm not willing to go as far as some of the Reformers did when they openly questioned God's tendency to specifically guide us and speak to us. John Calvin was so suspicious of direct listening to God that at times he even seemed to question private Bible study. I know, I know — who am I to question John Calvin? While he has undeniably been a great teacher to me, he's still not my God, and in this instance, by virtually limiting God's speaking to trained preachers, he may have inadvertently helped create the personality-centered church that has existed for so long, a one-man show that can undercut the priesthood of all believers. In this case, there must exist a happy middle, where we base our understanding on God's Word, appropriately studied and applied, while occasionally receiving personal instruction, comfort, and advice that must be tested before it is received; and even then these things are always held secondarily, perhaps even somewhat suspiciously, as possible applications of God's written Word.

The Third Test: A Holy Life

Another condition for hearing from God is a holy life. Sin may not block our salvation, but it does tend to stop up our ears. It leads us down a path of deception and hinders further understanding and direct hearing. If we are serious about listening to God, we must take seriously the words of God in Leviticus: "Be holy, because I am holy" (11:45). If you haven't dealt with your pride, your own voice and ambition will begin sounding suspiciously like God's. And if you haven't gained some mastery over your emotions, you'll mistake your moods for the Holy Spirit's confirmation.

Transformation is a process; growth in one area helps us grow in other areas as well. Augustine honestly faced the consequences of sin. He clearly believed that "true understanding depends on moral uprightness, for an evil will does not comprehend the truth."[12]

The listening life must therefore be a devout life. Hypocrisy stops up our ears and tends to lead to self-justification and empty rationalization rather than humble hearing. Klaus Bockmuehl makes this observation:

> If we look at the recipients of God's guidance, and remember, for instance, the calling of Cornelius or the characterization of Simeon in Luke 2, we see clearly that piety and probity ("whoever fears Him and works righteousness" — Acts 10:35 NKJV) are conditions for receiving divine communication. Indeed, as the book of Acts spells out in general, God gives the Holy Spirit "to those who obey him" (5:32). Obedience to what we already know of God's will prepares us to receive the gift of the Holy Spirit and his instruction.[13]

Obedience becomes an essential component of maintaining ears that hear.

The Fourth Test: Growing Familiarity with God's Voice

Finally, if you talk to those who are practiced in listening to God — those who invite his guidance and then heed it, who seek his wisdom and then apply it — they testify that, over time, God's voice becomes "familiar" in a way that nothing else can match. We begin to experience Jesus' promise in John 10:4–5: "His sheep follow him because they know his voice. But they will never follow a stranger; in fact, they will run away from him because they do not recognize a stranger's voice."

God's voice has a certain style and tone that mark it as genuine. Just as those who catch counterfeit money makers train by becoming obsessively familiar with the real thing, so we build walls between ourselves and deception by patiently, perseveringly, and faithfully, over time, practicing the presence of God.

A Tribute

No doubt you've noticed my reliance in this chapter on one of my mentors, Dr. Klaus Bockmuehl, and his excellent book *Listening to the God Who Speaks*. In my college-student lingo, Dr. Bockmuehl was a "spiritual giant" who challenged me to take seriously the call to listen to God. He blessed his students with his deep intellect. Trained in the German model (he was Karl Barth's teaching assistant), he could be brutal with ill-prepared students in seminars, but he joined his intellect with a spiritual passion and availability to God that still inspire me today, two decades after his death.

On several occasions, Dr. Bockmuehl invited me to his home. As we discussed life issues, he frequently said, "Well, let's listen to God and see what he says." For any who may doubt the wisdom of such a practice, all I can say is that unless you put your faith entirely in coincidence, God answered our prayers in amazingly specific ways. In public, Dr. Bockmuehl's lectures were steeped in Reformational and biblical thought; but in fact, each well-prepared lecture was prefaced with a gem from Dr. Bockmuehl's private "listening time" that had taken place earlier that morning — and it was sometimes difficult to say which was more valuable, the lecture or the devotion. By giving us both, Dr. Bockmuehl offered a tremendous gift and legacy of faith: train your mind, but keep your spiritual ears open.

I close this chapter with one of my mentor's characteristic reflections:

Let us pray that, above all, God would make us listeners to himself, so that we may be neither idle nor self-sufficient; not rash in our deeds, but ever pausing to listen, and then to follow him, moving in consonance with his will.[14]

ॐ **Looking Back** ॐ

- The Bible is filled with accounts of God speaking directly to individuals through various means — including but not limited to Scripture.

- John Stott calls the church to an appropriate balance when he writes, "Some honor the Word and neglect the Spirit who alone can interpret it; others honor the Spirit but neglect the Word out of which he teaches." Christian life is based on understanding God's written Word, but we also need God's active voice to appropriately apply his written Word.

- We are called to listen carefully to God's truth. Poor listening has serious negative spiritual consequences.

- Every time God's word is proclaimed, our priorities are tested.

- If we listen, God will give us words to "sustain the weary" — it may be a word that sustains us, or it may be a word God gives to us to sustain others.

- Classic writers teach that while "turning" to hear God usually begins as an act of the will, this turning, over time, becomes our normal bent. At this point, we become what the ancients called "turned" Christians.

- We can and should draw a distinction between authoritative revelation — that is, Scripture — and subjective inspiration, where we sense God's Spirit leading us to apply authoritative revelation in a particular way. "Listening to God" doesn't mean we must blindly follow personal impressions or others who claim to be speaking on God's behalf.

- Tests for accurately hearing God include Scripture, the church's witness, a holy life, and an increasing familiarity with God's voice.

Chapter 8

Minds That Think

Suppressing the knowledge of God will make you a casualty of corruption.

John Piper

It is funny how mortals always picture us [demons] as putting things into their minds: in reality, our best work is done by keeping things out.

C. S. Lewis

He who often thinks of God will have a larger mind than the man who simply plods around this narrow globe.

J. I. Packer

Behind most wrong living is wrong thinking.

John Piper

Then he opened their minds so they could understand the Scriptures.

Luke 24:45

"They're blocking Highway 99? In front of the airport? During rush hour?" My pointed questions betrayed my disbelief and frustration.

"It's a funeral procession, sir. A police officer died here last week."

"So can I take a taxi to the parking lot instead of waiting for your shuttle to pick me up?"

"A taxi won't be able to get through either."

I had been gone for a week. Forty-five minutes crawled by while I waited for a parking shuttle to take me to my car so I could go home. My desperation grew by the second, as the forty-five minutes became an hour.

"What if I just walked there?"

"Even if you walked," the attendant explained, "I don't think you could get out of our parking lot."

"They shut down 99?" I asked again.

"I'm afraid so."

"During *rush hour*?"

Once I finally arrived at my car, God had a few words for me. Yes, my trip home had been delayed by more than an hour. Yes, it was a frustrating inconvenience at the end of two plane trips that, combined, equaled six hours of flying. Yeah, I had woken up on the East Coast fourteen hours earlier and only now was in Seattle, still two hours from home (with traffic).

But the police officer being honored would *never* come home again. He wasn't just late; he was *gone*, removed for all of earth's time from ever greeting his wife or children at the end of a long day.

And I had gotten upset that I had lost an hour.

I believe that my self-absorbed attitude offended God every bit as much as if I had picked up a *Playboy* magazine at the airport, cussed out the attendant who kept telling me that the shuttle would be there "soon," drained my frustration with a pint of whiskey, or took the paycheck I had earned on the trip and stopped at a casino on the way home, putting all my family's money on red.

True transformation takes us beyond the limitations of traditional understandings about morality and expands it to include deep issues of the heart. Not only do I need to "behave" outwardly, but inwardly I must begin thinking like Christ. Christ grieved for the fallen officer. Christ expressed empathy for the family that lost a husband and father. Christ mourned with a city that lost a servant in the line of duty.

And I had fumed about being delayed for an hour.

If somebody had watched me, they wouldn't have seen any "sin." I didn't yell at anyone. I was rather polite, in fact. I didn't curse when told the news about the road closure. But my self-absorbed thinking was unconscionably selfish, anti-Christian, and vile.

When God made this clear to me, I started praying for the city, the officer, and the family he left behind, realizing how far I have yet to go to fully experience the blessed mind of Christ.

The mind is a key arena in the Beautiful Fight of transformation. As J. P. Moreland brilliantly observes, "The spiritually mature person is a wise person." The mind of Christ and God's wisdom are something we are given (1 Corinthians 2:16) *and* told to cultivate (Proverbs 4:1 – 13), the product, as Moreland puts it, "of a life of study and a developed mind."[1]

True transformation requires transformed minds: "Be transformed by the renewing of your mind. Then you will be able to test and approve what God's will is — his good, pleasing and perfect will" (Romans 12:2).

Increasingly Stupid

"It's difficult to watch someone throw off their faith and become increasingly stupid. *That's* the most difficult client to turn around."

Dr. Mitchell Whitman, a clinical psychologist, is a delight to talk to, and in this instance, he was describing his frustration over some people's tendency in midlife to suddenly reject the moral dictates of faith and proceed to destroy their families, their children, and their character. They make themselves and everyone around them miserable. They become increasingly misguided and seem to make ever-worse choices, until they are buried under an ever-cascading avalanche of stupidity.

Those who study human nature understand that foolishness begets foolishness. We *can* become "increasingly stupid" when we start making unwise choices; the snowball effect of darkened thinking can be quite destructive. When Paul writes, "Do not conform any longer to the pattern of this world, but be transformed by the renewing of your mind" (Romans 12:2), he's declaring, as C. E. B. Cranfield observes, that "when Christians allow themselves to be conformed to this world, what takes place is not just a disguising of their real nature but an inward corruption."[2]

We are fallen creatures who are radically dependent on God's continuing mercy and grace. When we shut God off, we become vulnerable to any foolish whim; our emotions and passions may rule us and degrade us. Worse, we even lose the spiritual perception that otherwise can warn us about what is happening. Solomon — who started out so wisely — is the poster child for this sad phenomenon, and his life provides a grave warning to all of us who grow careless that no matter how far we may have progressed, we can lose it all if we start sliding downward.

Confusion — lack of perception — breeds further uncertainty. Jesus' disciples experienced this growing uncertainty. When Jesus fed the five thousand, even those closest to him didn't fully understand the true nature of the miracle. So when Jesus conquered the waves and the storm — no greater feat than feeding so many with such a small amount — "they were completely amazed, for they had not understood about the loaves; their hearts were hardened" (Mark 6:51–52).

When they later missed Jesus' point about the "yeast of the Pharisees," Jesus seemed almost exasperated: "Do you still not see or understand? Are your hearts hardened? Do you have eyes but fail to see, and ears but fail to hear?" (Mark 8:17–18).

For their sake, he becomes literal:

> "When I broke the five loaves for the five thousand, how many basketfuls of pieces did you pick up?"
>
> "Twelve," they replied.
>
> "And when I broke the seven loaves for the four thousand, how many basketfuls of pieces did you pick up?"
>
> They answered, "Seven."
>
> He said to them, "Do you still not understand?"
>
> Mark 8:19–21

You can see Jesus' point: they *saw* what happened, so how could they not *see* his point? They were using their physical eyes, but their hearts were hardened to the spiritual implications — and so their minds remained dim.

In short, we can either develop or lose our ability to discriminate. I've seen churchgoing adults suddenly act as though feelings are all that matter and thus obliterate their families in order to follow their new emotional fancy. Then, five years later, they are genuinely surprised at how costly their choice has been for their children and their checkbook — and they're surprised again at how those intense feelings have faded, and they find themselves once again in the middle of a relationship that is going to take commitment and daily decisions to develop.

Paul warned about the intellectual frustration of living without God when he wrote to the Ephesians:

> So I tell you this, and insist on it in the Lord, that you must no longer live as the Gentiles do, *in the futility of their thinking.* They are darkened in their understanding and separated from the life of God because of the ignorance that is in them due to the hardening of their hearts. Having lost all sensitivity, they have given themselves over to sensuality so as to indulge in every kind of impurity, with a continual lust for more.
>
> Ephesians 4:17 – 19, emphasis added

Christianity exalts the role of the mind as a necessary part of right living, but our faith is unique in stressing how our behavior and our minds influence and act on each other. When our thinking goes, our behavior doesn't lag far behind. And when our behavior slips, our minds begin to slip as well. This aspect of the Beautiful Fight requires a one-two punch.

The Connection between Holiness and Right Thinking

Neurologists tell us a startling truth that has major implications for spiritual formation: Our choices and experience shape our brain, both literally and physiologically. What we choose cognitively helps make us into who we are. People talk about having an "addictive" mind (being prone to addiction), but the evidence is still inconclusive. At least one neurologist I've read has made a compelling case that it's more appropriate to speak of an addict*ed* mind; that is, the brain has been *shaped* by the addict's choices rather than a faulty brain has been leading him to make those choices in the first place.

In a neurological sense, our character is the sum total of the moral decisions we have made. In a theological sense, our behavior and our thinking are interconnected. Here's how the apostle Paul describes it:

> Those who live according to the sinful nature have their minds set on what that nature desires; but those who live in accordance with the Spirit have their minds set on what the Spirit desires. The mind of sinful man is death, but the mind controlled by the Spirit is life and peace; the sinful mind is hostile to God.
>
> Romans 8:5–7

To have a mind set on God, my entire life must be God-focused and God-directed. I can't live in hostility to God and think God's thoughts; surrendering to God opens up my mind to increased understanding and wisdom, while persistently wallowing in immorality will chip away at the insight I already possess.

Charles Hodge, the famed nineteenth-century Princeton professor, understood this interplay of understanding and character long before scientists could scope a brain. During a two-year trip to Germany, Hodge grew appalled at the poverty of spiritual life in Luther's homeland. He blamed the lack of what he called "vital religion" for this decline: "Holiness is essential to the correct knowledge of divine things and the great security from error. Wherever you find vital piety, there you find the doctrines of the fall, of depravity, of regeneration, of atonement and of the deity of Jesus Christ."

He followed this up with an impassioned plea to his students: "Keep your hearts with all diligence, for out of them are the issues of life.... When men lose the life of religion, they can believe the most monstrous doctrines and glory in them."[3]

I saw this in action when a Christian celebrity was asked about her recently troubled personal life. The question was almost demonically clever: "Would you recommend that your fans do as you did?" The camera zoomed in on her conflicted face until she finally shrugged her shoulders with an "I don't know" gesture. She knew she was caught. To say no would be to admit she had sinned; to say yes would be to endorse what she knew did not glorify God. So instead she opted for "I don't know."

Is "I don't know" the best that God's people can offer regarding clear moral choices? Is the sum total of our prophetic function to respond, "Your guess is as good as mine"? When we live in a state of moral failure, sidestepping the Beautiful Fight and allowing ourselves to give in to our lowest and our least, we lose the authority and the will to speak prophetically.

I have seen men who don't practice holiness start preaching nothing but grace — forgetting all about real change and transformation. I have also seen men who are deeply convicted about unrepented sin preach with anger and venom, forgetting all about forgiveness and mercy. Both camps miss the totality of God's grace, because they see it from only one side. They are led into either misunderstanding forgiveness, which exalts "tolerance" over transformation, or misunderstanding God's judgment, which leads only to condemnation. Because their souls have grown weak, their minds can't grasp the full reality of grace that pardons *and* transforms.

What we do affects how we think. There is no getting around this truth. Right living supports right doctrine; right doctrine helps us to keep living right. We desperately need both.

A Call for New Minds

A saint of a woman named Macrina lived in the fourth century (AD 327–380). She spent her entire life seeking to live the life of Christ and to think the thoughts of Christ, so that even on her deathbed, she showcased a compelling Christianity.

Gregory of Nyssa, Macrina's brother, visited her as she lay dying in deep pain. Gregory was a Cappadocian Father of significant renown, but he held his sister in even higher esteem than his followers held him. Another famous brother, Basil, had recently died, and as Gregory talked to Macrina about their loss, he slipped into a deep, soul-wrenching sorrow: "My heart sank, my face fell in sorrow, and the tears poured from my eyes."

Macrina, *in pain and on her deathbed*, comforted her brother with divine wisdom. Here's how Gregory himself described it:

> But she was so far from being downcast by our sorrow that
> she made our mention of the holy man [Basil] a starting point

111

for the higher [teaching of Christianity], and she expounded arguments of such excellence, explaining the human situation in terms of natural causes, unveiling to reason the divine providence hidden in sad events, and recounting in detail events of the life to be hereafter as if she were inspired by the Holy Spirit, that my soul seemed to be ... uplifted ... by her words and set down inside the heavenly sanctuaries by the guidance of her discourse.[4]

Because Macrina had dedicated her mind to think the thoughts of Christ, even in her weakness, even in her sickness, even in her human sorrow, she became a transforming presence through which the ascended Christ could speak brilliant words of comfort and wisdom.

Macrina grew up as a strikingly beautiful young woman, but her brother wrote about her, not because of her physical beauty, which had faded, but because of her mind and faith, which grew ever stronger and greater. We marginalize women when we value most that which they will surely lose as they age; we honor them as made in the image of God when we value that which can only grow as it submits to the workings of Christ.

Gregory felt so awestruck by his sister's insights that he wrote several treatises, trying to recount her discourses as closely as he could remember them.[5] In an age when not many women were allowed to write books, and even fewer to actually publish them, Gregory captured this gift of Christ by presenting his sister's thoughts under his own esteemed name (though giving Macrina full credit as the source).

Cultivating the mind of Christ gives the church great potential to showcase penetrating insight and compelling truth. The truth is, cultivating such a mind can require great effort, self-denial, and persistent study. How sad it is when people called to the ministry take a shortcut and, instead of calling people to a higher truth, try to mask their lack of understanding with cleverness or lighthearted entertainment.

This is by no means a new temptation. Well over fifty years ago, theologian Helmut Thielicke insightfully critiqued those who were turning church services into "shows," suggesting that "a preacher who can draw enough attention to his vestments may suppose that he can divert attention from the poverty of his thought."[6]

The Christian church has thrived for more than two thousand years because it has largely outthought its opponents. When we fail to cultivate the mind and wisdom of Christ, we are forced into adopting shallow substitutes — movie clips, clever PowerPoint productions, funny jokes — to mask the emptiness of our thinking. I'm not suggesting there is no place for movie clips, or that PowerPoint can never be an effective aid, or that humor has no place — I incorporate all three at various times in my own ministry. But I am suggesting that our presentations should be carried first and foremost by persuasive truth and heart-penetrating insight. Teachers must give their minds to God so that God can give his thoughts to the congregation.

Minds Gloriously Remade

Kit DesLauriers made worldwide headlines when she became the first person to ski from the summits of the highest peaks on all seven continents. Not just *climb* the peaks, mind you, but *ski* down them. Her last descent was Mount Everest in October 2006.

The danger of such a quest is incalculable; Kit recounts her thoughts as she looked down from twenty-nine thousand feet on Mount Everest: "This was the most serious ski descent we had ever attempted.... One mistake, and you would be unrecognizable at the bottom. It was very, very intense."

Her husband, Rob, concurred: "It was one of the few times in my ski career when it was, 'If you fall, you die.'"

How do you face, much less overcome, such a daunting challenge? What do you do with your fear? Kit's thoughts are illuminating: "I don't make any claims to not being scared. It's important, and it's healthy. I've been scared enough that I'm comfortable with it. When you experience fear, the next thing out of people's minds is, 'I can't.' *We are in control of our minds.* As much as our minds try to control us, it is important to not let your mind run too far."[7]

I greatly appreciate Kit's affirmation that we can control our minds. Our minds need not rule us; they can be ruled. When Scripture tells us that God will transform our minds, it's clear that we *can* grow and develop in this area. In fact, the apostle Paul suggests that a Christ-molded mind is the foundation of transformation. Consider this familiar passage:

> Offer your bodies as living sacrifices, holy and pleasing to God — this is your spiritual act of worship. Do not conform any longer to the pattern of this world, but be transformed *by the renewing of your mind*. Then you will be able to test and approve what God's will is — his good, pleasing and perfect will.
>
> Romans 12:1–2, emphasis added

This verse confirms what I have been saying repeatedly throughout this book: God is the agent of change, but we have a responsibility to surrender ourselves to God's change. This is the Beautiful Fight. As C. E. B. Cranfield puts it, "The use of the imperative [be transformed] is consonant with the truth that, while this transformation is not Christians' own doing but the work of the Holy Spirit, they nevertheless have a real responsibility in the matter — to let themselves be transformed, to respond to the leading and pressure of God's Spirit."[8]

"Brothers and sisters," Paul is saying to us, "let God have his way with you. Do not resist him. Do not give in to the patterns of the world. Allow God to transform you." The grammar in this passage suggests that this is to be a lifelong process.

To some, this may sound like a heavy obligation; in reality, it is a revolutionary message of liberation. We don't have to be hapless victims of tyrannizing passions, self-destructive patterns of living, and faulty thinking. We have a God who will splash his glory on us as we present ourselves to him — and this baptism often begins with our minds.

A holy mind is a mind captive to God. Paul's goal here is that our minds "will be able to test and approve what God's will is — his good, pleasing and perfect will." A sanctified mind is a mind that yields to what God says is holy. The Christian celebrity we mentioned earlier grew flummoxed because she didn't know what was right — but all we have to do is ask God and apply his Word as we discover that what he says is right. We surrender to God's definition of right living. A darkened mind wants to be accountable only to itself; an enlightened mind realizes that, regardless of where our feelings or passions try to lead us, our highest calling is to surrender to the illumination of God's higher truth: "Solid food is for the mature, who by constant use have trained themselves to distinguish good from evil" (Hebrews 5:14).

So how do we allow God to transform our minds? What are our points of cooperation?

1. Become Diligent Students

Every month, without fail, I eagerly read *Runner's World* magazine. It's not an obligation for me. Because I love running, I want to read about the latest training techniques and running gear. I revel in the inspiring personal stories. I check my calendar against upcoming races. I want to know about the latest shoes. I even pore over the ads.

The Bible could well be called *God's World*. If we truly love God's world, Bible study will be a joy. We will eagerly embrace the filling of our minds with his inspired words, and we'll also want to read the insights of others as they interact with God's Word, which is why being a diligent student also usually means reading other books.

Is it possible to be a faithful disciple and not be a diligent student? No. Contemplative prayer, social activism, fellowship, and enthusiastic worship all have their place; but if Paul declares that transformation includes the renewal of our minds, I don't believe it is possible for us to be serious disciples of Christ if we do not also become serious students of his truth.

I realize I'm probably preaching to the choir here; you wouldn't be reading a book like this if you weren't a serious "student." I say this more to spur you on with those you influence. We must not allow someone's laziness or lack of fondness for reading, discipline, and study to imprison them in spiritual immaturity. Someone may prefer not to exercise, but if they are fifty pounds overweight and fighting off diabetes, high blood pressure, and clogged arteries, then they had better get over it. They will never get healthy until they find a way to exercise.

In the same way, if someone is ignorant of God's Word, then they will reflect that ignorance in their beliefs, their speech, their purpose in life, their motivations, and in all sorts of spiritual illnesses. They need to get over their distaste of disciplined study. We have many ways to "study" these days, so we have less excuse to remain ignorant than ever before in the history of the church. That's not hyperbole; it's simple fact.

Christianity is not like some Eastern religions that try to circumvent the mind with meditations designed to put the mind in a state of paralysis (such as meditations on the sound of "one hand clapping"). Christianity is a reasonable and rational explanation of the universe and our relationship with the God who created us. Ignorance isn't just sin; it leads to ever-increasing sin. And it has no place in a maturing believer's life.

2. Sit at the Feet of Proven Teachers

Humility reminds us that we all need help. All of us are products of our own prejudices, personal blinders, and lack of experience. Thankfully, God has gifted many women and men with insights that can take us to new heights. We are fools if we ignore their companionship.

My writing career launched with the publication of *Seeking the Face of God* — an exploration of the most common themes of Christian spirituality according to the great Christian classics. C. S. Lewis explains that any new book (including this one) is "still on its trial," needing to be tested.[9] But many books have come down through the ages to help us understand the ways of God.

If you're a man, read some classic books written by a woman — perhaps Teresa of Avila, Julian of Norwich, or Madame Guyon. If you're a woman, go to the books of testosterone-laden teachers such as William Law or John Climacus. The classics allow us to step out of our century, and even out of our traditions, so that our minds can be stretched and expanded beyond their current limitations. Spiritual director R. Somerset Ward put it well: "Herein lies the great justification of the practice of devotional reading. It is, in fact, the use of, and cooperation with, the great process of inspiration which is forever going on in the world: a process whereby the power and wisdom of God is continually flowing out into the world to aid the growth and development of man's soul."[10]

Ward goes on to explain how devotional classics "act, like the starting handle of a motor, by drawing in some of the living power of God to enliven our lack of life." If you're not particularly challenged or inspired by people in your own community, or even in your own century, you are invited to mine the passion, conviction, and deep insight of brothers and sisters who lived in earlier times and in different places.

3. Redeem the Time

Ernest Hemingway didn't suffer fools. The great novelist once dismissed what he considered to be a silly interviewer by saying, "The fact that I am interrupting serious work to answer these questions proves that I am so stupid that I should be penalized severely."[11]

Notice the focus: Hemingway had the sense that he, also, was engaged in a beautiful fight — in his case, to create great literature — so he resented unworthy interruptions.

Do we have the same passion, the same guardedness, the same zeal, to join the Beautiful Fight of cultivating the mind of Christ? Since, in Christ, such a pursuit is possible, how faithfully are we taking advantage of it? Are we so steeped in cultural amusements that we allow ourselves to get lazy?

Certainly, we all need downtime. Recreation is a good thing, as my wife reminded me one day: "You can't read twenty hours a day." But has the "good" thing begun to crowd out the "best" thing — a determined focus to study and "present [ourselves] to God as one approved" (2 Timothy 2:15)? Are we redeeming the time, aspiring to receive and develop a mind marked by God? Will this amazing invitation — to have the mind of Christ — so captivate us that we will give up lesser pursuits to seize it?

4. Pivot

The biblical instruction is clear: we need to take charge of our minds. On their own, minds can be instruments of anxiety, doubt, worry, fear, and romantic fallacies. Paul urges us to exert ourselves more strongly in the arena of our minds than in any other area of the spiritual life: "Finally, brothers, whatever is true, whatever is noble, whatever is right, whatever is pure, whatever is lovely, whatever is admirable — if anything is excellent or praiseworthy — think about such things" (Philippians 4:8). He is even more forceful when writing to the Corinthians: "Stop thinking like children. In regard to evil be infants, but in your thinking be adults" (1 Corinthians 14:20).

We need to mature to the point where we take charge of our minds, Paul insists, because God holds us accountable to do so. Jesus challenged some teachers of the law for their faulty reasoning when he said, "Why are you thinking these things?" (Mark 2:8).

Some Christians act as if they are helpless victims of their own thinking, as if they can't stop certain fantasies, infatuations, negative thinking, rumination on fears, or hateful prejudices. This simply doesn't square with a biblical worldview that tells us to "pivot" toward pure thought. We are taught to stop thinking about evil and to start thinking about what is pure and admirable and excellent.

For understandable reasons, we give our brains a little more power than they deserve, but ultimately, the Bible tells us we must not allow any organ to rule over us — not our stomachs, not our genitalia, and not our brains. We must take dominion over each aspect of our humanity, surrender it to God, and allow it to be transformed by God.

Father, forgive me for failing to cultivate my mind. You have created an incredible instrument for your glory, yet I have all too often corrupted it with impure thoughts and judgments that do not square with your own. This day, I offer back to you my mind for your pleasure, your purpose, and your work on this earth. May you penetrate my mind with your truth, your insights, and your perspective. Grant me the discipline to properly take dominion over

my mind under your guidance, and help me to be faithful to study to present myself as one approved. Lord, please continue the process of sanctifying me by sanctifying my mind. I offer it to you without reservation in the name of Jesus Christ. Amen.

◎ Looking Back ◎

- True transformation takes us beyond the limitations of traditional understandings about morality and expands it to include deep issues of the heart. Not only do we need to "behave" outwardly, but inwardly we must begin thinking like Christ.

- Stupidity can be progressive; we begin to act with ever-increasing foolishness when our minds become strangers to God's truth.

- Christianity stresses how our behavior and our minds influence and act on each other. When our thinking goes, our behavior doesn't lag far behind. And when our behavior slips, our ability to discern is also negatively affected.

- We need to cultivate the mind and wisdom of Christ and avoid the temptation to adopt shallow substitutes in order to mask the emptiness of our thinking. The church's teaching should be carried first and foremost by persuasive truth and heart-penetrating insight.

- We are not at the mercy of our minds. The Bible teaches us that we can take control of our minds and offer them to God for his service and transformation.

- Maturity requires us to become students; ignorance of God's truth handicaps our spiritual growth.

- The call to be transformed by the renewing of our minds includes becoming familiar with the wisdom God has given to others, redeeming our time to give appropriate effort to study, and learning to take charge of our minds, "pivoting" to maintain our focus on the purposes and presence of God.

Chapter 9

Hands and Feet Used by God

Man is so made that he cannot find genuine satisfaction unless his life is transcendent in at least two ways. It must transcend his own ego in that he cares more for a cause than for his own existence, and it must transcend his own brief time in that he builds for the time when he is gone and thereby denies mortality.

Elton Trueblood

Here then is the decisive difference: we can attempt to spread and strengthen the faith by our own effort, or we can allow ourselves to become part of God's greater design.

Klaus Bockmuehl

The world is anxiously waiting to see what Jesus Christ can do in, by, for, and through one man wholly given to him — God-led. You can be that man.

Frank Buchman

The black cloud which hangs over many a dying brow means the stain of an influence lost for Christ.

Henry Drummond

For we are God's workmanship, created in Christ Jesus to do good works, which God prepared in advance for us to do.

Paul, in Ephesians 2:10

Walking through Narita Airport in Tokyo, Japan, my daughter spoke one of her classic "Allison" phrases: "I feel like such an outsider," she said.

I laughed and replied, "That's because you *are*."

Our trip eventually took us to Singapore, an impressive, cosmopolitan country. As we strolled past the Clarke Quay, I began praying for the people, including those who would hear me speak in a few days.

My mind wandered to an article I had read about a rising "sexual tourism" in Thailand in which young women and men were often lured into the country with promises of false jobs and then virtually imprisoned and forced to sell themselves into sexual service for tourists. Because I was an outsider in Singapore, I thought of what I was bringing to the country: truth, I hoped; encouragement; a manifestation of the risen Christ; a passion for God. All of these things would be good gifts, precious splashes of glory that I prayed God would spread through me.

But a war also rages within me. Like the "sexual tourists" in Thailand, I could bring something much different: my lust; my pride; my selfishness. It brought me up short to think about it. I really *can* bring lust into a country with me, as well as greed, arrogance, prejudice, and condescension.

Or I can bring Christ.

Because of the ascension of Jesus and the ongoing work of the Holy Spirit, I can literally bring Christ into a country, if indeed Christ is real in me. Paul wrote, "I no longer live, but Christ lives in me" (Galatians 2:20).

What a thought!

But let's bring it home. Every time you enter a room, you bring *something* with you. Is it lust? If you allow your thoughts to roam into impure places, at that moment you are both creating and bringing lust into your environment.

When you walk along a sidewalk, stroll through the marketplace, or enter a church, what are you bringing with you: lust, or the Spirit of Christ?

When you walk into your house following a long day at work, do you bring selfishness, negativity, harshness, condemnation — or the meekness and gentleness of Christ?

When you go to church on Sunday, what marks your manner more than anything else? Christ, or some spiritual failing? Do you bring encouragement or criticism, judgment or grace?

It was a stunning thought for me to realize that wherever I go, I can spread splashes of glory or showers of sin. What do I want to leave behind?

In this instance, walking toward the famous Mer Lion statue in Singapore, it dawned on me what a force each of us can be in this world. Our "private" battles have a very public effect, for what we cultivate in secret shapes the world we live in.

When we talk about Christ making a real difference with our hands and feet, we must come to grips with the fact that, by God's decision, we are forceful beings. We shape this world. We impact it. We mold it. In fact, it is impossible to walk on this earth and not make a difference of some kind.

God's Grace in Various Forms

The point of Christian ministry is not personal fulfillment. It is not to gain a sense of importance, relevance, or significance. The primary purpose of having hands and feet that reach out to others is to display God's glory. This reality necessitates a focus on God's empowerment as opposed to human giftedness.

The apostle Peter writes about this:

Each one should use whatever gift he has received to serve others, faithfully administering God's grace in its various forms. If anyone speaks, he should do it as one speaking the very words of God. If anyone serves, he should do it with the strength God provides, so that in all things God may be praised through Jesus Christ. To *him* [*not* to the believer] be the glory and the power for ever and ever. Amen.

1 Peter 4:10–11, emphasis added

One October, several years ago, I was in Nashville with my oldest daughter. The next day, *Focus on the Family* would air my first interview with them, creating a platform I hadn't had before. As I went to bed and prayed, anticipating what was to come, I sensed God saying, "I have waited forty-two years for this day."

I cried at the impact of those words.

For years, people had badgered me with the question, "Why haven't you been on *Focus on the Family*? Your stuff on a sacred marriage is the best I've heard." What was I supposed to say? It's not like I didn't want to be on the program, but I could hardly call Dr. Dobson, introduce myself, ask him to join me for a cup of coffee, and then start talking broadcast dates.

But finally, about three years after the book came out, the producers contacted us to set up the interview that would reach millions of people. As I thought about the absurdity of it all, it dawned on me that I may have been their most unlikely guest. What do *I* know about marriage? I'm not a trained therapist, and at one point I practically destroyed my own marriage with my selfishness. Nor am I a particularly gifted writer. Early on, I went through *eight years* of rejection from publishers and magazine editors, including one very painful string of 150 straight rejections. Experts in the business told me I either had nothing to say or couldn't say it well enough. If I was a naturally gifted writer, I can't imagine it taking nearly that long to break through.

And yet, as I lay in that bed, realizing that the message from one of my books would soon go out to numbers I had only dreamed of, it dawned on me that only God can create a platform like this.

Through it all, God *knew*. He had a plan, and he worked out that plan. When I doubted after the tenth rejection, then the twentieth, then the hundredth, then the hundred-fiftieth, God knew what was coming. When I cried about the lost hours typing out words that never made it into print, God knew what lay ahead. When I thought I was wasting my time, God knew otherwise. He had mapped out my life and marked this day on the calendar, and somehow — through all my tantrums, doubts, and accusations — he had brought me to it. It took him forty-two years, but he made it happen.

And doing so brought him great joy.

Looking at the event through this prism — that God had waited more than four decades for this day — cut short any sense of pride.

On the contrary, it sent me into amazement and appreciation and worship: *God, you've outdone yourself this time. You really pulled it off!*

What a joy to work *with* God instead of just *for* God, to see him operate *in spite* of us instead of *because* of us. Have you ever realized that God purposely sets up our lives to reveal his glory? Speaking of one man's healing, Jesus told his disciples, "This happened so that the work of God might be displayed in his life. As long as it is day, we must do the work of him who sent me" (John 9:3–4).

Your limitations can bring glory to God as they provide platforms for him to do something that has no other explanation but God. If I was a naturally gifted writer and a naturally loving husband, you could look at my ministry and say, "What a great guy!" But knowing the truth, you can come to only one conclusion: "What an amazing God, who can use someone like that!" The apostle Paul testifies to this reality this way: "But we have this treasure in jars of clay to show that this all-surpassing power is from God and not from us" (2 Corinthians 4:7).

I put a high premium on service. Since I'm not a particularly musical person, my concept of worship goes well beyond singing praise and worship songs; in fact, at times I may be more dismissive of this form of worship than I should be. I listen to myself and those around me sing songs of incredible commitment, making seemingly heartfelt promises — but how many of them will we actually keep? Yes, in some sense music helps us rest and revel in God's presence, but too often we walk out of church and go our own selfish ways.

 I can find no verse in the New Testament in which Jesus commanded his disciples to sing songs for at least a half hour once a week. But I can hardly go two pages without coming across Jesus' call to commitment, a call he applied and fulfilled in glorious fashion. Jesus prayed to his heavenly Father, "I have brought you glory on earth *by completing the work you gave me to do*" (John 17:4, emphasis added). It's not necessary or even helpful to pit musical worship against service; the two should go hand in hand. But if we lack Jesus' sense of giving God glory by completing the work he gave us to do, our worship will suffer accordingly. Consider how often Paul calls believers "fellow *workers*" (see 1 Corinthians 3:9; 2 Corinthians 6:1), *not* "fellow singers."

Have you ever thought of your own life from God's perspective, as if God were saying to you, "I've waited twenty-five years ... thirty years ... thirty-five years ... fifty years for this day"? What would that day be for you? God has a purpose for you, and he's working to make this purpose come true. And because it's *his* purpose and because *he* is doing it, it's never in doubt. It's going to happen. God knows that it is so. When you see things through that lens, life becomes an exciting adventure of anticipating what God is going to do next rather than participating in a spiritless and desperate rat race in which we try to make something happen.

Thy Will Be Done

My son's middle name comes from a courageous, passionate, and sometimes embarrassing Old Testament king. Astute readers will immediately know I'm talking about David. Who else?

The young shepherd grew into a powerful leader who could be totally right and utterly wrong (sometimes almost simultaneously). But what marks him most is when Scripture calls him a man after God's own heart — and says it more than once. Here's how the New Testament records this description: "After removing Saul, [God] made David their king. He testified concerning him: 'I have found David son of Jesse a man after my own heart; he will do everything I want him to do'" (Acts 13:22).

Did you catch that last line? "He will do everything I want him to do."

My prayer for my son, my daughters, myself, and you is that we will do everything God wants us to do. Henry Drummond waxes eloquent when reflecting on this charge:

> The general truth of these words is simply this: that the end
> of life is to do God's will. Now that is a great and surprising
> revelation.... One man will tell you the end of life is to be true.
> Another will tell you it is to deny self. Another will say it is to
> keep the Ten Commandments. A fourth will point you to the

Beatitudes. One will tell you it is to *do* good, another that it is to *get* good, another that it is to *be* good. But the end of life is in none of these things. It is more than all, and it includes them all. The end of life is not to deny self, nor to be true, nor to keep the Ten Commandments — it is simply to do God's will. It is not to get good nor be good, nor even to do good — it is just what God wills, whether that be working or waiting, or winning or losing, or suffering or recovering, or living or dying.[1]

This makes it all so easy, doesn't it? If it is true that I am to offer my hands and feet back to God, then all of life becomes about finding out and then fulfilling God's purpose for these hands and these feet. This is service in the big things as well as the little things, in the "winning or losing" and even in the "living or dying." Let's say, for instance, that God wills for me to face an illness. How can I be faithful in the midst of that illness? If God wills for me to be poor, or wealthy, or famous, or anonymous, or influential, or ignored, my call is to be faithful in the midst of God's will for me.

Drummond offers further insight about the will of God:

> That is the object of your life and mine — to do God's will. It is not to be happy or to be successful, or famous, or to do the best we can, and get on honestly in the world. It is something far higher than this — to do God's will.... [By this I don't] mean, are we doing God's work? — preaching or teaching or collecting money — but God's *will*. A man may think he is doing God's work when he is not even doing God's will. And a man may be doing God's work and God's will quite as much by hewing stones or sweeping streets as by preaching or praying. So the question just means this — Are we working out our common everyday life on the great lines of God's will?[2]

As believers in Christ, we will search in vain to find happiness outside of his will. I don't pretend, of course, that God's will is always easy to discern. I'm also not certain that God's will is always the narrow road we sometimes make it out to be; if a man loves working with wood and offers up that skillful passion to God, who is to say that his working with wood doesn't become God's will? But one thing I do know: Almost without question, the happiest, most joy-filled people I meet are those who believe they are exactly where God wants them to be. And the most frustrated people on this planet tend to be those who are fighting God rather than surrendering to him.

Offering our hands and feet to God has to do with far more than what we do, however. It also affects *how* we do it.

Struggling with All Christ's Energy

From my childhood, I've wrestled with the reality championed by Paul in a number of places, including Colossians 1:29, where the great apostle writes, "To this end I labor, struggling with all [Christ's] energy, which so powerfully works in me."

This is not merely an imitation of Christ; it is an ongoing *reliance* on Christ, almost (dare I say it?) a mystical dependence (there, I did say it). I once checked two commentaries on Colossians 1:29, both written by well-known and well-respected evangelicals, and was astonished by how little they had to say about this reality. They not only failed to consider what "struggling with all his energy" actually means; they barely even mentioned it, as if it has nothing to say to us today. We evangelicals experience a huge gap between the mystical force of God promised in the New Testament and our actual experience of it. Our focus on imitating Christ may have blinded us to how we are to *appropriate* Christ, receiving his ongoing power. Other traditions can help us gain insight. An Eastern Orthodox monk looks at Christ's presence and power this way:

> Not only Paul but the author of the book of Revelation, the Alexandrine exegetes, martyrs like Ignatius of Antioch, Felicitas, and Perpetua, and many others have witnessed — (the "cloud of witnesses") — to the Spiritual Christ, to the actual charismatic presence of the Lord, as the great fact behind the whole Christian movement. Do *we* believe as intensely in the reality of the Spiritual Christ? ... We, in our day, should endeavor to take the possibility of direct communications from the Risen Lord

most seriously, to become more vividly aware of the absolute reality of his presence, to open our eyes and ears more readily to the deeds and words of the Spiritual Christ. The Christ of the Spirit is no figure of speech, no mere symbol of a surviving influence; he is forever alive and present.[3]

Christ lives through us as we align ourselves with the purposes of God, becoming available to serve him and his kingdom. This, in turn, gives a spiritual depth to our lives and efforts that otherwise would be missing. Klaus Bockmuehl makes this observation:

> Here then is the decisive difference: we can attempt to spread and strengthen the faith by our own effort, or we can allow ourselves to become part of God's greater design. The apostles did not attempt to pursue God's purpose by their own means, interpretations, or strength. They did not separate the *what* and the *how*, consigning the one to God, the other to people. In this way, they arrived at obedience, which is the reason for the deeply spiritual quality of their lives.[4]

It's not as if I'm called to find out the will of God and then accomplish it in my own strength. On the contrary, not only does God call me; he also equips me, sustains me, and empowers me. Anything less is a Christless Christianity.

Bockmuehl helpfully adds, however, that the apostles also do not appear to be "helpless puppets dangled from strings." God, he says, "leaves plenty of room for human initiative."[5] It's a picture of being available to God, of being ready to be used by God, through divine direction and basic wisdom — not an either-or, but a both-and. God will use our natural strengths, but success and initiative are not limited to those strengths — they become infused with God-power.

I can't tell you how many times I have stood up in front of a group feeling tired or sick or defeated and then watched in awe as God's Spirit literally carried me through the day or evening. Self-empowered ministry is so limiting. We're rarely at our best — fully rested, fully prepared, highly energetic, feeling strong. Usually, something niggles at us that will hold back natural-based ministry:

a sinus headache, insomnia, family concerns, an overly busy schedule, nervous anxiety, financial problems — you name it. But when ministry flows out of God-reliance, when our service issues from supernatural dependence, then a full night of sleep, a clear head, or even a clear conscience matters far less than allowing God to do what he does best, namely, glorify his name through us.

How do we open ourselves up to this kind of ministry?

First, we open ourselves up by believing in Christ's empowering presence. The Bible certainly teaches it, so we have to accept it as a possibility. Too many believers don't even consider it; they rely on natural means for a supernatural ministry.

Second, we open ourselves up by humbly asking God to fulfill his word in us. I'm fond of using the following prayer: "Lord, you've created this moment, you've created these people, and you've created me. Not only have you created me, but you've shaped me and prepared me for such a time as this. You've brought us all together, and now I ask you to release your life-giving power to accomplish your aims and your purpose. May the ascended Christ manifest himself through me today."

Because there are relatively few role models within our own tradition, we may need to strike out as pioneers, learning by trial and error and God's direction how to yield to the work of his Holy Spirit.

Third, we prepare for such a ministry by cultivating our relationship with Christ and by living daily in the reality of his indwelling power. We don't turn this relationship on and off; it has to remain the tenor of our lives. I can't ignore God for days on end and then get in front of a group and expect to rest in and rely on his empowering presence. But when my life becomes a prayer, when my service becomes an act of worship, when God-granted humility becomes my companion, then relying on God becomes the only thing I know how to do. There is no other way.

The more I live this way, the more my heart sings with Paul when he calls Christianity a *beautiful* fight, "the only race worth running" (2 Timothy 4:7 MSG).

Soul Salsa

Those who have heard me talk know of my wife's penchant for all things organic. She shops at stores that sell products that boast low salt, no trans fats, no poisonous preservatives — products that somehow bear the name "tortilla chips" — and no taste. My savior when downing these insipid delicacies?

Extra hot salsa.

Service is salsa to the soul. People often talk about the blessings of being a believer, usually referring to financial provision, physical healing, reunited families, and the like. Without denying that God indeed offers such gifts, we would do well to remind ourselves that service is among the most cherished blessings that God bestows. What was true in the time of Moses is just as true today: "I [the LORD] am giving you the service of the priesthood as a gift" (Numbers 18:7).

Without this sense of mission, our lives become intolerable. In the words of Elton Trueblood, "Man can bear great physical or spiritual hardship, but what he cannot bear is the sense of meaninglessness."[6] To further explain, Trueblood talks about one of the ironies of war: "Evil and horrible as war is, there is no doubt that it brings tremendous zest and even mental health to multitudes whose lives normally have no element of victory in them. In the pain of all, they tend to forget their own tiny problems, and in the excitement of the total struggle, each life is lifted temporarily to a higher plane.... War gives significance to little lives."[7]

Our greatest foe is what we most often seek — unencumbered lives and unbroken leisure, lives free from any care or concern. Trueblood believed this would destroy us: "The ultimate enemy is not pain or disease or physical hardship, evil as these may be, but triviality."[8]

We have tried to overcome triviality with sports, but even as a fan, I have to admit that following the latest sporting achievement is still too small of an aim to nurture a soul. After he won the U.S. Open, one of the most prestigious events on the professional golf tour, Johnny Miller found himself saying just days later, "Is this it? Is this really all there is?" Tom Brady, quarterback of the New England Patriots, said something similar after winning one of his several Super Bowl titles.

Perhaps both men heard the whispers of Trueblood's insight: "If a man begins each day as just another unit of time in which he wonders what to do with himself, he is already as good as dead. The man who really lives always has vastly more to do than he can accomplish."[9]

Though it isn't the main point of the parable of the vineyard in Matthew 20:1–16, I think it's interesting how Jesus often calls us "to work in his vineyard" (verse 1) and contrasts that with others "doing nothing" (verse 3). Elsewhere Jesus says, "Ask the Lord of the harvest ... to send out workers into his harvest field," for "the harvest is plentiful" (Matthew 9:37–38). It's good to be reminded that Christianity does involve a call to work. Being a Christian is an honor and joy and comes to us as undeserved grace, but it also entails a responsibility and a task to fulfill.

In the parable of the tenants, Jesus points to exactly what his work will include: being betrayed, mocked, flogged, and crucified (Mark 12:1–12). This was Jesus' *work*. It's so easy to think of Christianity for all its benefits while forgetting the work aspect. And the thing about work is that you don't always get to choose your job. Our employer has the right to tell us what we're going to do; he assigns the jobs. Kingdom work is kingdom *work*.

In fact, that work is the doorway to our greatest satisfaction. Trueblood reminds us, "The greatest unhappiness ... comes from focusing attention on ourselves."[10] If your comfort, fame, and success are the indicators of your happiness, then you will be perpetually frustrated, for who among us can be comfortable enough? Famous enough? Rich enough?

Do you feel frustrated with God? If you do, chances are you've turned your faith on its head. You're likely frustrated because God isn't ordering your life in the way you would choose; he's not answering your prayers like you want him to. You must ask yourself, "Do I really want a fulfilling life?" Remember, satisfaction isn't found in cajoling God to adopt your agenda but in surrendering to God's agenda. Instead of accusing God for what he's not doing, spend time asking him what you're supposed to be doing.

That's what Gene Easley did.

Why Doesn't Somebody Do Something?

Gene Easley lived on the second floor of a Guatemalan apartment. One day he noticed a young girl walking with an elderly woman. Some time later, the pair passed his window one more time, but on this occasion, the young girl carried a bundle of sticks on her head. Gene describes it this way: "The girl particularly caught my eye because of her physical condition. She looked undernourished, very weak in her body, and, in reality, at the very point of collapsing."[11]

As the days passed, the young girl's condition worsened, to the point where Gene began to fear for her life: "She was almost stumbling as she walked. She looked ill, and I seriously wondered if she would survive. Her little arms and legs were so thin that no one had to ask if she was eating right. It was apparent that the girl was suffering from a serious case of malnutrition."[12]

Seeing such a pitiful sight made Gene wonder, *Why doesn't somebody do something?* And then it hit him. God seemed to turn the tables on him: "Why don't *you* do something?"

Gene reflects on the experience this way:

> This is the condition of much of the church world. We are sitting, looking out the windows of our nice churches, seeing the pitiful sights of a world in turmoil; and we are asking the question, "Why doesn't somebody do something?" And God is trying to speak to us and motivate us. He wants us to be active in the harvest fields. No child of God was meant to be just an onlooker. When God shows us the need, we become responsible for that part of the harvest.[13]

I love that phrase: "When God shows us the need, we become responsible for that part of the harvest." Another way to say this is that we are to become the feet and hands of Jesus, which is what Gene and his wife did that afternoon when God's question confronted him. They drove to a grocery store, bought such staples as beans and rice — but also a few treats, including strawberry preserves and some candy — and drove around until they found the elderly woman and her ten-year-old granddaughter.

This was the first of many visits the Easleys made, giving authenticity to Gene's charge to Christians: "God has not called the church to sit and gaze out the window and wonder why situations are so bad. He has called the church to go out and do something."[14]

The Intimate Side of Sweat

When we work *with* God instead of *for* God, our sweat creates an intimacy. In fact, it becomes an act of adoration and worship.

One wintry morning, Francis of Assisi was praying in a cold church when a passerby noticed the famous saint. "Look," he said, "there's Francis. Ask him if he won't sell you a penny's worth of his sweat!"

Francis broke into a smile. "It's not for sale," he replied. "I prefer to keep it for God, who will give me a much better price for it than you."[15]

One June morning, I was feeling worn out from having endured a busy spring schedule. I remember sitting in my office, opening my Bible for morning devotions, and suddenly feeling washed clean by Luke 8:1: "After this, Jesus traveled about from one town and village to another, proclaiming the good news of the kingdom of God." My sense of dislocation ("If it's Friday, I must be in Grand Rapids"), the experience of meeting people and then moving on ("No, that's not Jim; Jim was in Nashville — it must be Aaron"), waking up in the middle of the night, groggy and disoriented ("I thought the bathroom was *that* way") — Jesus knew all that. He could relate to it. Even in what I usually consider the least enjoyable part of what I do (the travel), Jesus can relate. I had almost unwittingly built a new sense of intimacy and sharing with him. How good God is to let me know him this way, to allow me to identify with him like this! Almost immediately I saw joy where just minutes before I had felt only a heavy burden.

Why?

Because I could relate it to Jesus.

My joy reached even greater heights when I read N. T. Wright's description of Jesus' ministry:

> The fact that Jesus was an *itinerant* prophet means, clearly, that he went from village to village, *saying substantially the same things* wherever he went. Local variations would no doubt abound. Novelty would spring up in response to a new situation or a sharp question or challenge. But the historical likelihood — and it is very likely indeed — is that if he told a parable once he told it dozens of times, probably with minor variations; that if he gave a list of (what we call) "beatitudes" once, he gave such a list, probably with minor variations, dozens of times; that he had regular phrases with which he urged repentance, commended faith, encouraged the desperate, rebuked those he considered hard-hearted, spoke words of healing.[16]

You may not travel in your ministry, but you can still use aspects of your ministry to identify with our Lord. Maybe your family misunderstands your passion for service and even belittles you. Jesus can certainly relate to that.

Maybe you work with incompetent people who embarrass you — well, think about what Jesus had to put up with as he loved his disciples day after day.

Maybe you aren't appreciated in your hometown. Whatever the challenge, you can usually find a connection with Jesus — and for your heart's sake, it is a very helpful spiritual exercise to do.

The best ministry is always but a shadow of Jesus' ministry, a reflection of his prior work, the ongoing service of Jesus building his church through us.

Here's the exciting part: such service not only builds intimacy between us and our Savior, but it gives God great joy. Only one place in the New Testament declares that Jesus "rejoiced." (The NIV translates it, "full of joy.") What occasioned such exuberance in our Lord?

The service of the seventy-two ambassadors (Luke 10:21).

Jesus commissioned thirty-six pairs of followers to go out into the towns as workers, because the "harvest was plentiful" (10:1–2). The workers came back bubbling over with accounts of God's power at work. Jesus' near-rapturous response gives ample testimony to the true happiness such labor brought to him. Remember, this is the *one* place where the Bible describes Jesus — the man "familiar with suffering" (Isaiah 53:3) — as "full of joy."

On a Mission

Have your hands been too idle? Have your feet been too stationary? Have you truly offered up your body for active service? Remember Paul's words: "You are not your own; you were bought at a price. Therefore honor God with your body" (1 Corinthians 6:19–20).

When you work for yourself, you can be as careless as you want. As a self-employed person, how I spend my days is up to me. But when I work for someone else, when someone is literally buying my time, that's a different matter entirely. Then I must take great care to account for every minute.

In the Bible's worldview, none of us are self-employed; all of us have been bought with a price. Passivity is an offense to the God who saved us. Consider Jesus' words to Zacchaeus: "The Son of Man came to seek and to save what was lost" (Luke 19:10). Seeking is an *active* word. Jesus wasn't passive; he initiated on our behalf — and as the ascended Savior, he wants to remain active through us.

It's worth noting that following the account of Zacchaeus, Jesus tells the parable of the minas (see Luke 19:11–27). One man gets ten minas and doubles his investment; one gets five and also doubles his money; the last man receives just one mina, hides it, and finally returns it, unused and unmultiplied. Jesus faults the man's passivity. This man didn't steal somebody else's minas or lose his one mina, but neither did he increase it.

Service reminds us that Christianity isn't about *keeping* our faith as much as it is about *spreading* our faith. Religious meetings are the means, not the end; they don't define us as Christians but help us to be faithful as Christians. Henry Drummond warned of a "worship which ends with the worshiper, a religion expressed only in ceremony, and a faith unrelated to life."[17] He goes on later to make this observation:

> The great use of the church is to help men to do without it.... Church services are "diets" of worship. They are meals. All who are hungry will take them, and, if they are wise, regularly. But no workman is paid for his meals. He is paid for the work he does in the strength of them. No Christian is paid for going to church. He goes there for a meal, for strength from God and from his fellow-worshipers to do the work of life — which is the work of Christ.[18]

If all you do is sing to God but never offer your service to him, then you're living on your lunch hour. And what kind of faithfulness is *that*?

Drummond once again shares insight into the difference we can make in the places where God has put us as we stay attuned to his will:

> No man can do more with his life than the will of God — that though we may never be famous or powerful, or called to heroic suffering or acts of self-denial which will vibrate through history: that though we are neither intended to be apostles nor missionaries nor martyrs, but to be common people living in common houses, spending the day in common offices or common kitchens, yet doing the will of God there, we shall do as much as apostle or missionary or martyr — seeing that they can do no more than do God's will where they are, even as we can do as much where we are — and answer the end of our life as truly, faithfully, and triumphantly, as they.[19]

True Christian life is filled with true ministry. True ministry is the ascended Christ ministering to his people, building his church, and accomplishing his will.

Once, as I prayed just before I got up to speak, I remember feeling assured by God that his purpose would be accomplished. It's hard to describe, but I had the sense that the work was *already done* before I even stood up. Since I was totally depending on God, the outcome was never in doubt. My hands were his hands; my feet were his feet. Those nail-scarred limbs still bleed on our behalf.

Mark ends his gospel with precisely this picture. Notice how he bases it on the ascension and the ongoing reign of Christ: "After the Lord Jesus had spoken to them, he was taken up into heaven and he sat at the right hand of God. Then the disciples went out and preached everywhere, *and the Lord worked with them and confirmed his word* by the signs that accompanied it" (Mark 16:19–20, emphasis added).

This is not a picture of a passive historical Jesus. It testifies to a reigning, ruling, active, dynamic Christ, still present today, still working today, using our hands and our feet to complete his task.

Father, forgive me for ever thinking that my hands are my own or that my feet are servants to do my bidding. Make them holy instruments, willing apostles, of your kingdom work. Help me, Lord, to experience what your servant Paul wrote about when he said that your energy worked so powerfully in him. I no longer want to work for *you, Father; I want to work* with *you. I want the power of the risen Christ to lift me above my limitations and set me free to glorify your name above and beyond all I can think or imagine. Lord, take my hands, take my feet, and make them yours. Sanctify them for your service. In Jesus' name. Amen.*

∞ Looking Back ∞

- What we cultivate in secret shapes the world we live in. We can bring the presence of Christ, or we can bring a destructive attitude, everywhere we go.

- Jesus brought his Father glory by completing the work he was given to do. Authentic Christianity involves working diligently with God.

- Understanding that we are called to do God's will helps us move toward surrender and provides a proper context through which to view current frustrations. Whatever situation we're in, our call is to be faithful to God's will in that moment.

- Evangelicals have had a tendency to become so focused on *imitating* Christ that we've lost touch with being mystically *empowered* by Christ. Christianity isn't just concerned about the *what* of God's will; it is equally concerned about *how* that will is accomplished.

- Triviality buries our God-given thirst for fulfillment. We need to be actively engaged in the larger work of building God's kingdom.

- God often makes us aware of a great need as a call for us to become part of the solution. Instead of asking why God doesn't do something, we should ask God, "What do you want me to do?"

- An effective way to build increased intimacy with Christ is to take one of the greatest challenges or frustrations in our current ministry and relate that challenge to something similar that Jesus experienced.

Chapter 10

Hearts That Feel
What God Feels

Whenever a man feels kind compassion with love for his fellow Christian, it is Christ within him.

Julian of Norwich

Jesus demanded of, and offered to, his hearers that renewal of heart which would characterize them as the restored people of YHWH.

N. T. Wright

The greatest difficulty in conversion is to win the heart to God, and the greatest difficulty after conversion is to keep the heart with God.

John Flavel, seventeenth-century Puritan

The LORD your God will circumcise your hearts and the hearts of your descendants, so that you may love him with all your heart and with all your soul, and live.

Deuteronomy 30:6

Have you ever been called to a ministry for which you knew you had lost your heart?

Maybe you've lost your heart for your marriage — even though you still believe God wants you to persevere. Maybe you've lost your heart for your parents or for one of your children — you've been hurt so many times, you just can't care anymore. Maybe you've lost your heart for your congregation, your business, or your small group.

Is it possible to get God's heart back?

Following a trip to Philadelphia, I returned to the West Coast, up in Canada, to do a Sacred Parenting weekend seminar. Because of the time shift, I didn't sleep well at all, and after doing a full Friday night and Saturday morning and afternoon seminar, I came back to the church on Saturday evening for the first "Sunday" service.

When I woke up on Sunday, I felt tired, but prayer, adrenaline, and a venti cup of chai tea from Starbucks got me through the first two services. Just before the third Sunday morning service (four overall), I sat by myself in an office and finally had to admit something I'd never faced before: I *just didn't care* about the fourth service. The travel schedule, combined with the time change (and the fact that I'd been running for two weeks straight), just took my heart away. Besides, how compelling can a sermon be when you've already preached it three times in a row?

At first, I was appalled — how could I go into that pulpit when I really, honestly, just didn't care? Yet how could I *make* myself care?

So I prayed a simple prayer: "Lord, before I came here, and again this morning, I asked you for your words. Now, please, give me your heart. I don't merely want to give a 'lecture.' I want to share your passion for these people and preach out of that power."

Nothing happened.

I picked up my notes and walked back into the church. As I stood up front, one of the pastors leaned over and asked if I would pray for people as they came forward during worship. "We're a bit short on elders and pastors for this final service," he explained. "It's pretty packed, and we may need some help."

I stood up front, and four people came directly to me for prayer, one right after the other. Three left in tears after I had prayed for them. As the final one walked back to the pew, I realized that God had restarted my heart. He reminded me that I was not preaching to a crowd but to real hurting people with concrete problems, who sometimes desperately needed his wisdom. In a brilliant turn of events, God had given me a renewed heart.

I smiled as I sat back down and got ready to take the pulpit. God knows what he's doing! I hadn't been asked to pray for anybody in the first three services. If this was just a "coincidence," it's the one millionth coincidence of my life — all of which occurred after prayer.

God can — and *does* — take hearts that have stopped feeling and imbue them with his passion, purpose, and concern.

The All-Important Heart

It is difficult to overstate the importance of a heart captured by and settled on the things of God. Proverbs 4:23 reads, "Above all else, guard your heart, for it is the wellspring of life."

Above all else.

Did you catch that "above all else"? It's really important. Our hearts can be led astray, and when they are, we become blinded, deaf, and stupid. We are so made that our passions set our course; they shape who we become. The great nineteenth-century preacher Andrew Murray put it this way:

> We know that whatever a man sets his heart on exercises a mighty influence on the life, and leaves its stamp upon his character. He that follows after vanity becomes vain. He that trusts in a god of his own fancy will find his religion an illusion. He that sets his heart upon the loving God will find the living God take possession and fill his heart.[1]

I've seen this happen in a negative way many times. I knew a man who walked in godliness for several decades. He was a solid believer with a strong moral character and a willingness to speak out when others started going astray. Two years after his wife died, I noticed a change in his churchgoing habits. When I asked about his absence from church the previous week, initially he remained silent but then said he had been doing something that, while it might meet his own needs and desires, "could also advance God's kingdom."

"That's great," I said. "Pretty early for evangelism, though."

I could feel his discomfort.

"I'm guessing your evangelism involved a woman," I offered, and he nodded. The meek look told me even more.

"And the reason it started early," I surmised, "is because she actually arrived at your house the night before."

"That's about it," he admitted.

"And this advances God's kingdom *how*?"

"I think I can be a good influence on her."

"By sleeping with her when the two of you aren't married?"

"You know, sometimes you have to meet someone on their own level before they'll hear the gospel."

"So I need to get drunk with alcoholics before I can share the good news with them?"

My friend eventually came around, but I never, ever expected to hear him, of all people, rationalizing something that he had criticized others for doing while his wife was still living. Did his mind suddenly stop thinking? Did his eyes stop seeing? Did his ears stop hearing?

Yes, yes, and yes — but it all began when his heart was led astray.

Perhaps this is why when Jesus went on the attack, he addressed the heart first and foremost:

- "It was because your hearts were hard that Moses wrote you this law" (Mark 10:5).
- "Isaiah was right when he prophesied about you hypocrites; as it is written: 'These people honor me with their lips, but their hearts are far from me'" (Mark 7:6).
- "For from within, out of men's hearts, come evil thoughts, sexual immorality, theft, murder, adultery, greed, malice, deceit, lewdness, envy, slander, arrogance and folly. All these evils come from inside and make a man 'unclean'" (Mark 7:21–23).
- "This people's heart has become calloused" (Matthew 13:15).

Thankfully for us, Christ's death, resurrection, and ascension fulfill a prophecy given long ago: "The LORD your God will circumcise your hearts and the hearts of your descendants, so that you may love him with all your heart and with all your soul, and live" (Deuteronomy 30:6).

Through what Christ has done, our guilty, shame-ridden hearts can be spiritually defibrillated, jump-started to once again beat with Christ-passion and heavenly adoration. The Bible declares this:

Therefore, brothers, since we have confidence to enter the Most Holy Place by the blood of Jesus, by a new and living way opened for us through the curtain, that is, his body, and since we have a great priest over the house of God, let us draw near to God with a sincere heart in full assurance of faith, having our hearts sprinkled to cleanse us from a guilty conscience.

Hebrews 10:19–22

Yet once sprinkled, our hearts still need to be maintained — and even guarded.

Spiritual Intoxication

The book of Revelation warns us how intoxicating sin — and particularly lust — can be. Rebellion against God prevents our hearts from adoring him. Referring to "the great prostitute," the apostle John writes, "The inhabitants of the earth were intoxicated with the wine of her adulteries" (Revelation 17:2). That's what sin does — it intoxicates us with a distorted view of reality. I've seen this when people first get into the throes of a marital affair, or when singles get sexually involved in a premarital relationship. They can become spiritually inebriated. They literally stop seeing things as they really are and become fixated on a fantasy that doesn't actually exist. They can even convince themselves that God approves of what they're doing because it "feels so right."

Heart-blindness goes far beyond sexuality. In fact, the prostitute of Revelation represents a city — Babylon — and the judgment pronounced against her focuses more on her materialism than on her sexual immorality:

- "The merchants of the earth grew rich from her excessive luxuries" (18:3).
- "Give her as much torture and grief as the glory and luxury she gave herself" (18:7).
- "The merchants of the earth will weep and mourn over her because no one buys their cargoes any more" (18:11).
- "The fruit you longed for is gone from you. All your riches and splendor have vanished, never to be recovered" (18:14).

The people react with astonishment that a city so rich, so luxurious, so seemingly glorious, could be brought to such desolation so quickly:

> "Woe! Woe, O great city,
>> dressed in fine linen, purple and scarlet,
>> and glittering with gold, precious stones and pearls!
> In one hour such great wealth has been brought to ruin!"
>
> Revelation 18:16–17

This luxury and materialism acted like a spell on Babylon's citizens: "Your merchants were the world's great men. By your magic spell all the nations were led astray" (18:23).

What are the practical implications of this? Sexual and materialistic sin can make us spiritually drunk. We lose our footing. Our minds go fuzzy. We can't see clearly, feel clearly, or pray clearly. And then, as surely as the wind picks up a stray piece of paper, we get blown here and there by our sin. If we allow the world to steal our hearts, we have all but lost the battle.

The real danger is not just the sin but the fact that the sin has so intoxicated us that *we don't even know we're intoxicated.* This sin inebriation starts to feel normal; some even write books justifying it as an element of basic Christianity.

Jesus warned about this issue in Matthew 13:13–16. I've quoted from this passage already, but notice in this case how it addresses the heart:

> "Though seeing, they do not see;
>> though hearing, they do not hear or understand.

In them is fulfilled the prophecy of Isaiah:

> "'You will be ever hearing but never understanding;
>> you will be ever seeing but never perceiving.
> For this people's *heart* has become calloused;
>> they hardly hear with their ears,
>> and they have closed their eyes.
> Otherwise they might see with their eyes,

> hear with their ears,
>> understand with their hearts
>>> and turn, and I would heal them.'

But blessed are your eyes because they see, and your ears because they hear."

Matthew 13:13–16, emphasis added

Another danger of "intoxication" is worth mentioning here. In the wake of another nationally known evangelical pastor's fall into scandal, I visited the church's website. The former pastor had a recommended reading list; intrigued, I clicked on the button and looked at the pastor's list of suggested books. Every book dealt with organizational, sociological, political, or leadership issues. Not one book focused on intimacy with God, the safeguarding of the heart, or the formation of the spiritual life. And this was a *pastor's* recommended reading list.

It's a cheap shot for someone who writes books about the spiritual life to say, "Well, look at what he was reading! Where was the spiritual food?" But it is fair to ask pastors, lay leaders, and parents to examine whether organization and family successes so intoxicate us that we lose our first love — our heart for God. If we don't keep our heart, which means continually feeding our heart's affection — if we allow the running of a business or the raising of a family or the maintenance of a church to keep us so busy that we don't take time to cultivate intimacy with God and to keep our hearts burning with passion for our first love — then we shouldn't be surprised if our souls collapse into the false intimacy of scandalous sin.

Remember, Jesus said the problem arises not when our hearts become totally blackened but when our hearts become *calloused*. That's what stops us from hearing, seeing, and understanding. A callus builds up over time; it doesn't appear instantaneously. This brilliant image depicts spiritual truth regarding the heart (but we wouldn't expect anything less from God himself).

Over time, as duties press, are you allowing your heart to become calloused?

Above all else — above running a church or business, raising a family, earning a living, keeping your finances afloat — above *all* else, guard your heart, for it is the wellspring of life.

A Rightly Ordered Heart

How do we cooperate with God's work to cultivate and maintain a pure heart? Jeremiah tells us, from God's perspective:

> "I will give them singleness of heart and action, so that they will always fear me for their own good and the good of their children after them.... I will inspire them to fear me, so that they will never turn away from me. I will rejoice in doing them good and will assuredly plant them in this land with all my heart and soul."
>
> Jeremiah 32:39–41

Here's what we need to know so that we can cooperate with this amazing work of God:

1. A Rightly Ordered Heart Lovingly and Joyfully Fears God

"Lovingly and joyfully fearing God" may seem like a contradictory phrase, but only because we misunderstand the true meaning of love, joy, and reverent fear. Love without respect — emotion without discipline — is tragically weak. Sentiment isn't a strong anchor but a fickle visitor. Just ask any formerly infatuated couple now seeking a divorce. If we base our faith only on sentiment with little reverence, we'll be inconsistent at best and (eventually) completely deluded at worst — though, sadly, perhaps even "happy" in our delusion.

Our old hearts, quite frankly, aren't good enough. They're broken, dead, and insufficient for life in the New Way. This reality explains why Old Testament followers lived such dysfunctional lives and raised such dysfunctional families; their faith was largely about following laws and not about God inhabiting them by his Spirit. But God has promised *us* much more: "I will give you a new heart and put a new spirit in you. I will remove from you your heart of stone and give you a heart of flesh. And I will put my Spirit in you and *move you to follow my decrees and be careful to keep my laws*" (Ezekiel 36:26–27, emphasis added). God's Spirit gives us an urgency based in respect. When we receive our new hearts, we will be moved to "be careful to keep [God's] laws."

It amazes me that I still meet many Christians today who think that "the fear of God" is an outdated concept. Without wanting to sound condescending, I'm tempted to ask, "Haven't you ever prayed? Are you really that much of a stranger to God's dynamic presence?"

The book of Acts tells us that the early church exhibited an appropriate fear: "Everyone was filled with awe" (2:43). After two Christ-followers were disciplined most severely, we're told, "Great fear seized the whole church" (5:11). Acts 9:31 gives us a picture of a *healthy, vibrant* community of believers: "The church throughout Judea, Galilee and Samaria enjoyed a time of peace. It was strengthened; and encouraged by the Holy Spirit, it grew in numbers, living in the fear of the Lord."

At root, this is a ridiculous debate. The fact is, if God fully revealed himself to you or me right now, pulling back the veil of heaven and letting us see him as he is in all his glory, we wouldn't be debating the fear of God; we'd fall on our faces and start quaking in our shoes (that is, if we didn't die first). The argument would be all but over. Yes, we'd be in love with him; but just as much, we'd be in awe of him. His greatness would cause us to fear — not necessarily in a terrified sense, for our shared love and affection may well temper that, but certainly in a reverent sobriety. *Those who do not fear God do not live in the reality of God.*

Pastor and author John Piper has a brilliant take on this truth:

> Suppose you were exploring an unknown Greenland glacier in the dead of winter. Just as you reach a sheer cliff with a spectacular view of miles of jagged ice and mountains of snow, a terrible storm breaks in. The wind is so strong that the fear rises in your heart that it might blow you over the cliff. But in the midst of the storm you discover a cleft in the ice where you can hide. Here you feel secure. But, even though secure, the

awesome might of the storm rages on, and you watch it with a kind of trembling pleasure as it surges out across the distant glaciers. Not everything we call fear vanishes from your heart, only the life-threatening part. There remains the trembling, the awe, the wonder, the feeling that you would never want to tangle with such a storm or be the adversary of such a power.

And so it is with God. The fear of God is what is left of the storm when you have a safe place to watch right in the middle of it. Hope turns fear into a trembling and peaceful wonder; and fear takes everything trivial out of hope and makes it earnest and profound. The terrors of God make the pleasures of his people intense. The fireside fellowship is all the sweeter when the storm is howling outside the cottage.[2]

2. A Rightly Ordered Heart Sees Sin for What It Is

Consider Paul's heart against sin: "Who is led into sin, and I do not inwardly burn?" (2 Corinthians 11:29). Paul felt a repulsion toward sin, and his keen discernment immediately recognized its destructiveness. He saw sin for what it is — the great thief that steals our hearts away from God.

Today we have a softer view of sin. We call it an illness. A character foible. A family trait. But sin *repulsed* Paul. This kind of reaction leads to authenticity. One of the best ways to build a zero toleration for sin is to become repulsed by it — which is a *heart* response. Paul saw sin for what it was, and still is — a reprehensible, vile, hateful rebellion against God.

By God's grace, I am growing in my hatred for sin. I hate what it does to families. I hate what it does to churches. I hate how it imprisons individuals. I hate how it turns nations against each other. The very thought of God giving me over to sin (Romans 1:28) or giving our nation over to our sin makes me sick to my stomach and compels me to cry out for God's mercy and grace.

The ancients, particularly the ascetics, grew to know the sin in their own hearts to such an extent that they could truly understand the pitiful human condition and thus be enraptured by God's remedy. Many of us gloss over the evil that lies within us; we excuse our wretchedness or try to overpower its foul stench with religious perfume. In so doing, we unwittingly undercut the glory of God's redemption. If somebody saves me from stubbing my toe, that's one thing; if someone saves me from falling off a cliff, that's something else entirely. The more I hate sin, the more I truly love the grace of God that saves me from such a hideous existence.

Augustine's famous prayer, "Grant me chastity and continence, but not yet," reveals a heart that does not truly see sin correctly (as he himself admitted).[3] How can I be grateful to God for delivering me from doing something that I truly enjoy?

The ascetics looked into the full darkness of their sin and out of horror awoke to hearts filled with divine mercy, grace, and gratitude to God for lifting them out of the muck and the mire. Paul tells us that when we fail to glorify God or give him proper thanks, our thinking becomes futile and our foolish hearts are darkened (see Romans 1:21). We can't fully give thanks unless we realize the depth of God's forgiveness and his astonishing gift of mercy.

3. A Rightly Ordered Heart Is in Love with God's "Eternal Pleasures"

After growing in our reverence for God and seeing sin for what it truly is, we are ready to move on to the third step, namely, renunciation. A caution is in order here, because I'm using *renunciation* in a way many moderns don't. The mere moralist looks at renunciation exclusively through the lens of what we are called to give up, while the incarnationalist sees renunciation as a *transfer of affections*. We don't just "let go"; we find something even better.

The psalmist testifies, "You have made known to me the path of life; you will fill me with joy in your presence, *with eternal pleasures* at your right hand" (Psalm 16:11, emphasis added). God can rightfully ask the person caught in a besetting sin, "Are my pleasures not good enough for you? Why then will you not embrace them?"

Now, eternal pleasures belong to a much broader category than Bible study and worship choruses.[4] When I go for a run with my daughter, that's an eternal pleasure. When you hike beside a mountain stream, enjoy a romantic weekend with your spouse, share a latte at Starbucks with a friend, or read a novel that rocks your worldview — all of these can, in the right context, be "eternal pleasures" — gifts of God's grace — because they can point to his presence. They invite God into our lives in a healthy and holy way.

But how are these *eternal* pleasures? I was made to live in authentic relationship. Building relationships now prepares me for heaven. We will spend eternity surrounded by God's creation. Enjoying the wonders of his creation *now* prepares our hearts for what's in store *then*.

Here's the powerful truth of eternal pleasures: we can begin shaping our hearts now to thirst for and enjoy the things that most mark heaven. In the same way, the choices we make on earth can also block our thirst for heaven. If we fail to embrace the soul-enriching pleasures of God, we'll look for quick fixes.

There is great pleasure and fulfillment, for example, in true relational intimacy. An abusive person tries to take a shortcut. He doesn't want to slowly cultivate a relationship built on trust, transparency, forgiveness, and grace; instead, he wants to get his way by shouting at and abusing others. In doing so, he shuts himself off from the pleasures of God.

A stressed-out mother with no time to herself, perhaps ignored by her husband and isolated from laughter and friends, may soon wonder why she feels so drawn to the refrigerator. She was made to enjoy eternal pleasures; if the poor woman is not experiencing healthy pleasure, she's likely going to start searching for *any* kind of pleasure.

A narcissist who hasn't learned the joy of being used by God to serve and encourage others instead tries to find solace in drawing all attention to himself every time he enters a room. He doesn't know the joy of selfless, nurturing love and thus gets distracted by a fruitless, constant search to get more and more attention.

Pick a sin, and you can find a holy opposite: giving instead of stealing, encouraging instead of gossiping, building up instead of tearing down. The path of life is filled with *eternal* pleasures that lead to steady fulfillment. The path of death throws pitiful substitutes at our feet while inevitably leading us to disappointment and occasionally even into various soul-shrinking addictions.

Here's the well-known trap: temporal pleasures can easily crowd out eternal ones. We are told to let go of cheap substitutes for the same reason that our parents told us not to eat a bag of potato chips a half hour before dinner. If we want to truly relish genuine spiritual nutrition, we must be willing to grow just a little bit hungry without immediately running toward a sin substitute.

If someone is caught in a sin, the mere moralist will say, "You must stop." Fair enough; we *should* stop all rebellion against God. But for the incarnationalist, stopping is merely the *beginning* of transformation, not the end. It's the threshold of entering into something even better.

What does the stay-at-home mom truly desire instead of that cheesecake? Those who have tasted "eternal pleasures" gradually develop souls that cannot feel satisfied by anything less than God's best.

The ancients, better versed than most moderns in the reality of the human heart, talked about three stages of maturity. In the beginning, we may keep the law out of fear; we want to do something, but we refrain because we don't want God to punish us. This is a *willful* obedience. In the next stage, our obedience grows and flows out of love and gratitude; we don't want to hurt the God whom we love and to whom we owe so much. This is a *relational* obedience. We reach the highest state when we are truly *satisfied* with the good, when we obey because our heart desires only what God desires. This is a *transformed* obedience.

This evolution takes time, and there are no shortcuts. True transformation of the heart is a chosen, focused, intentional, and lifelong journey of surrender, repentance, and renewal. And the longer we keep choosing cheap substitutes, the more obstacles we create in our journey toward transformed obedience. That is why we are told, *above all else*, to guard our hearts.

Please, let's avoid the moralist's trap. A heart for God isn't just a heart that's *against* something; on the contrary, it stands out in what it is *for*. If I don't lust, steal, gossip, slander, murder, or covet, *but also fail to love*, I am far from having the heart of God. It is such a trap to focus on avoiding the negative; to do so is to mistake the means for the end. The end is a heart that loves as God loves, that is satisfied in the things of God, and that revels in the glory of God.

Here, more than anywhere else, is where we need God to be active.

A Father's Face

Scene 1: It had been a long weekend. The enterprising organizers had figured out a way to squeeze in a Sacred Parenting conference after the end of a Sacred Marriage conference. Finally, after all the talking ended, people queued up to get their books signed. An engaged woman walked up and asked me a question or two, and then I prayed for her. Afterward she sent me an email, briefly thanking me for the content of the seminar but focusing mostly on that prayer: "Why would you take the time to pray for me when there was a long line of people behind me?"

You know why? Because even when she stands in a long line of people, her spiritual welfare is very important to God. I believe God wanted me to pray for her with a very specific prayer, and so I did. Out of a forty-eight-hour weekend, that was about half of 1 percent of my time — but to her, it constituted the main message.

These seemingly insignificant acts of service help people realize that God is a God of love who is passionate about his people. When we go to God, he gives us his heart for others.

This is not something inherent in me. It's not natural for me to care. But the more I open my heart to God's heart, the more he pours in his passion for real individuals. There was a time when I would focus almost exclusively on the public impression I made while teaching. But I have discovered that God often shows himself even more powerfully in the private, one-on-one conversations; it's just the way he is.

Scene 2: A young man, eager to be a writer, asked if we could get together. I prayed before our meeting that day, sensing that God was moving in this man's life. I asked God to help me be his conduit.

We talked for almost two hours. As I walked away and looked at my watch, my selfish natural heart said, "I can't spend two hours in the middle of the day like this. I've got tons of work to do at home!" But immediately, God challenged me with *his* heart: "This young man has a future. You're investing in my kingdom, and that's a wise use of your time. You were put in this place so that you could provide some needed inspiration and a listening ear."

What changed my heart? Looking at the situation from God's standpoint. Perhaps because I'm so selfish, I don't even try to pretend that my own heart is sufficient. I just don't care about people as much as I should. I'm way too self-centered and self-absorbed. But God has a way, when I allow him, to give me a new passion, a real empathy, a genuine concern.

I think we gain God's heart by gaining God's mind. Marriage is a great exercise for building on this reality. We've already talked about how God is our Father-in-law. If someone married one of my daughters but did nothing but complain about her, my father's heart would shout, "Everything you say may be true, but have you noticed *this* about her? And *that*? And how she excels in this area as well as that area?"

If you feel disillusioned in your marriage, go to your heavenly Father-in-law and let him fill your mind with what you aren't seeing. You may have lost your heart for your spouse, but God hasn't lost his heart for his child. You may have lost your heart for your congregation or your business partner or a sibling or a city, but God, the great Father of all, remains passionate about their welfare.

It might just be the way I'm wired — I tend to be conceptually oriented — but the quickest way for me to gain God's heart is to gain God's thoughts. God's perspective breeds God's passion. Thus I have to spend time in Bible study and listening prayer, allowing God to transform me so that he can conform my heart to his.

Freed from Self-Obsession

Living passionately in the world with God's heart can be profoundly liberating on a personal level. I was asked to speak at St.

Stephen's United Methodist Church in Albuquerque, New Mexico, one February weekend. Steve Roberts, one of the church's pastors, picked me up from the airport and commented on how odd the brown landscape must look to me since I had just flown in from the evergreen (and ever-*wet*) city of Seattle.

"How often *does* it rain here?" I asked.

"Hardly ever," he replied.

I had my running gear with me and was looking forward to a dry run; as a runner in the Pacific Northwest, I own two pairs of running shoes and two raincoats so that one can dry out before my next run.

I spoke on Saturday, beginning at 8:30 a.m. and ending late in the afternoon. As I left the church, clouds had darkened the skies and the heavens had opened up. It was *pouring*.

I have to confess that part of me was thinking, *Great! I run in the rain every other day at home and finally visit a place where it almost never rains — except when I'm visiting!*

But looking at the situation with God's heart, I offered a different prayer: "Lord, thank you for sending this rain to Albuquerque. Steve mentioned to me how much they need it. He even said that officials were calling the need for more rain 'extreme.' Thank you for your goodness in sending this much-needed rain."

Instead of wallowing in resentment, I came out of that prayer with great joy in God's goodness. That's what happens when we live an incarnational spirituality. As we feel with God's heart, he frees us from defining every event only as it relates to us.

A few years ago, an atheist who conceived a child out of wedlock and who never even lived with his daughter sued the United States government on his daughter's behalf to get the words "under God" removed from the Pledge of Allegiance. He explained to a reporter that he was worried his daughter would think less of him if she and her classmates were to "endorse a supreme being."[5]

Notice the concern — it wasn't that the nation may be better served believing in God or that his daughter may benefit from a life of faith. No, he was motivated to act because he didn't want his daughter to think less of him for being an atheist.

That's the kind of self-interest that sours our souls. But please don't let this story about an atheist draw attention away from your believing heart — let us use his weakness as a spotlight to search our own hearts. In what way are *we* distracted by self-interest?

This is true even in a nationalistic sense. By all means, may God bless and preserve the United States of America (or Canada, Australia, South Africa, Korea, or many other countries); but from God's perspective, the kingdom of God does not depend on any one political system. In the book of Revelation, John is told, "You must prophesy again about many peoples, nations, languages and kings" (Revelation 10:11). Peter had to have his prejudice blown away until he could say, "I now realize how true it is that God does not show favoritism but accepts men from every nation who fear him and do what is right" (Acts 10:34–35). God is at work all over the world. His impact on this planet is not reserved for one political party, one government, one continent, or even one world.

The Bible makes it clear that any hatred of others amounts to a form of spiritual blindness. Hatred blinds us to the way things really are:

> Anyone who claims to be in the light but hates his brother is still in the darkness. Whoever loves his brother lives in the light, and there is nothing in him to make him stumble. But whoever hates his brother is in the darkness and walks around in the darkness; he does not know where he is going, because the darkness has blinded him.
>
> 1 John 2:9–11

I cannot feel with God's heart and at the same time hate another person. When you see through the eyes of love, nothing can make you stumble — no prejudice, no envy, no resentment, no arrogance, no selfish motives. You can see clearly, accurately, and objectively. If you do not love, you do not see. As soon as you give your heart over to hate, you stop seeing things accurately.

This is what so often happens during a divorce. People stop loving, start hating, and create caricatures of each other (not always, of course, but much too frequently). They stop seeing their own failings and then exaggerate their spouse's failings. They see neither themselves nor their mate with accuracy. Think about it: when someone initiates a divorce, isn't this, at its root, a statement that "you're not good enough for me"? How dare I tell God's daughter, "I deserve better than you"? (Please understand that I'm speaking generally here. I'm not suggesting that the victims of adultery or abuse were either flippant or shallow if their marriages ended as a result of the sin.)

Sometimes my hard-heartedness results in hatred; other times it's simply a matter of indifference — which isn't acceptable either. God is not indifferent to anyone, and his heart is to imbue us with his passion. In his excellent book *Second Guessing God*, Brian Jones writes this:

> Having Jesus' heart for people keeps us from turning people in our lives into "it" people. You know what I mean by "it" people. When we treat the bank teller no differently from an ATM machine, we have turned that person into an "it." When the cashier who takes our order at a drive-thru doesn't even have a face, we've turned them into an "it." Sometimes we even live in the same house with "it" people. Jesus never met an "it" person. Jesus noticed everyone.... Every interaction he had with another person meant something to Jesus.... When we have Jesus' heart, we see what he sees as if we're borrowing his eyes.[6]

While I heartily applaud Jones's emphasis on learning to see poor and "invisible" people,* I've also found that God's heart helps me to more accurately see and serve wealthy and influential people. I've been blessed with the opportunity to occasionally minister alongside Norm and Bobbe Evans, who head up a wonderful ministry called Pro Athletes Outreach. As I prayed before one of their conferences, God gave me his heart for these men and their wives. While my natural heart felt tempted to envy their financial security, God helped me see the burden behind this supposed freedom:

---

*To be sure, the Bible places a priority on reaching out to the poor, but stressing our need to minister to the downtrodden doesn't mean God wants us to ignore the rich and powerful.

Somebody always wants something from them. Their careers are based entirely on recent performance — what have you done for me lately? — and fans who pay high ticket prices expect autographs, an occasional piece of clothing or equipment, and the right to interrupt a family dinner at a public restaurant. Churches can exploit their athletes to build their congregations; charities bombard them with requests for signed memorabilia and large donations; some family members expect regular "loans." Because these professional athletes often earn millions of dollars a year, few people even think about empathizing with them.

But God does.

I believed, through prayer, that God wanted to give these couples a restful place where he could give gifts back to them — gifts of encouragement, instruction, insight, hope, and laughter. God doesn't write off the poor and lowly, but neither does he lack love and concern for the wealthy and famous.

God's heart keeps us balanced because God's heart overflows with love. It's easy to ignore the poor because they can't do anything for us; on the other hand, it's also possible to go to the other extreme and so focus on the poor that you start to hate, resent, and therefore act unfairly toward the rich. You can score a lot of political points by doing that, but your political persuasion may be blinding you to the benevolent absolutes of God's love. Christ's presence helps us to have God's heart for *all* people, because with God's heart we can be freed from our cursed self-obsession. We no longer discount some people because they can't give us anything; nor do we make selfish demands of others because they *can* give us something. Love remains entirely free of such self-absorption. God's love "does not envy, it does not boast, it is not proud. It is not rude, it is not self-seeking" (1 Corinthians 13:4–5). It is benevolent toward all.

Willing Worship

Since the heart is all-important, worship becomes an essential discipline of the Christian's life. We need to keep celebrating God's gigantic generosity, embracing God's goodness as evidenced through the small pleasures of the world.

Thankfully, we are doubly blessed in that God empowers us to worship him. The risen Christ who lives in us glorifies and worships the Father through us. Here's the marvelous way that Gerrit Scott Dawson describes it:

> This means that in the midst of every sanctuary, Jesus is leading our praise. In the tiniest church in the remotest region to the grandest cathedral in the heart of the city, Jesus is worshiping his Father, bringing his brothers and sisters with him into the presence of God. For the Son of God who became man is still fully human, still in the flesh, still incarnate. As a man he worships God. He has blazed the way before us. He has pioneered the path in his own flesh. And he collects us up, gathers us in his arms, and presents us in praise to God the Father as those whom he has cleansed and redeemed and sanctified. All of that is going on in the midst of our sanctuary when we are there, sitting some mornings like bumps on a log, sleepy, distracted, bored, confused, and waiting for lunch. We may call the people to worship with the astounding news that Jesus is here with outstretched arms declaring to us the name of God.[7]

Worship, prayer, obedience, love — God empowers it all. You cannot name one element of life for which God fails to equip and sustain us. He never leaves us alone. God will give us his heart if we will just go to him and receive it.

Father, there is no heart as large as yours, no heart as pure as yours, no passion as persevering as yours. I humbly ask that you would replace my hardened heart with your genuine compassion. Teach me to hate the things that you hate and to love what you love. Grant me the grace to care, the power to persevere, and a heart that feels content only when it becomes aligned with yours. I pray this in Jesus' name. Amen.

◈ Looking Back ◈

- When we "lose our heart" for a person, a ministry, or a calling, God can renew our passion if we go to him for that purpose.

- It is essential that we learn to guard our hearts. We are made in such a way that our passions set our course; they shape who we become.

- Christians need to be careful about slowly becoming "spiritually intoxicated" with disobedience, which leads to a calloused heart.

- To love God is to fear God; it is essential for Christians to maintain an appropriate reverence for God.

- In addition to fearing God, we should grow in our repulsion toward sin without becoming judgmental of others. To have our hearts set on God is to eventually become repulsed by what is repulsive to God.

- If we're dealing with habitual sin, we should consider how our hearts are being stolen away from God and what "eternal pleasure" we can grab on to that will help us let go of the sin substitute.

- Having God's heart means there are no "it" people in our lives. God gives us his concern, compassion, and love for everyone.

- Cultivating God's heart helps set us free from self-obsession in which we view everything only as it relates to us and our comfort.

- Regular worship is essential for developing and maintaining the heart of God.

Part 3

Embracing the High Call and Duty of Personal Transformation

The deepest mark of committed Christianity is the difference it makes.

Elton Trueblood

Let catechumens spend three years as hearers of the word. But if a man is zealous and perseveres well in the work, it is not the time but his character that is decisive.

Hippolytus

And we, who with unveiled faces all reflect the Lord's glory, are being transformed into his likeness with ever-increasing glory, which comes from the Lord, who is the Spirit.

Paul, in 2 Corinthians 3:18

Chapter 11

Holy Available

At the heart of the logic of all renewal is the recognition that there is no changed Church without changed lives among the members.

Elton Trueblood

Jesus is remaking you into a person who actually loves people and who begins to consider their best interests. Our opinions and impulses no longer reign.
What he has begun, he will complete.

David Powlison

If you are wise and understand God's ways, live a life of steady goodness so that only good deeds will pour forth. And if you don't brag about the good you do, then you will be truly wise!

James 3:13 NLT

Nepal was in an uproar. A fifteen-year-old boy named Ram Bahadur Bomjon had spent the better part of 2005 meditating underneath a pipal tree, reportedly without taking any food or water for months on end.

It's fair to say that Nepal was ripe to believe in a miracle. An ongoing war between Maoists and the monarchy had spawned atrocious and inflammatory conditions, with more than ten thousand casualties in the past decade. Journalist George Saunders describes it this way: "The country is scared, wired, suffering, dreading an imminent explosion that will take a catastrophically poor country and turn it into a catastrophically poor country in a state of civil war."[1]

Begin with a small, troubled village near the Indian border and drop in a miracle-working child twice bitten by poisonous snakes, who refused all medication and yet survived, allegedly has taken

163

no nourishment to speak of for up to seven months, and sits trance-like underneath a "Buddha tree," all but motionless — and *voila*! You have an immediate shrine.

Visitors in the thousands arrived daily, up until March 2006, when the now popularly described "Buddha boy" disappeared in the middle of the night. Rumors spread like wildfire for more than a week, until the BBC reported that "the boy had briefly reappeared for a secret meeting with the Chairman of the Village Committee. He said he was going into hiding and would reappear again in six years."[2]

Quite predictably, Ram Bahadur Bomjon has spawned his own Elvis-like kitsch. Devout Buddhists will no doubt count down the months until his promised return. He followed the classic Buddhist prescription — meditating to achieve a high level of "enlightenment," allowing him to overcome basic bodily needs. Among those seeing such a display, the whispers started out slowly, then built into a crescendo: *This must be a visit from God in the form of a boy.*

And boy, do we need a visit from God!

Every country and every faith are hungry for some visit, some sign, some evidence, that God is really acting on this world, visiting this world, impacting this world. From a Christian worldview, I obviously have significant differences with those who practice Buddhism, including the things they most value. My faith is based on God as our Creator, the physical birth of Christ, his death and resurrection, his ascension, and the sending of his Holy Spirit to empower us. Nevertheless, the Buddha boy does raise an interesting question: What does it mean to be holy?

God declares, "Be holy because I, the LORD your God, am holy" (Leviticus 19:2). But how many Christians know what "be holy" really *means*? "I don't know" was the most common reply to a recent Barna study asking participants what holiness meant.[3]

Holiness through the Ages

If we were to travel back about eighteen hundred years, extreme holiness meant dying for your faith. Both Origen and Tertullian taught that "the life of a Christian ought to be a preparation for martyrdom."[4] Martyrs and even would-be martyrs took on a supreme status, even above the clergy, forcing some concerned mothers to virtually tie up their sons and daughters to keep them from pursuing a martyr's sanctity. To be supremely holy meant to be willing to give up your life prematurely.

Felicity, Perpetua's servant and fellow martyr, actually gave birth to a child just three days before her walk into the amphitheater, where she would be executed for her faith. It is astonishing to read how she had prayed fervently that God would cause her child to be born, because it was against Roman law for pregnant women to be made sport of. She considered it an answer to prayer that the birth came when it did, allowing her to express her full faith commitment to the world (knowing that her sister would care for her newborn child).

A few centuries later, popular holiness involved living a heroically ascetic life — fleeing to the desert, living in solitude, walking around in camel-hair shirts, or camping out on a pole. In essence, this became a self-inflicted martyrdom, since the social acceptance of Christianity made actual physical martyrdom unlikely.[5] The willingness to live in poverty and in absolute obedience became a hallmark of a Christlike spirit, the very picture of holiness in that day.

By the Middle Ages, "holy" and "miracle worker" became virtually synonymous. And it wasn't just working miracles while you lived. To be *really* holy, your bones had to do the trick. Your corpse would be divided up, and if your former finger brought a woman out of her fever or stopped a boy from bleeding — well, then you were holy indeed. Even today, formal canonization in the Roman Catholic Church requires at least one verified miracle after death (not via relics, but through prayer).

Traveling on a few hundred years, in the time of John Wesley and George Whitefield, and in some sense leading up to Aimee Semple McPherson and Billy Graham, the "extremely holy" were those who had powerful ministries of evangelism. Their lives and testimonies drew people into the faith by the thousands.

Today, we often define holiness as "victory in recovery" — former alcoholics and drug abusers breaking free from their addictions, greedy consumers finally gaining control of their spending, broken families learning how to reunite in love. Contemporary believers tend to have a highly moral definition of holiness.

Behind every definition lies an ancient hunger. We all want to see God's power, God's reality, God himself, break through into our natural world. We hunger for splashes of heavenly glory on this earthly stage. Whether these splashes of glory transform what we value most about life, make sick people well, or set addicted people free, we want to experience the reality of a God who acts in this world. And *holy* is the word we use for those who seem most marked by this God-activity.

Two Sides of the Same Face

I've spent the first two-thirds of this book trying to make the case that a big part of our holiness is surrendering our members to God, allowing his Holy Spirit to manifest himself through us, transforming us to see, hear, think, and feel as the ascended Christ sees, hears, thinks, and feels.

But to what end?

That's what the next two chapters are about. And here's my quick answer: so that we can be available to God and thus give glory to God.

Once I begin surrendering my body to be transformed, I become a living and breathing center of possibility. I become a force that God can use to impact the world. This truth teaches me to see my life as a call to represent Christ wherever I go, whether it's at a high school basketball game, a family get-together, the dreaded Department of Motor Vehicles office, a local Starbucks, or my own home. Regardless of my location, I can live with a sense of offering myself up to God so that he can encourage his children and reach out to the lost.

So often, previous generations made morality seem to be an end in itself rather than a means to know, understand, honor, and serve

God. The word *sanctification* literally means to be "set apart," that is, *available*, for God's service, so once I enter the Beautiful Fight, I need to keep myself available.

One of the great dangers of sin is that it keeps us selfishly preoccupied and shut up to the reality of God's working in and through our lives. Some people become preoccupied with sin by becoming addicted; they get to the point where they can't think of anything else. They're not available to be used by God, because their fight is focused on their own plight — *will I or won't I fall?*

Others, however, become preoccupied with sin through a more religiously acceptable route, namely, legalism. These poor souls, strangers to mercy and grace, live their lives largely trying to avoid "making a mistake." Ironically, they can be just as consumed with thoughts of sin as someone given over to it. They may not gamble at a casino on that business trip, overindulge in drink or food, or get involved in some sexual addiction, but they define the success of their business trip largely by what they *didn't* do while away from home. They are just as obsessed with *not* doing something as others are with *doing* something: "I didn't gamble! I didn't get drunk! I didn't order an 'adult' movie!"

And neither dissatisfied soul is fully, wholly, and eagerly available to God.

Jesus Christ sets us free to find new lives made pleasant by grace and mercy and strengthened by purpose. Even more, we live in a way charged with experience and personal encounters with an out-of-this-world God who is still very much in it.

God didn't design us to feel captivated by sobriety, chastity, or financial responsibility; he created us to be captivated by *him*. Paul tells us that the law was replaced by a person (see Galatians 2:16; 3:24–25). Instead of mere obedience, we are called to a passionate relationship. Father Lev Gillet (whose well-known pseudonymn is A Monk of the Eastern Church) observes, "The secret of every spiritual victory is to look at the Lord Jesus, not at temptations and obstacles."[6] At the risk of sounding embarrassingly adolescent, the foundation of the Beautiful Fight is a compelling craziness for Christ.

Even Francis of Assisi, as great a soul as he was, came perilously close to falling into this error of mistaking the means for the end. There can be no doubt about Francis's passion for our Lord, yet he so idealized and personified "Lady Poverty" that the praise he heaped on this cherished aspect of his faith left him — or if not him, then at least his followers — in danger of mistaking the means for the end.

"Availability to God" reminds us of the all-essential relational component of holiness; it's all about being in tune with God, ready to be used by God, and living for God on a moment-by-moment basis.

It is vital to recapture this notion of holiness, particularly if we do not want to lose our young people. When we reduce holiness to mere moralism — which is how most young people view the Christian faith today — Christianity becomes a list of prohibitions. You know what most captured my sixteen-year-old son's heart? Being used by God. Entering an environment in which God's empowering presence used him to bless others solidified his faith far more than years of abstaining from alcohol or sexually explicit movies ever could. It's one thing for young people to learn not to cuss someone out; it's another thing entirely to learn how God can use their tongues to bless, encourage, strengthen, and build his church. It's one thing to close their eyes to something vile or salacious; it's another thing altogether to have God use their eyes to spot a need and then be used by God to minister his presence.

The gospel of transformation is a far more powerful and inviting journey than the religion of prohibition. If we teach primarily that Christianity is about learning how *not* to do something, we will raise seriously frustrated children, because James promises us, "We all stumble in many ways" (James 3:2). A merely prohibitive faith will seem at first frustrating and eventually impossible. But when we teach how Christ transforms us and uses us, including sharing insights on how to experience God, know him, and be used by him; when we rouse people to join the Beautiful Fight — then each battle scar will build assurance, confidence, and joy. Every moment becomes pregnant with possibility, as I discovered one night in a local hospital.

Unexpectedly Available

While I was writing this book, my daughter became seriously ill with pneumonia. At the time of her diagnosis, I felt pretty wiped out myself — but when your kid is sick, you just can't afford the luxury of illness.

The doctor checked Allison into the hospital. After we were settled into the room, the nurse came in and then left. A few minutes later, she stopped in again. The third time she came into our room, she paused and looked at me.

"I know you from somewhere," she said.

"Do you go to church?" I asked.

A big smile crossed her face. "You're Gary Thomas! Oh, we love your books. Wait until my husband hears I met Gary Thomas."

We talked as she came in and out of the room, but I never saw her after that night until Allison was discharged five days later. She stopped in just to say hi. The nurse explained that she didn't normally work on that floor, but the hospital had been unusually busy on Allison's first night. We chatted for a little while longer, and then she added, "I think God just knew I needed to meet Gary Thomas."

I didn't remember any particularly significant conversation that had taken place, certainly nothing I would consider "ministry." In fact, I had felt rather ill myself and was preoccupied by thoughts about the implications of my daughter's illness.

"It's not what you said," the nurse went on to say. "You always had a smile. And you were so calm."

And that's when I felt another splash of God's glory. I caught a glimpse of how his presence — and my being available to him — helps transform not only me but also others around me. At that moment, whether I gambled or not, got drunk or not, or did any of the things people usually think of as an offense to holiness didn't really come into play. When I felt sick and my daughter was ill, at that unexpected moment, was I available to God?

Don't get me wrong. The moral choices we make — the rejection of greed, the cultivation of a Christlike spirit — lead up to these moments of being available. But their chief value lies in making us available to God so that he can inspire others.

We need to spiritually train, which includes repenting of our sins and cultivating the virtues; but these actions aim to prepare us for the ultimate race of service and interaction with others. Throughout Scripture, God points us toward others and cleanses us to reach out to others. We may enter solitude to become available to God in social situations, but if we enter solitude in order to escape society, we've made the means the end.

Are you available to God when you least expect to be called on? That's what prayer, Bible study, worship, fellowship, and similar spiritual disciplines point toward — being available to God. Are you — pun fully intended — holy available?

Perhaps you've found, as I have, that private ministry requires an authenticity often lacking in public ministry. Public ministry — preaching, administration, and other up-front ministries — is largely based on gifting and doesn't necessarily require a corresponding life. I remember one man who greatly challenged me in one of his sermons, so much so that the main point of his powerful, moving sermon still echoes in my mind nearly a quarter century later. Yet I later discovered that he was in the midst of an affair while delivering that sermon.

But private ministry is different. Spontaneous, God-directed private ministry doesn't usually come to me when I'm not spiritually healthy. By "tuning in" to God, God tunes me in to people, bringing them my way.

I want to stay spiritually fit, first to honor God but also so that I can help people. The more I give in to lust, the less I'll see women as they truly are — and I'll miss the holy, pure intimacy that comes from getting to know God's daughters. The more my heart gets captured by greed, the more money will influence the way I think about and treat people, whether they're rich or poor. The more I crave recognition and power, the more I'll be blinded to the selfless service that spawns a joy nothing else matches. Sin makes me blind (lustful or power-hungry), deaf (self-centered), and mute (apathetic) — in other words, wholly unavailable to God.

Holiness, then, involves becoming not only more aware of but also more available to God.

On Call

A young man, a good friend of my son, suffered a sad injustice. I felt heartsick at this turn of events and woke up early the next morning and started to pray. "God," I asked, "can I do anything about this? Can you move creatively here? Would you inspire me to do something to make right this obvious wrong?"

I had been sharing a hotel room with my son and three of his friends. While they slept, I figured I would pray better outside than inside, so I went for a walk beside a river. Once again, I poured out my heart to God, asking him to use me to intervene in some way. I waited for God's quiet leading, which led to nothing.

Absolutely *nothing*.

I share this rather uninspiring story for an important reason: just because we make ourselves available to God doesn't mean we'll experience an unending string of miraculous encounters and exciting celestial conversations. God moves as he wills, where he wills, when he wills. But it was still an act of worship to present myself before God, saying, "Here I am. If you want to do something through me, I'm ready."

Maybe you're about to go to a family reunion; you can pray, "Lord, make me sensitive. I'm offering my ears, mind, tongue, hands, and eyes. Fill them with your presence so that I'll be your servant."

Maybe you know a couple going through a difficult time in their marriage, or a rebellious teenager, or a hurting church, or a troubled coworker. Will you at least present yourself to God and make yourself available to be used by him? He may or may not take you up on your offer, but offering yourself is an important step, a holy act of worship.

Consider a few questions we can ask to help rid ourselves of mere moralism and begin to embrace the gospel of transformation:

- Are my eyes free from lust — but also blind to compassion and opportunities for private encouragement and ministry?
- Are my hands innocent of shedding blood — but also shamefully uncalloused from never reaching out to others?

- Are my ears protected from the vile words that often spew out of cable television — but also deaf to the cries of hurting souls?
- Is my mind free from hate — but also a stranger to God's kingdom plans?

The foundational question is this: Are you available? Is God using your eyes, your mind, your ears, your hands and feet, to build his kingdom? Have you ever offered them up as an act of worship? If not, why not do so now? Why not become an active participant in the Beautiful Fight?

Let me reiterate how exciting and fulfilling a life this is. It's exactly what Paul was talking about when he called Christianity "the only race worth running" (2 Timothy 4:7 MSG). When every moment becomes pregnant with divine possibility, and when each situation provides opportunity for God to manifest himself through us, well, there's nothing else like it. There really isn't! Please don't see this as a heavy obligation or a spiritual "duty." It's an amazing gift of grace, a merciful offer, and a glorious invitation.

◈ Looking Back ◈

- Holiness has been defined in various ways throughout the centuries. Contemporary views of holiness most often revolve around morality, but behind every definition lies an ancient hunger: we want to see God's power break through into our natural world.

- An essential component of holiness is being set apart for God, that is, being *available* to God.

- God didn't design us to be captivated by success in ministry, sobriety, chastity, or financial responsibility; he created us to be captivated by *him*. We must never mistake the means for the end.

- Availability assumes that we are offering ourselves up to God to be used by him in his ministry to others. This requires a certain "spiritual fitness."

- Making ourselves available doesn't necessarily mean an unending string of miraculous encounters; we are called to be faithful as God chooses to use us, but we can't make things happen, nor should we grow angry with God if he has other plans.

Chapter 12

Holy for God

The church is not a tribe for the improvement in holiness of people who think it would be pleasant to be holy, a means to the integration of character for those who cannot bear their conflicts. It is a statement for the divine intention of humanity.

Harold Loukes

The greatest ethical challenge is so to live that men don't glorify you for living that way, but God.

John Piper

Finally, brothers, we instructed you how to live in order to please God, as in fact you are living. Now we ask you and urge you in the Lord Jesus to do this more and more.

Paul, in 1 Thessalonians 4:1

Joe Belzer woke up to the screams.

Late in the night of March 18, 2006, an intoxicated woman driving the wrong way on the highway plowed head-on into the van that was carrying Joe, two of his children, and twelve college students from Truman State University. Joe had been sleeping two rows back in the van, with his legs under the seat in front of him, which is why his right leg snapped when the vehicles collided.

He remembers the screams first. Then the awful scraping of metal on the pavement. It was so loud. That was followed by the curious sensation of road debris and glass that had worked their way into Joe's scalp.

And then the muffled sobs and cries, the shock, as everyone began to realize what had happened. As a campus minister, Joe's first concern was for his children and the college students: Were they alive? Were they OK?

Medical help arrived surprisingly soon. Joe was sprawled out on the roadway; emergency personnel took off all his clothes, right down to his boxers — and that's when Joe heard the best news of the day. A paramedic took one look at him and said, "Looks like this guy is the worst of the bunch. Let's take him first."

"Praise God," Joe whispered. "I'm the worst one in the bunch."

Most people might not take comfort in the fact that they were injured the worst, but then again, most people aren't like Joe. He's the father of ten children, for starters. He's still in campus ministry, even though he's closer to fifty than forty. And while he has enough kids at home to field two basketball teams, he spends his life helping other people's kids grow in their faith at Truman State.

Some people might pass through such an ordeal and ask, "Why me, God?" Joe passed through that event in awe of God's kindness, praying, "Thank you, God!"

"First off," Joe explains, "the van was packed, so there was a lot of cushioning. Second, we had gotten lost earlier, which meant that when the accident did occur, we were at just the right spot — within a quarter mile of the highway patrol headquarters, directly in front of a mile marker, which one of the students mentioned in order to tell the 911 operator where we were, and in the middle of three major trauma hospitals."

In fact, Joe calls the accident "a God thing." "There were people in Oklahoma City who needed to see the glory of our heavenly Father, and God chose to shine the light there. He then had it broadcast over the airways all across this country, and then to hundreds, maybe thousands of churches who prayed for us at their services the next day."

The nurses, doctors, and medical technicians who took care of Joe all listened to him recount "God's miracle." Getting your legs permanently injured might not be the "miracle" most of us would pray for, but from Joe's perspective, a deeper work broke through.

"I felt God say, 'Your comfort is not my highest ambition, Joe. I have made you to give me glory, and sometimes that happens in the midst of suffering.' Through the pain pills that made my thinking fuzzy, my heart understood full well that we were in the middle of something far bigger than we could grasp: *to give him glory*. The week before the accident, I sang, 'To you be all the glory,' but did I mean it now that it meant a physical setback for me?"[1]

Joe's attitude revealed a heart and mind that have been spiritually transformed into those of a mature believer. Joe's highest aim is God's glory, not his own comfort.

This should be true of us, not just in how we handle adversity, but also in how we embrace transformation. We are called to grow in holiness, first and foremost, *to glorify God*.

For the Sake of God's Name

The Pharisees practiced religious righteousness in order to exalt themselves; that's *not* what I'm talking about. A hundred times over, I reject any pride-centered, legalistic false piety based on a list of arbitrary rules. If avoiding certain sins makes us proud and self-righteous, then all we've done is act like an alcoholic who thinks he's superior to another because he gets drunk on vintage wine instead of malt liquor.

There's a far more glorious motivation for embracing real character growth than selfish piety: "[The LORD] guides me in paths of righteousness *for his name's sake*" (Psalm 23:3, emphasis added).* If my transformation can bring glory to God and comfort to his people, I'm going to take it that much more seriously. Jesus picked up this theme in the Sermon on the Mount: "Let your light shine before men, that they may see your good deeds and *praise your Father in heaven*" (Matthew 5:16, emphasis added).

Throughout my youth, I heard sermon after sermon decrying the negative effects of sin, describing how it would do this to me and that to me and make me miserable and so forth. All of that is true, but all of that is also secondary. The highest motivation for striving to grow in holiness is to honor the God who has saved us.

---

*See Isaiah 43:25: "I, even I, am he who blots out your transgressions *for my own sake*"; 1 John 2:12: "Your sins have been forgiven *on account of [Jesus'] name*" (emphasis added in both quotations).

Ezekiel 36:23 magnifies the outreach aspect of this truth: "I will show the holiness of my great name, which has been profaned among the nations, the name you have profaned among them. Then the nations will know that I am the LORD, declares the Sovereign LORD, when I show myself holy through you before their eyes."

Jeremiah chimes in with his take: "'I bound the whole house of Israel and the whole house of Judah to me,' declares the LORD, 'to be my people for my renown and praise and honor'" (13:11).

Walking Billboards

True experiential faith is not an exercise of self-glorification but rather the pathway to giving glory to God. Our transformation proclaims his reality. Luke put it this way: "When [the Sanhedrin] saw the courage of Peter and John and realized that they were unschooled, ordinary men, they were astonished and they took note that these men had been with Jesus" (Acts 4:13).

When we allow God to mark our manner, alter our attitudes, and burnish our behavior, people will naturally ask, "What is it about him? What is it about her?" They'll take note that we have been with Jesus — and have undergone dramatic change. This gives glory to God as we become walking billboards that proclaim his reality and redeeming power.

The reverse is also true: if people take note that we claim to be with Jesus and *haven't* changed, that we're still driven by fear of others and our own passions, then the gospel gets robbed of its glory.

Our motivation for calling God's people to embrace experiential, realized holiness is based on upholding the glory of God's name. In Romans 1:5, Paul clearly lays out the driving force behind his spiritual effort: "Through [Jesus] and *for his name's sake*, we received grace and apostleship to call people from among all the Gentiles *to the obedience* that comes from faith" (emphasis added).

It is for God's sake, first and foremost, that we are obligated to call people to obedience and to preach the practice of holiness. When I allow God to change the way I view people, talk to people, hear people, and feel about people, I become a conduit of ministry, an encourager of faith, and a walking advertisement for God's transforming grace. When I wear the label "Christian" but live in such a way as to deny its truth, I become a stumbling block instead of a stepping-stone to the faith of others. This behavior does not honor or glorify God.

Making It Real

So what does this mean, practically, to you and me?

God's grace empowers and motivates us to live holy and transformed lives for his glory. To complacently continue in sin is not to rest in grace but to deny its continuing power.

To a lesser but still important degree, sinful living also represents hard-hearted ungratefulness. God has forgiven, redeemed, and empowered us, but we're often too lazy and self-absorbed to receive his transforming work in a way that brings glory to his name. We willingly accept the benefits of kingdom living but shirk the responsibilities. We take God's kindness and mercy for granted. We mistake grace as a past reality rather than a present and future friend. We know we don't have to study the Scriptures to earn our salvation, so our Bibles stay closed. It's not necessary to become familiar with the spiritual disciplines to get to heaven, so we ignore them. We don't have to confess our sins to others and spend the time in prayer necessary to mature, so we skip these exercises.

This diminishes our outreach, poisons our Christian communities, frustrates our families, and can even assault our own physical health. But even more than all this, it robs God of his rightful glory.

If we bear his name, we must also show his face.

It's all about giving glory to him.

Think about how God has loved you. Consider the fearful cost he paid to win your salvation. Reflect on his patient mercy and his gentle manner whenever you have gone astray. Meditate on the reality that this perfect God gives to his imperfect children his very name. We are called *Christians*, "little Christs."

Can we not, in the face of such love, embrace the grace of God that teaches us and empowers us to say no to the passions that war against our souls and yes to the invitation to transformed living?

Will we not surrender to the weight of such compelling and compassionate care? Will we still insist on living our own lives our own way and according to our own dictates?

You may not care what that substance or neglect does to your body, but won't you care about what it does to God's body, the church? You may not care what that attitude or response does to your reputation, but won't you care about what it does to God's reputation? You may not care how remaining unchanged reflects on your personal destiny, but won't you care about how it affects God's eternal purposes?

We have found, or been found by, all we could ever want, all we could ever hope for, more than we could ever dream up on our own. Loved with such love, forgiven with such mercy, strengthened with such power, taught with such wisdom, emboldened with such courage — dare we remain the same?

God's grace is not lost in history; it is just as powerful in its ability to deliver us from present and future sins as it was to win our pardon from past sins. True grace continues to transform. We may grow weary, but grace will not. We may become tired and complacent, but God's grace will not. We may momentarily become blind to God's glory, but this can never be true of grace. The grace that saved you is the grace that continues to transform you — they are one and the same.

Consider what the apostle John wrote generations ago:

> And how can we be sure that we belong to him? By obeying his commandments. If someone says, "I belong to God," but doesn't obey God's commandments, that person is a liar and does not live in the truth. But those who obey God's word really do love him. That is the way to know whether or not we live in him. Those who say they live in God should live their lives as Christ did.
>
> 1 John 2:3–6 NLT

In many ways, that is the entire message of this book: "Those who say they live in God should live their lives as Christ did."

For God's glory.

∞ **Looking Back** ∞

- A Christian's highest aim should be God's glory; we are called to embrace transformation, first and foremost, to glorify God.

- Our transformation in holiness proclaims the reality of God and his work in our lives to a disbelieving world.

- Sinful living represents hard-hearted ungratefulness.

- We should consider how our lack of holiness affects God's church, the spread of his kingdom, and his eternal purposes. Out of gratitude for all he has given us and in awe of all he is, we are invited to embrace his transforming work.

Chapter 13

Pursuing Perfection

His humanity is the revelation of what we can be; his divinity the pledge that we can be it.

Andrew Murray

They became changed men themselves before they went out to change others.

William Penn

Men of our way of life should be redolent, not of perfume, but of perfection, and women should be fragrant with the odor of Christ, the royal chrism, not that of powders and perfumes.*

Clement of Alexandria

"Be perfect, therefore, as your heavenly Father is perfect."

Jesus, in Matthew 5:48

On a recent wintry weekend, four dads and four teenage boys (ages sixteen and seventeen) went on an overnight trip. We four dads planned a mix of fun and serious events. We brought a tape of a challenging talk given by a former NFL quarterback to listen to and discuss, and then we prayed for our sons, specifically that the last year and a half they spent in high school would witness their growth as leaders and Christian men.

On the morning of that event, I woke up early, as I'm inclined to do, and read from Joshua 14, one of the most strikingly original and

---

*I can't resist completing Clement's thought, because it's kind of funny: "Yet, let us not develop a fear of perfume.... Let the women make use of a little of these perfumes, but not so much as to nauseate their husbands, for too much fragrance suggests a funeral, not married life."

inspirational passages in the Old Testament. Caleb approaches his old friend and colleague Joshua, telling him, "So here I am today, eighty-five years old! I am still as strong today as the day Moses sent me out; I'm just as vigorous to go out to battle now as I was then. Now give me this hill country that the LORD promised me that day.... The LORD helping me, I will drive them out" (Joshua 14:10–12).

As I prayed, God challenged me; the whole day before, my prayers had focused on helping my son to grow, to step up in his faith, to be bold and strong and Christlike — but now God was putting the spotlight on *me*. Did I think I was done growing? Would I, like Caleb, be just as zealous for God's work in my eighties as I am today in my forties? Would I grow cold in my faith? Would I start to think I'm close enough, even good enough, to stop making "every effort" to add to my faith (see 2 Peter 1:5)? While I may give some occasional effort, am I earnestly striving to grow in Christlikeness?

It is so easy to focus on our children, isn't it? It is so easy to challenge those over whom God has given us authority, whether you're a teacher, pastor, parent, coach, or business owner. But have you and I lost our vision to become more and more Christlike all the way into our eighties? Or do we, God forbid, think we've come "close enough" and can now relax a little as we challenge others?

It's this continuous creep toward complacency that leads me to read those classics that awaken me from my slumber. One such writer is John Wesley, who generated a lot of criticism when he dared to talk of Christian perfection. While I'm not a Wesleyan, I have tremendous respect for Wesley and his teachings, because he was courageous enough to confront the Christless Christianity of his day. One woman, troubled by the phrase "Christian perfection," wrote to Wesley about her concerns. Here's how the great evangelist responded:

> By Christian perfection, I mean, 1. Loving God with all our heart. Do you object to this? I mean, 2. A heart and life all devoted to God. Do you desire less? I mean, 3. Regaining the whole image of God. What objection to this? I mean, 4. Having all the mind that was in Christ. Is this going too far? I mean, 5.

Walking uniformly as Christ walked. And this surely no Christian will object to. If anyone means anything more or anything less by perfection, I have no concern with it.[1]

With all due respect to Wesley, sadly, today there *are* Christians who strongly object to the notion of actively devoting ourselves to "regaining the whole image of God" and the mind of Christ. It's considered an exercise better suited for the Pharisees than modern Christians, maybe even a dangerous doorway to legalism.

To be sure, legalism is a real and serious threat to true faith and devotion. But so is complacency. We must not fall into the latter while we fight the former. Paul told the Corinthians that he prayed for their perfection (2 Corinthians 13:9) and then urged them, "Aim for perfection" (verse 11).

I've included in this book references to a wide variety of authors throughout the ages to demonstrate what Christianity has taught historically, namely, that experiential transformation can be the norm of contemporary Christian life — accounts by the first-century *Didache*, the premedieval Francis of Assisi, the medieval Teresa of Avila, the eighteenth-century Methodist John Wesley, the nineteenth-century Scottish evangelist Henry Drummond, and the twentieth-century Anglicans R. Somerset Ward and Austin Farrar, among others.

In more contemporary terms, John Piper has eloquently suggested that, by God's grace, today's believers can be more obedient than those who lived under the old covenant:

> The old [covenant] is not deficient because it was a *commanding* covenant, or because it commanded wrong things. It was deficient because it was not accompanied, by and large, with inner, transforming, enabling divine power (see Romans 8:3). But what that means practically is that we can go back and profit immensely from the instructions of the Old Testament, *since we now have this transforming, new-covenant power at work within us.*[2]

I am trying to remind us in this book of what Piper appropriately calls "this transforming, new-covenant power at work within us." To receive the grace of forgiveness and to shun the grace of obedience and personal transformation is to misunderstand grace completely. It is a false split concocted by modern minds that view mercy only through the lens of weakness, never through power.

Wesley was so attuned to "the way" that he cared little about denominational distinctions. In one marvelous passage from his journal in 1773, the seventy-year-old founder of Methodism recounts how he "went on, through a most dreary country, to Galway; where, at the late survey, there were twenty thousand Papists and five hundred Protestants. But which of them are Christians, have the mind that was in Christ, and walk as [Christ] walked? And without this, how little does it avail, whether they are called Protestants or Papists!"[3]

In Wesley's mind, whatever creed we ascribe to is called into question if our lives don't reveal the mark of Christ. It's not just John Wesley who looks at us this way, however; it's also our children.

The Letter

One day I found a letter in my office, written by my youngest daughter, Kelsey. It went like this:

Dear Papa,

I want to thank you for checking my English papers so often without a complaint and for being such a good example for me. I have never seen you blow up at us kids or Mom, you never lose your temper! I have never heard you use bad language. Those things have made a huge impact on me. I love how you laugh so much. You make me feel cheerful. You are such an optimist. I'm sorry for losing my temper at you so much. Your attitude and how you react to stuff has shown me a lot. I have grown a lot closer to God this year, and you have helped. You are the best dad I can imagine. I love you so much.

Your affectionate daughter,
Kelsey Thomas

For the record, Kelsey displays a selective memory here. I have lost my temper on occasion, and I don't always treat my wife with the respect she deserves. Sometimes I'm so self-absorbed that I forget to walk in joy, discounting God's goodness and living with a heavy heart. And I do not think I am even remotely close to being the best dad Kelsey can imagine — hardly a day goes by when I don't grieve over some lost opportunities for exemplary parenting.

Even so, Kelsey has noticed her dad displaying some admirable qualities, and she makes a direct connection between those qualities and God. My kids know that prayer and Bible study have been staples for virtually my entire life. If, knowing that, they see that I lose my temper with the same regularity as someone who doesn't seek God; if they notice that I treat my wife no better than anyone whose heart has never been convicted by God; if they witness that I do not possess the joy of one who has experienced God's grace and salvation; if they see that my religious disciplines make no discernible difference in how I live — then the only conclusion they can be expected to reach is that all this "God stuff" doesn't really matter.

In fact, if they regularly see me praying and studying my Bible but acting no differently from anyone else, you could make the case that my religious devotion is more harmful to them than helpful. Religious hypocrisy is like an inoculation that gives a minute fraction of faith but just enough to develop sufficient antibodies so that those around us never come down with the real thing — true devotion.

It's like telling my kids, "God is powerful enough to change my mind but not powerful enough to change my life." But what affects them more — how I believe, or how I act? A child who lacks developmental abstract thinking is going to be much more concerned with how I act.

Perhaps this is why Paul writes, "Watch your life and doctrine closely. Persevere in them, because if you do, you will save both yourself *and your hearers*" (1 Timothy 4:16, emphasis added). One reason it is so essential for my faith to take root in my behavior is so that those who hear about my faith don't turn away through my lack of example.

The challenge, of course, is that none of us — no one — can be a perfect example. But not being able to reach perfection doesn't excuse us from surrendering to and receiving God's enabling grace to grow. Some elements within contemporary Christianity seem to fear effort more than complacency, as if legalism is a bigger threat than our lackadaisical lives. But Paul didn't wear our cultural blinders when he wrote to Timothy, "Be diligent in these matters; give yourself wholly to them, so that everyone may see your progress" (1 Timothy 4:15).

The key here is that last phrase — "so that everyone may see your progress." Paul is saying, "Timothy, you can't be a perfect example to your churches, but you can be an *authentic* example, and any authentic believer is growing in holiness and Christlikeness. Others should see progress in your life. You should be kinder today than you were five years ago. You should have more courage, more gentleness, less self-absorption, and a greater willingness to serve and sacrifice. And you should be humbler five years from now than you are today."

In one sense, prayer and Bible study *are* ends in themselves; I receive no greater joy than meeting God through them. But in another sense, they are very much the means to an end. If I am not changed through practicing them, I'm not providing much of an advertisement for their personal value.

When we use grace as an excuse instead of as inspiration, we hurt others. Yes, God will forgive me if I lose my temper, but my kids will suffer for it — and I don't want that. Yes, God will forgive me if I speak disparagingly to my wife, but she will still be wounded by my words. Yes, God will forgive my pessimistic, self-absorbed attitude, but those around me will have to endure it.

It is selfish to use God's grace as a reason not to grow in godliness. Our sin has real consequences — not just for us but for others as well. I can't think of a single sin that doesn't have severe repercussions for others. I cannot steal without denying someone something that belongs to them. I cannot abuse alcohol or substances without endangering someone by my intoxication. I cannot lust without dehumanizing someone. I cannot display arrogance without belittling or dominating someone. To say, "Oh, but God forgives me, so what does it really matter?" is to completely discount everyone but myself.

Grace does more than earn our forgiveness; it moves us to practice holiness. Consider what Paul wrote to Titus: "For the grace of

God that brings salvation has appeared to all men. It teaches us to say 'No' to ungodliness and worldly passions, and to live self-controlled, upright and godly lives in this present age" (Titus 2:11–12). This then is also part of the Beautiful Fight: say no so that you can say yes to God. And then walk in his service.

Paul goes on to make the direct connection between grace and realized experiential holiness, speaking of "our great God and Savior, Jesus Christ, who gave himself for us to redeem us from all wickedness and to purify for himself a people that are his very own, eager to do what is good" (verses 13–14).

A Gift of Character

A good friend of mine puts so much effort into his anniversary gifts that his wife has learned to anticipate them with much excitement. One year, he looked at her and said, "My gift to you this year is going to be practicing on a daily basis kindness and gentleness."

The tears of gratitude in his wife's eyes erased any notion that this gesture hid a pathetic attempt to avoid spending money. In fact, his wife's reaction helped my friend realize what his tendency toward harshness was costing his wife; his commitment to practice gentleness and kindness was without question the best gift she could imagine.

The last thing I want to do is call us back to legalism or a Pharisee-type faith. But notice, Jesus never faulted the Pharisees for making an effort to practice kindness, mercy, humility, and sacrificial love. He faulted them for putting religious traditions that were empty of real faith — public displays of prayer, ostentatious fasting, arrogant offerings, and the meticulous minutiae of human traditions — above the weightier matters of love. Paul attacked ethnic religious rules that served only to exclude Gentiles and other undesirables.

Sadly, some Christians take Jesus' condemnation of the Pharisees' religious acts and Paul's attacks on religious laws that exclude Gentiles as license to all but give up making any effort to grow in true holiness. Jesus doesn't condemn the desire to grow in godliness (in fact, he says, "Be perfect, therefore, as your heavenly Father is perfect" [Matthew 5:48][4]); rather, he condemns what the Pharisees defined as *godliness* — meaningless religious rules that did not conform to God's view of godly behavior.

I wonder if our misreading of this has caused us to look at the New Testament from the wrong end of the telescope. I believe in the unity of Scripture, including the letters of Paul and James. Both writers obviously use some of the same words (*faith* and *deeds*, for instance) somewhat differently. The problem is that the contemporary church tends to read James ("Faith without deeds is dead" [2:26]) in light of Paul. I think this is backwards. James lived with Jesus; James was the undisputed leader of the early Jerusalem church. We should read Paul in light of James, not the other way around. Paul expected us to exhibit love and do good deeds, as did the writer of Hebrews: "And let us consider how we may spur one another on toward love and good deeds" (10:24). Paul fought against the notion of religious rituals having value for salvation, but in refuting the saving power of religious rites, he never intended to imply that genuine Christians can forget about the poor and about being kind and generous and doing good deeds. Mere belief without evidence of love never passed the first-century test — and it shouldn't pass the test today.

I'm not suggesting that James is more reliable or authoritative than Paul; rather, I'm pleading for us to not minimize James's inspired words the way Luther did when he called the letter of James an "epistle of straw." James and Paul are not at war with each other; on the contrary, they complement and even explain each other. My main point is this: James is essential to keep us from taking Paul's words out of context and to an extreme that would have horrified Paul himself. Without truly understanding James, we are likely to misunderstand Paul and complacently excuse our wallowing in sinful behavior.

In fact, the apostle Paul clearly joined Jesus and James in calling us to actual growth in character. Look at the absolute nature of his words to the Ephesians (in all cases, emphasis added):

- "Be *completely* humble and gentle" (4:2).
- "Make *every effort* to keep the unity of the Spirit" (4:3).

- "So I tell you this, *and insist on it in the Lord*, that you must no longer live as the Gentiles do" (4:17).
- "You were taught, with regard to your former way of life, to put off your old self, which is being corrupted by its deceitful desires; to be made new in the attitude of your minds; and to put on the new self, created to be like God in *true* righteousness and holiness" (4:22–24).
- "Therefore each of you *must* put off falsehood" (4:25).
- "He who has been stealing *must* steal no longer" (4:28).
- "Do not let *any* unwholesome talk come out of your mouths" (4:29).
- "Get rid of *all* bitterness, rage and anger, brawling and slander, along with *every* form of malice" (4:31).
- "Be imitators of God" (5:1).
- "But among you there must not be *even a hint* of sexual immorality, or of *any kind* of impurity, or of greed, because *these are improper* for God's holy people" (5:3).
- "For of this you can be sure: No immoral, impure or greedy person — such a man is an idolater — *has any inheritance* in the kingdom of Christ and of God. Let no one deceive you with empty words, for because of such things *God's wrath comes* on those who are disobedient" (5:5–6).
- "For you were once darkness, but now you are light in the Lord. *Live as children of light....* Have nothing to do with the fruitless deeds of darkness" (5:8, 11).

These aren't the words of moderation; they are words of an ardent enthusiast. No discussion is allowed — "you must"; "make every effort"; "get rid of all bitterness and every form of malice." Paul loved mercy, but he saw living in the light as central to Christianity. Indeed, when testifying before King Agrippa, Paul declared, "I preached that they should repent and turn to God and *prove their repentance by their deeds*" (Acts 26:20, emphasis added).

Do we feel this same passion for sanctification today? Are we concerned about the quality of our character? Or are we content just to be "declared" righteous?

God Is on a Mission

The fact is, God cares more about true transformation than we do. I can live quite contentedly with certain blind spots, but every now and then, God has a way of shining his light on the weaknesses that war against my profession of faith. One season, God challenged me through his Word to be "completely humble and gentle" (Ephesians 4:2). It's the word *completely* that revealed my pathetic immaturity. You see, *completely* doesn't mean being gentle only with my wife, kids, and coworkers; it includes driving my car in a selfless manner.

There's something about getting inside a car that brings out the worst in me. When I'm tired, I'm even worse, which was the case on a recent trip home to Bellingham, Washington, from Portland, Oregon, where I occasionally teach at Western Seminary. Eager to get back, I was driving in the left lane, being conservative to keep my speed less than five miles over the limit. A car pulled out in front of me and proceeded to drop its speed to about five miles *below* the speed limit. I clicked off the cruise control, and a few minutes later, the car in front of me signaled its intention to slip back into the middle lane. I waited until it started to make the lane change and then clicked my cruise control back on. My car jumped forward — but the vehicle in front of me took about forty-five seconds to move over. I've never seen a car straddle two lanes for that long. Since my cruise control was increasing my speed, I came up on the car's rear end and had to click off my cruise control again to avoid hitting it.

A policeman had observed this encounter and pulled me over. The policeman knew I wasn't speeding, but he thought I had been riding this guy for a long time to try to force him over. My brain was so fried from a full weekend of ministry that I couldn't offer much of an explanation. So I got a ticket — my first one in almost two decades — which I thought served me right. I was thinking only of myself and my desire to get home, which made me far from being "completely humble." And even if the guy was taking a ridiculous amount of time to move to a new lane, I wasn't driving "gently."

Five days later, I was driving home from lunch when another policeman pulled me over.

"How fast were you going?" he asked.

"I'm guessing about forty," I said.

"Actually, you were going thirty-eight."

"You pulled me over for going three miles over the speed limit?"

"Sir, it's twenty-five miles per hour through here."

The limit on every nearby street was thirty-five; I'd driven this stretch a million times and never really paid attention to the actual limit.

Now I had two tickets — in less than a week.

My kids loved this, to be honest. Seeing their dad held accountable created an undeniable and even gleeful sense of satisfaction.

Three weeks later, I was returning from a weeklong trip that had sent me to three states. Once again, I was eager to get home. I could smell home, taste home, and even picture myself walking through the front door.

Less than a mile from my house, I cut through a grocery store parking lot to avoid a traffic light. I came up on a parking lot stop sign, where a car signaled a driver's intention to turn left. He had arrived a little ahead of me, so the polite thing to do would have been to let him take his turn first, but my eagerness to get home got the better of me. I drove forward and saw the driver wave at me as I cut him off.

I expected a frustrated wave, but his was polite and friendly. And then I saw the face connected to the waving hand.

It was my senior pastor.

I had cut off my senior pastor!

These three events occurring so close together helped shake me out of my complacency behind the wheel. If Paul urges us to be "completely humble and gentle," there's really no room for aggressive driving — or aggressive board meeting tactics, or harsh treatment of the kid who's refereeing your son's or daughter's soccer game. In the original Greek, "completely" means *completely*.

If we believe in a providential God, then we also must believe in a God who so orders events that he may allow us to become occasionally overwhelmed so as to arrest our attention. Maybe it's a series of illnesses or mishaps, a string of confrontational relationships in which the issue is remarkably the same, or a succession of events that strike us as too specific and too direct to be mere coincidence (you might even call them "splashes of opportunity"). In such moments, will you pause long enough to ask God, "OK, what am I not getting? What are you trying to build in me? What strengths do I lack? What weaknesses are you confronting?"

It took three events for me to finally get it. The law wasn't enough, but humiliation in front of my spiritual shepherd was. By saying "No" to selfish, forceful driving and "Yes" to gentle, thoughtful driving, I invited God back into my car. I can hear his voice when I drive. I can pray for others. I'm available to be used and even in this small, seemingly uneventful area to rejoin the Beautiful Fight. My car becomes a sanctified place, a holy sanctuary, instead of a forceful tool of selfishness and possible hurt.

May I suggest something you may think is ridiculously pious or even dangerously legalistic? As Christians, we should drive like Christians. We should resolve disputes with our neighbors in a Christian manner. Our marriages should be marked with the spirit and love of Christ. Our kindness toward others should mirror the concern of Christ. If no one sees anything different about us, then we're not taking Scripture seriously. What part of Ephesians 4:17 — "I tell you this, and insist on it in the Lord, that you must no longer live as the Gentiles do" — don't we understand? Will we surrender ourselves to God's mission as he transforms us, little by little, into his perfect image?

Toddler Teachers

An author I know answered the phone one day and heard a very nervous voice on the line. It was someone from her publishing house. Someone had made a mistake, and it was about to make my friend's life a little more difficult. She listened to the news, dealt with the reality of what it meant, and moved on. The publisher's representative sighed and said, "You know, that's why we like working with you so much. A lot of writers wouldn't be nearly as gracious."

Can I bore you with the obvious? We're talking about a *Christian* publisher who presumably publishes *Christian* authors. If Christian authors are just as self-centered and resentful when someone makes a mistake as anyone else, then what marks them as Christians?

Admittedly, when James wrote, "We all stumble in many ways" (James 3:2), he was specifically talking about teachers; but I do think we need to expect a higher standard for those who are called to testify publicly to God's truth. I think that many teachers (and parents) stop persevering in their Christian growth. They stop making progress, and when they do, their character usually goes backwards.

Brother Giles, a companion of Saint Francis, warns us of this danger:

> Many men who did not know how to swim have gone into the water to help those who were drowning, and they have drowned with those who were drowning. First, there was one misfortune, and then there were two. If you work well for the salvation of your soul, you will be working well for the salvation of all your friends.... I believe that a good preacher speaks more to himself than to others.[5]

At the foot of the cross, we are all toddlers. But on behalf of the cross, we must press on, persevere, and mature in the faith. We may never in this world grow past being spiritual teenagers, but is it asking too much for teachers to move beyond the toddler stage? The people who hear us have a right to expect that we are growing out of ourselves, moving past our natural self-absorption, and growing in the grace and sweet mercy of our gentle Savior.

It is spiritually toxic and personally disastrous to assume that we have ever arrived, that we can stop making progress.[6] Relying on a misunderstood notion about "grace" is even worse; now we're entangled in theological error as well as in lapsed living. If you're not making progress, you're not really standing still — you're probably going backwards. That's why it's so dangerous to speak only of resting and never of pursuing perfection.

Admittedly, one of the great challenges in writing a book such as this one is how miserably short I fall of its implied reality. I want

God's power but all too often feel spiritually impotent. I want God's authority but all too often cower in fear and doubt and self-loathing. I want God's victory but am often defeated on a daily basis.

And yet — *yet* — there are glimpses, tiny splashes of glory, that reflect a power, a wisdom, a work not my own, that must have its genesis in heaven. I am too old and too spiritually frail to believe that "spiritual perfection" will ever come close to describing me. Whatever John Wesley was talking about, it's not a label I could ever claim.

Yet in the midst of ten of my failures, God is gracious enough to give me one victory, and that one victory is so sweet that I lose all taste for anything else. I have found that God's presence, visits, and mercy are much more wonderful than my sin and limitations are horrible.

I may indeed get it wrong far more often than I get it right — but oh, the glory when, in spite of me, God shines through and does something so wonderfully out of this world!

As this chapter comes to an end, let's take a moment to ponder Caleb's challenge: Will we be fully engaged and vigorously participating in the Beautiful Fight until the end of our lives? What decade will see us slip back into complacency? If you're in your twenties, will you be just as zealous in your forties? Fifties? What about during "retirement" in your sixties or seventies?

Will we begin coasting in our transformation, or will we take up the call to persevere in righteousness — and even be so bold as to pursue perfection, though it will inevitably elude us? The point of this chapter is this: even if perfection as a destination can't be reached in this world, the journey toward it is well worth taking.

∽ **Looking Back** ∾

- Spiritual maturity requires us to guard against the continuous creep toward complacency. Experiential transformation should be the norm of contemporary Christian life.

- One of the reasons it is so essential for our faith to take root in our behavior is for the benefit of those who hear about our faith and may be influenced by our faith and progress, or lack thereof.

- We can't ever provide a perfect example of what it means to be a Christian, but overall we should make progress in our spiritual growth toward Christlikeness.

- Both Jesus and Paul attacked empty religiosity and any notion of earning our salvation through religious observance, but both also urge us on toward character growth and good deeds. We must not mistake condemnation of empty religion as condemnation of true devotion or religious effort.

- God may providentially order certain events and circumstances to wake us up to character issues we are blinded to or complacent about. We need to face such revelations with open, humble hearts.

- When we stop focusing on growing, we usually regress. That's why, even though perfection may not be possible, the journey toward it is still well worth taking.

Chapter 14

What If It's Not Easy?

The cross which stood at the foot of my bed, it was bleeding hard.

Julian of Norwich

A little commitment turns out to be the same as none.

Elton Trueblood

*When all around us the air is full of vague rumors of a newfound faith
which is free of effort and tolerant of everything save toil and pain, it
is time to speak out boldly and to say that true Christianity is the most
costly possession in the world, that it still knows but one road, which
leads over Calvary, and still has but one symbol, which is a cross.*

R. Somerset Ward

*Of this gospel I was appointed a herald and an apostle and a teacher.
That is why I am suffering as I am.*

Paul, in 2 Timothy 1:11 – 12

My friends know that if it's OK to have heroes, then Teresa of Avila
is certainly one of mine. Marginalized because of her gender — even
though she was far more competent administratively and far more
mature in character than many of the men through whom she had
to lead — Teresa was nevertheless as humble as she was wise. In
fact, you never see a single power play in her history. Instead, her
spirituality and her relationships are marked by an extraordinary
intimacy and humility.

Teresa came to the Carmelites at a time when convents were
often little more than holding pens for unwanted or recalcitrant
daughters. The monasteries were comfortable places of luxury and
idleness, and Teresa had the gall to seek a new form of spirituality

that stressed discipline, humility, and service. In spite of fierce opposition and sometimes brutal repression, the Discalced (shoeless) Carmelites that Teresa founded shaped Christian spirituality for centuries to come.

Because of Teresa's leadership, people encountered Christ. Her way of prayer and the Christian life was anything but easy; it was filled with discipline, toil, and sacrifice — everything some modern Christians would categorically dismiss as part of a legalistic, human-centered effort. Because her teachings confronted the soft Christianity of the time, she made many enemies. Some of Teresa's closest associates, such as John of the Cross, were jailed because of their allegiance to her teaching.

But Teresa paid the price because she saw how powerful it was for people to embrace a soul-transforming renewal. Nuns and monks, dedicated to prayer, became women and men of power marked by intimacy, relying on a grace buttressed by self-denial and exhibiting great joy in the midst of suffering. All of the things that our world often considers self-contradictory were joined in a holy unity as these women and men gave themselves over to Christlikeness.

Any movement that stresses Christlikeness comes with a cost. While we often laud Dietrich Bonhoeffer's classic *The Cost of Discipleship*, I sometimes wonder how many Christians still read it and, even more, how many truly believe it. What I'm about to say may sound like heresy, but I believe it will be truth medicine for Christ-followers: character transformation, though dependent on grace and God's empowerment, requires a lot of hard work, vigilant oversight, rigorous thought, self-discipline, and a life marked by repentance. It also entails surrendering to a God who is more concerned with our character than with our comfort.

I want to encourage you, but I also want to be honest. If you think the Beautiful Fight is an easy life, you've been misled. Yes, Jesus said, "My yoke is easy and my burden is light," but he also said, "Take up [your] cross," and "In this world you will have trouble" (Matthew 11:30; 16:24; John 16:33).

This chapter is about courageously facing and even using the "cross" and the "trouble" as you walk the road of a transformed life.

Vague Rumors and Ancient Truth

R. Somerset Ward (1881–1962), one of the Anglican Church's most influential spiritual directors, asks a question that spiritual theologians have wrestled with for ages:

> How comes it that saints are still looked upon as a class apart instead of being normal examples of membership of the church? The answer to that question is to be found in the cost of saint-hood. It cannot be too often or too clearly proclaimed that Christianity is something for which a big price has to be paid. When all around us the air is full of vague rumors of a new-found faith which is free of effort and tolerant of everything save toil and pain, it is time to speak out boldly and to say that true Christianity is the most costly possession in the world, that it still knows but one road, which leads over Calvary, and still has but one symbol, which is a cross. If a saint is one who ap-proximates to the life of Christ, it is self-evident that he is one who suffers in the endeavor to come to God. There were many ways in which our Lord could have saved the world, but he was limited in his choice, for God can but choose "the best," and the way he chose was the way of suffering, of hard discipline, and severe tests. The man and the woman who are not prepared to pay this price cannot attain the profession of sainthood to which they are called.[1]

I've placed this chapter near the end of this book because it speaks such a sobering truth, yet an absolutely essential one. I hope by God's grace that in this book you've been inspired by the splen-dor of a more realized life in Christ. The flip side, however, is that such a transformation comes with a heavy cost, and "the man and the woman who are not prepared to pay this price cannot attain the profession of sainthood to which they are called."

Others will try to tell you there's an easier way. This message is precisely what Ward warns us about when he writes that "all around us the air is full of vague rumors of a newfound faith which is free of effort and tolerant of everything save toil and pain,"

There's Pain Either Way

The reason I receive Ward's admonition as an encouraging invitation is because I've experienced the other side. I've come to realize that when I refuse to face the pain of transformation, eventually I must endure the misery of my immaturity. I can drive like a Christian, or I can fork over hundreds of dollars for traffic fines. I can eat and drink in moderation, or I can spend time in a hospital. I can be selfless and loving toward my family, or I can endure the cold scorn and lack of respect of my wife and kids.

I have found, from far more experience than I care to admit, that sin overpromises and underdelivers. It shouts its promises but then mockingly reneges on its pledge. Obedience whispers its alternative but then shouts its affirmation.

Just talk to an addict who must spend more energy than you can imagine trying to avoid a self-destructive response to any number of life "triggers." Look into the eyes of two hurting spouses whose sin has destroyed their family. Spend just five minutes in the presence of a pastor whose sin has been exposed and who has lost much respect and his vocation, ministry, and reputation.

Words can hardly describe such agony. We've all felt it in our own ways and at our own levels. The truth is, sin eventually makes us feel miserable. The best way to unleash stress in our lives is to rebel against God's plan. The surest path to unrest is ungodliness. There is no greater weight we must bear than the heaviness of our own sinful choices. Whether our unrestrained anger leads us to a heart attack, our unrestrained greed leads us to debt, our unrestrained passions threaten our family, or our unrestrained appetites threaten to cut short our lives, the result is always the same — misery, frustration, and angst.

I love John Piper's concise take on this: "Not knowing God puts you at the mercy of your passions — and they have no mercy without God."[2] Or Charles Spurgeon's insight: "To be a believer in God early in life is to be saved a thousand regrets."[3] Or, even better, God's word of truth: "'There is no peace,' says the LORD, 'for the wicked'" (Isaiah 48:22).

Having faced the personal misery and relational pain of doing things my way, having experienced the futility of living life to be noticed, and having carried the heavy burden of making pleasure my idol, I'm far more willing to pay the price for transformation. There's pain in either direction. I may as well embrace the pain that leads me *to* God instead of suffer the pain of being drawn *away* from him.

So I hope you'll take these words as an encouragement. Pain in this world is a foregone conclusion. The only question is whether we choose to live a life of redemptive pain or of self-destructive pain. I pray you'll choose redemptive pain.

A Difficult Road

"I'm thinking of running the Grandma's Marathon in Duluth, Minnesota."

"Duluth? I thought you were going to run San Diego. Why in the world would you want to fly out to *Duluth*?"

"I'll tell you why. I've run three marathons in Washington State, including two in Seattle, which happens to have a monster of a hill about twenty miles into the race. San Diego throws a big hill at you about five miles in. Overall, Duluth goes *downhill*. I think I'd like that."

Call me a wimp, but I was just on the cusp of qualifying for Boston — and always while running very hilly, relatively local races. I thought if I could run an easier one, I could eventually end up on the starting line of every marathoner's holy grail — the famous Boston Marathon. Of course, I'd rather spend time in San Diego than Duluth, Minnesota; I love San Diego, and one of my closest friends lives there. But in this case, none of that could compare with a course that goes downhill.

It's human nature to seek the easiest course, in our faith as well as in our athletic endeavors. But when I read the ancients, I'm struck by their very different expectations about the Christian journey. They held up holy living as a glorious ideal, but they also warned how difficult it is to attain. Consider John Chrysostom, a late-fourth-century bishop of Constantinople. He's talking specifically about guarding a life of chastity, but the same principle applies to any form of transformed living:

> [The apostle Paul] shows and demonstrates to us that as long as we breathe and are clothed in this fleshly covering, the labors of the palaestra [place of gymnastic exercises] are necessary for us, and that temperance is never correctly practiced without difficulty; it is rather necessary to prepare for this trophy with quantities of sweat and weariness. Thus he says, "I mortify my body and keep it in subjection, lest in preaching to others I myself be rejected as counterfeit coin" (1 Corinthians 9:27). He made these remarks to indicate the rebelliousness of the flesh and the madness which stems from desire, to show that the battle was a constant one and his own life a contest.[4]

If indeed the Beautiful Fight is a beautiful *fight*, the best way to prepare you is to warn you of the "quantities of sweat and weariness" that it may entail. In fact, the battle may be a constant one. Elsewhere, Chrysostom issues this warning:

> I know the violence attendant upon this state [of holiness]. I know the strain of these deeds. I know the burden of the fight. You need a soul fond of strife, one forceful and reckless against the passions. You must walk over coals without being burned, and walk over swords without being slashed. The power of passion is as great as that of fire and sword. If the soul happens not to have been prepared in this way to be indifferent to its suffering, it will quickly destroy itself. We need iron will, eyes always open, much patience, strong defenses, external walls and barriers, watchful and high-minded guards, and in addition to all of these, divine help.[5]

I wonder how many people we have injured by promising that God can "heal" them of their addictions without warning them adequately of the dangers and effort that such freedom can entail. Is it possible that we've added to their sense of worthlessness, making them feel unusually weak because we're afraid to admit that we, too, struggle mightily, even daily, against the worst tendencies of our own nature?

Let's be honest: even sedentary, overweight people can eventually run a marathon — but getting to that point won't be easy. In the same way, pleasure-loving, weak-willed Christians can be transformed to more accurately represent the risen and ascended Christ — but getting there takes a lot of effort and constant focus.

Perhaps this is why Jesus told us we must take up the cross *daily*. True transformation isn't built on a onetime decision or on a spark of inspiration and motivation after attending a prayer meeting or reading a book. It's built on consistent choices. Small events eventually create big characters. R. Somerset Ward put it this way:

> The necessary materials for the building up of a saint are in every life; they need only to be used.... It is not necessary to be hung upon a cross in order to be crucified; an idle slander accepted meekly will do instead. It is not necessary to kiss a leper to secure self-discipline; a genuine effort to be kind and companionable to a person we dislike intensely will do as well. It is not necessary to face martyrdom before a heathen judge to secure a severe test, for the humble acceptance of a sudden insult or the true and instant forgiveness of a wrong will serve as well.[6]

My books *Sacred Marriage* and *Sacred Parenting* are built on this very foundation. The ordinary events of family life provide more than enough drama to increase and foster spiritual maturity if we will only embrace them as such. Christlikeness is born in us when we deny ourselves in the small tasks of life — seeking to understand instead of being understood, holding our tongue when before we would readily and openly criticize, having our will broken by forgiving and serving and listening. These are often the truest tests of spiritual discipline. They are rarely easy, but if we accept and engage them as tests, if we are willing to do the work required to maintain our relationships, we will be transformed in the midst of that process.

An Awful Task

Without perseverance, there is no maturity. James writes, "Perseverance must finish its work so that you may be mature and complete, not lacking anything" (James 1:4). Perseverance is perhaps the most difficult step. R. Somerset Ward makes this observation:

> Of all the tests of the saint, I suppose this is the hardest for us. To go on day by day without getting slack, without continual stimulus, is an awful task. Look back on life and you will see how often we have had the opportunities of sainthood, and how often we have lost them because we would not persevere.[7]

I don't want to be perceived as picking on divorced people, especially since in many cases, divorce is forced on a believer who, because of the laws in our country, really has no choice if one partner insists on bringing the marriage to an end. I've known some very godly people who eventually had to let the other person go. But isn't it often true that divorce is a refusal to keep working on the relationship? Isn't it, by definition, the refusal of at least one of the partners to persevere? It's saying, "Things have become too difficult, too frustrating, too hard. I want something easier, something more fun, something more pleasurable, so I'm going to try to start over with someone else."

What such people miss is the experience of God's power in doing a soul-scouring work in the midst of a very difficult relationship — and this goes far beyond marriage to include parenting, office politics, and even (or perhaps especially) church life. But this works only when we realize, as Ward reminds us, that the difficult relationships and situations we find ourselves in are really masked "opportunities of sainthood."

These qualities of a saint come at a premium price. We cannot wake up one day and suddenly see a saint looking back at us in the mirror. The tapestry of Christlikeness is laid down stitch by single stitch, as God weaves events, attitudes, relationships, and personal affliction through our daily experience. As we lovingly respond to him, he shapes us by his firm and gracious will. This wonderful, costly process produces a marvelous, even miraculous, return. There is nothing so dear, so rich, so utterly fulfilling, as to be God's instrument in the midst of our frailties. Ward captures it well:

> The church has been the wonder of the world, and the chief cause of that wonder has been that with all the feebleness of its constituents, it still is filled to overflowing with life. So long as it is God's means of manifesting Christ, it must be full of life, for every agent which God uses is provided with his life. Nor is it any different, save in degree, with you and me. If we are prepared to pay the cost and volunteer as God's instruments, we, in spite of all our frailty and failings, shall assuredly be filled to overflowing with the power required. Never yet was there a laborer in God's vineyard who was not overpaid.[8]

The cost doesn't sound so severe when we realize that the payoff is so grand. And isn't this the truth behind Peter's words: "These [trials] have come so that your faith — of greater worth than gold, which perishes even though refined by fire — may be proved genuine and may result in praise, glory and honor when Jesus Christ is revealed" (1 Peter 1:7)?

Keep On Paying

Before we become enamored with the end, however, we must take a hard and honest look at the process. If you want to become like Christ — if you would see with his eyes, hear with his ears, become available in every way — you will be asked to pay a price. Even more, you will be asked to keep on paying.

Teresa of Avila lived with constant migraines; she was reviled, hated, hunted, and hurt by her enemies. Francis of Assisi ended his life as a physical wreck. Outwardly, it is not an exaggeration to call his physical condition "pathetic." Francis finally slipped into heaven, leaving behind a broken body that had all but given out. He was virtually blind, could hardly walk, and may have suffered the bleeding wounds of the stigmata.

Madame Jeanne Guyon — praised by Fénelon, Wesley, and other historical leaders for her insights and writings — traveled this same journey. She was born in the hedonistic reign of Louis XIV in France, and her intellect, wit, beauty, and conversational skill placed her firmly within the most popular elements of fashionable society. She married a wealthy man but also gained a tyrannical mother-in-law, thus setting into motion an avalanche of tribulation.

It all began when Jeanne's husband lost much of his wealth, which helped turned Jeanne's bitter mother-in-law into a bitter, avaricious mother-in-law. A bout of serious sickness was followed by the death of a close, much-loved relative. Jeanne received these calamities as God's gift to her soul:

> Thou hast ordered these things, O my God, for my salvation!
> In goodness Thou hast afflicted me. Enlightened by the result,
> I have since clearly seen that these dealings of Thy providence
> were necessary in order to make me die to my vain and haughty
> nature.[9]

In a hagiography, Jeanne's biographer would have showed her as going "from glory to glory" — once she saw the error of her ways and the shallowness of her life and faith, she would never be the same — but the truth was far more complicated. Her conversion was certainly genuine, making her initially lose her taste for the frivolous entertainments of Louis XIV's court, but after a couple of years, Jeanne found herself slipping back into her former ways and appetites.

Haven't we all been there? God convicts us, and we earnestly turn back to him, resolving to change our ways, reform our behavior, and grow in grace. But then time passes, and the passion of our hearts cools. God has a way of using severe tests, coupled with good teaching, to bring back our focus.

In Jeanne's case, God helped solidify her heart and win back her allegiance with two major events — a conversation with a godly stranger on a Paris bridge and then the onset of smallpox, which all but wiped out Jeanne's famous beauty. In King Louis's court, appearance mattered far more than character, at least as far as women were concerned. Yet Jeanne received her permanent facial scarring as another divine gift: "The devastation without was counterbalanced by a peace within."[10]

In a move shocking to her intimates, Jeanne ordered her servant to bring a mirror. After studying her marked face, Jeanne confessed, "I was no longer what I was once. It was then I saw my heavenly Father had not been unfaithful in his work but had ordered the sacrifice in all reality."[11]

Freed from lesser concerns, Jeanne's sanctity reached inspiring levels, even heroic ones. Having realized that "soft touches" would not have shaken her out of her slumber, Jeanne embraced the severe road to transformation. Her own experience kept her from bringing false comfort to those whom God was in the process of breaking:

> Oh, adorable conduct of my God! There must be no guide, no prop for the person whom Thou art leading into the regions of darkness and death. There must be no conductor, no support to the man whom Thou art determined to destroy to the entire destruction of the natural life.[12]

By "destruction of the natural life," Jeanne was referring to our vanity, selfishness, and carnal desires.

Guyon left behind approximately sixty volumes of wisdom that have fed church leaders for centuries afterwards. Many of her writings are still read today.

One need only read the spiritual biographies of Teresa, Francis, Jeanne Guyon, Julian of Norwich, Richard Baxter, and countless others to discover that these servants reached the end of their earthly lives looking conspicuously like their Lord — broken, bleeding, hurting, and grieving — but transformed into an ever-growing Christlikeness. Julian of Norwich is typical of the classical Christian writers when she recounts, "Like a wretch I tossed and moaned with the feeling of bodily pain, and I thought it a great weariness that I should live longer, and I was as barren and dry, through the return of my pain and my loss of spiritual feeling, as if I had received little comfort."[13]

These brave, faithful saints testify to a truth that may have little appeal today, one that will probably never sell a lot of books or make it on any refrigerator magnets: we are called to the cross, not to a cruise. God will have his way with us; he will even be severe at times, because the journey, though difficult, is glorious. And the fight may be beautiful, but it is, nonetheless, a real fight.[14]

There really is no other way.

What Will You Pay?

Perhaps one of the reasons we so feebly bear the marks of Christ's promised transforming work in our lives is that we refuse to pay such a heavy price. We want to be delivered from our *troubles* instead of being delivered from our *sin*. We want to be like our affluent neighbor instead of like our rich Savior. We want to be surrounded by nice, polite, mature, and interesting people instead of having our prejudices and pride exposed by petty, small-minded, gossiping church members. We want to wear nice clothes instead of covering ourselves with godly virtue.

And what does it mean to pay the price? It means we need to start learning, listening, and surrendering. Don't waste your physical ills; learn from them. What does it matter whether God causes them or merely permits them? What truly matters is how he uses them to conform us to the image of his Son (see Romans 8:28–39). Don't run from social frustration or relational confusion; be humbled in the midst of it. Learn how to love in the messiness of human relationships — confronting, forgiving, and asking to be forgiven. Don't make a hassle-free life your primary pursuit; instead, listen to God to discern how he is using these interruptions to cleanse your soul and purify your attitudes.

Honesty demands directness: *God has to discipline us to transform us.* He did it with his Son ("Although [Jesus] was a son, he learned obedience from what he suffered" [Hebrews 5:8]), and he does it with us:

> "My son, do not make light of the Lord's discipline,
>   and do not lose heart when he rebukes you,
> because the Lord disciplines those he loves,
>   and he punishes everyone he accepts as a son."

> Endure hardship as discipline; God is treating you as sons. For
> what son is not disciplined by his father?
>
> Hebrews 12:5–7

God is a gentle God, but he can also be fierce and seemingly un-yielding. This, too, is an expression of his love; for while God loves the addict, he hates the addiction and would rather have us suffer than remain slaves to anything but him.

The process of transformation thus begins with the *fear of God*, recognizing that he is Lord and that, as Lord, he has the right to do whatever he thinks is best, regardless of our opinion, comfort, or complaining. As Solomon teaches, "The fear of the LORD is the beginning of wisdom" (Proverbs 9:10).

Transformation then takes root with the virtue of *humility*, the constant recognition that we need to grow, that we never arrive, and that there are always further lessons to be learned. The apostle Peter urges, "Clothe yourselves with humility toward one another, because, 'God opposes the proud but gives grace to the humble.' Humble yourselves, therefore, under God's mighty hand, that he may lift you up in due time" (1 Peter 5:5–6).

Transformation is next strengthened with *surrender*, the joyful acceptance of God's providential direction. The first-century disciples did not live with our accursed sense of entitlement. They had far different expectations from the ones we have. They encouraged each other with the words, "We must go through many hardships to enter the kingdom of God" (Acts 14:22).

Added to this already difficult task is the essential requirement of *perseverance*. Transformation is a longtime process requiring vigilance and rededication. Jesus tells us, "The seed on good soil stands for those with a noble and good heart, who hear the word, retain it, and *by persevering* produce a crop" (Luke 8:15, emphasis added). We will fail, but we must get back up and keep going. Paul reminds us, "To those who *by persistence* in doing good seek glory, honor and immortality, he will give eternal life" (Romans 2:7, emphasis added).

And then, finally, we must embrace *gratitude* — not just for what God has done but also for what he *is* doing and what he *will* do. The psalmist declares that gratitude is the keeper of spiritual intimacy, the preserver of spiritual passion: "Enter [the LORD's] gates with thanksgiving and his courts with praise; give thanks to him and praise his name" (Psalm 100:4).

Can I be honest with you? You may have been lied to, and you may have believed that lie. You've been taught a Christianity that has no cross; you've been sold a faith that, as John Piper puts it, "turns God into the spiritual embodiment of absolutely unconditional approval, which never says, 'should,' 'ought' or 'must.' "[15] You've been told that God loves you just as you are (which is true) and that it's therefore OK to stay that way (which is *not* true).

I want you to have the *whole* truth. The Bible (emphasis added in all quotes here) tells us that "Moses proclaimed to the Israelites *all* that the LORD had commanded him concerning them" (Deuteronomy 1:3). Likewise, "Joshua read *all* the words of the law — the blessings and the curses — just as it is written in the Book of the Law. There was not a word of all that Moses had commanded that Joshua did not read to the whole assembly of Israel" (Joshua 8:34 – 35). We are told, "Do not add to what I [the LORD] command you and *do not subtract from it*" (Deuteronomy 4:2).

Have some today been teaching a half-truth?

If I recognize that I am not like Christ, that I am proud where he is humble, that I am selfish where he is sacrificial, that I am greedy where he is giving, that I am lustful where he is pure, then mustn't I be broken before I can be remade?

Of course I must. And so must you.

The breaking can be painful, even excruciating. It hurts to die to certain dreams and desires. It sometimes feels as though we're being ripped apart when we let something go. But the pain is a *good* pain, the difficult journey is a *good* journey, and the Beautiful Fight is still a *beautiful* fight.

∿ **Looking Back** ୬

- Character transformation, though dependent on grace and God's empowerment, requires a lot of hard work, vigilant oversight, rigorous thought, self-discipline, and a life marked by repentance. It also entails surrendering to a God who is more concerned with our character than with our comfort.

- The previous truth can be an encouraging one when we realize that pain is inevitable. It's better to embrace redemptive pain that draws us toward God than to face the pain of rebellion, which creates distance in our walk with God.

- The ancients described the transformed life as a very difficult life.

- Common events and relationships can be God's tools to shape our character if we respond to them as such.

- Without perseverance, there will be no maturity: "Perseverance must finish its work so that you may be mature and complete, not lacking anything" (James 1:4).

- God will discipline us to help us grow.

- On a practical level, paying the price to grow in transformation begins with the fear of God, takes root with the virtue of humility, is strengthened with surrender, and embraces gratitude.

Chapter 15

Poor Logs,
Bound Together

*What could make me love my fellow Christians more than to see in God
that he loves all who shall be saved as though they were one soul?*

Julian of Norwich

*Close contact with a redeemed people makes us both weep and shout for
joy, and do both at the same time.*

Elton Trueblood

*We go to church services hoping that Christ will appear in the
"temple" — a church building — but all the while God is looking at us
and hoping that Christ will appear in us — the true temple of God.*

R. T. Nusbaum

*"You must not defile the land where you are going to live, for I live
there myself. I am the LORD, who lives among the people of Israel."*

Numbers 35:34 NLT

"Mark" (not his real name) took the courageous step of joining a
church group that encourages men who want to grow out of destructive patterns of living. We had talked several times before, and I had
gently urged Mark, "If you're really serious about growing out of
this sin, why wouldn't you take advantage of this group?"

So after Mark made the move, I told him how my respect for
him had risen. But as I looked with God's eyes, I saw a shadow in
his face, a touch of discouragement, perhaps even a hint of fear. He
needed some encouragement.

"But you know," I added, "when you read the classics, they stress
how once a believer begins taking God more seriously, Satan is likely

to unleash his most fierce temptations against that person, thinking that now's the time to try to pull him back."

The relief that flooded Mark's face was immediate, almost gushing. "Thank you for sharing that," he said. "Thank you. It helps me understand what's been going on."

Sisters and brothers, we need each other. Just hours before I talked to Mark, two of my friends had spoken to me, ministering God's presence and wisdom. If they hadn't lifted me up, I don't know if I would have been available to encourage Mark. True transformation is a *community* effort.

The Mystery of God's Presence

When the New Testament talks about the reality of God and puts it in a corporate context, the possibilities are staggering. For the apostle Paul, life in the Spirit was so real that through the Spirit, he could be present even when physically removed. Consider his words as he addresses the issue of a man who took his father's wife as his own:

> Even though I am not physically present, I am with you in spirit. And I have already passed judgment on the one who did this, just as if I were present. When you are assembled in the name of our Lord Jesus and I am with you in spirit, and the power of our Lord Jesus is present, hand this man over to Satan, so that the sinful nature may be destroyed and his spirit saved on the day of the Lord.
>
> 1 Corinthians 5:3–5

This is clearly more than Paul simply saying, "I'll be thinking of you, so why don't you think of me?" In a reality difficult for those of us living in the modern age to comprehend, Paul clearly understands himself as in some way present during this ceremony; his connection with the Lord and his adoption by God's Spirit were that strong. Somehow, through God, he was there. Even more important, "the power of our Lord Jesus is present." This isn't mere belief; this is real presence, real power, true experience.

Is that what we truly know and experience today?

This passage also speaks of the radical depth of Christian community. The unrepentant man's loss of Christian fellowship would be felt so deeply that it could be compared to being "handed over to Satan." Without the church as an ongoing, present reality, the man would live like one who has no connection to God; this, the apostle Paul believes, might lead him to repent and thus ultimately be saved.

Do our contemporary churches so capture the presence and power of God that to be cast out of them is like being separated from God himself? Or have we become so sidetracked with the business of running the church — paying the mortgage, filling the pews, advertising the programs — that we've neglected cultivating God's presence in the midst of community life? What is the "awe factor" in our contemporary congregations?

Once again, all of this resurrects the original question of this book: How real is God in our midst? How genuine and dynamic is the faith experience that we expect today and share in common? Paul urges us, "Examine yourselves to see whether you are in the faith; test yourselves. Do you not realize that Christ Jesus is in you — unless, of course, you fail the test?" (2 Corinthians 13:5).

But what is this test? Earlier in his letter, Paul clearly expresses one such "test," which provides clear evidence of God's presence in a Christian community:

> Now the Lord is the Spirit, and where the Spirit of the Lord is, there is freedom. And we, who with unveiled faces all reflect the Lord's glory, *are being transformed into his likeness with ever-increasing glory*, which comes from the Lord, who is the Spirit.
>
> 2 Corinthians 3:17 – 18, emphasis added

Transformation — the theme of this book — is one of the ways we know God is among us. If God is among us, then we will surely be changed with "ever-increasing glory."

So often when Paul talks of transformation, he addresses a *community*, not individuals. In the best-case scenario, cultivating God's presence is a *corporate* experience. Paul is also speaking of the church when he tells the Ephesians, "And in him you too are being built together to become a dwelling in which God lives by his Spirit" (Ephesians 2:22). Because the individual heart is sinful, we need the shelter of Christ's body through which we can be trained, restrained, occasionally confronted, and sometimes restored. In our arrogance, we may be tempted to use experiential Christianity to build our own kingdoms and our own reputations, but to do so is exactly the opposite of true Christian faith: "So neither he who plants nor he who waters is anything, but only God, who makes things grow" (1 Corinthians 3:7).

Powerfully Pathetic

The main problem when talking about corporate experience is that in the abstract it's inviting, while in reality it's frustrating. In theory, a group of people committed to sharing Christ together sounds like heaven; in practice, whenever you put a group of people together, you're going to face frustration, sin, and conflict. This fact need not stop our mission, however.

One morning I began reading Scripture and stopped cold after getting through just thirteen words: "When Jesus had called the Twelve together, he gave them power and authority" (Luke 9:1).

"That's what your church needs, Lord," I prayed. "That's what *I* need. Your power and your authority."

I wondered what it must have been like to receive such amazing gifts — *God's power* and *God's authority*. Imagine the gravitas, the weight, of God's imprimatur, the solid foundation of heavenly wisdom. I couldn't read any further, so caught up was I in the mere thought of such a reality.

Not until twenty-four hours later did I return to Luke to read what happened after the disciples received such remarkable gifts. Initially, my visions of glory were confirmed. As the disciples went out, they conquered both sickness and ignorance (see Luke 9:6). But as the days turned into weeks, these "authoritative" and "powerful" prophets proved almost pathetic. Three of the best of them witnessed the transfiguration and all but lost their minds trying to comprehend it. Peter makes a ridiculous suggestion, which Luke dismisses with, "He did not know what he was saying" (9:33).

Some authority!

Next, Luke tells us the disciples were incapable of healing a demonized boy (9:40).

Some power!

The very next snapshot shows the disciples arguing about who is the greatest (9:46). This sad picture transitions into yet another sorry example when a Samaritan village insults Jesus with their prejudiced judgment. The "powerful, authoritative" disciples know exactly what to do: "Lord, do you want us to call fire down from heaven to destroy them?" (9:54). Jesus promptly rebukes them.

After these glaring failures, you might think Jesus would pull the disciples away for another year of training. You might suppose he started thinking, "These guys aren't ready to play in the Jerusalem High School cafeteria, much less on Broadway," and therefore expect him to launch an all-out effort to educate, develop, and train these pathetic disciples.

Instead, we learn in Luke 10:1 that this is exactly when Jesus sends out seventy-two others. Rather than letting the disciples' meandering ministry give him pause, Jesus keeps pushing forward.

Even with God's power, we can be pathetic. Even with God's authority, we can be fearful, dim-witted, and stupid. And yet in the midst of our failures and spectacular limitations, God still sends us out and still allows his power to break through and accomplish something through us that we could never do on our own. Take note of Luke's account:

> The seventy-two returned with joy and said, "Lord, even the demons submit to us in your name."
>
> He replied, "I saw Satan fall like lightning from heaven. I have given you authority to trample on snakes and scorpions, and to overcome all the power of the enemy; nothing will harm you."
>
> Luke 10:17–19

The "you" is decidedly plural. Jesus is not exalting any individual here; he's dispensing God's ministry gifts corporately.

Interestingly, Jesus seems to rejoice that this power and this authority are given to such seemingly unworthy subjects. Jesus exults in prayer, "full of joy through the Holy Spirit," and says, "I praise you, Father, Lord of heaven and earth, because you have hidden these things from the wise and learned, and revealed them to little children. Yes, Father, for this was your good pleasure" (10:21).

What does this story tell us? First, it reminds us that even the most mature among us will display moments of sheer stupidity; even the best can show themselves powerfully pathetic. But Jesus entrusts his ministry to a body of believers, knowing that, *together*, we can exercise the weight of God's power and more properly proclaim God's authority.

Second, it teaches us that though we have different roles of service, we are all called to equal commitment and common ministry. Just three people witnessed the transfiguration of Jesus in this chapter — perhaps mirroring David's three mighty men.[1] Twelve disciples walked with our Lord, almost certainly mirroring the twelve tribes of Israel. But *seventy-two* set out to conquer sickness, sin, and ignorance.

You may not be the senior pastor of your church, one of the three "elders," or even one of the twelve "deacons." But you are still called to exercise God's authority and power. Jesus' kingdom is not built on one-man or one-woman rule. It is a corporate call and a joint effort. People talk about certain Christian celebrities who have a "special anointing," but that's primarily an Old Testament reality that existed before Jesus died, ascended, and sent his Spirit. Now the anointing is more likely to be corporate — a shared authority, a joint exercise of God's power, a communal call to proclaim the glorious reality that Christ lives and reigns even today.

Consider the words of the apostle John in his first letter:

But you [plural] have an anointing from the Holy One, and all of you know the truth.... As for you [plural], the anointing you [plural] received from him remains in you [plural], and you [plural] do not need anyone to teach you. But as his anointing teaches you [plural] about all things and as that anointing is real, not counterfeit — just as it has taught you [plural], remain in him.

1 John 2:20, 27

Reading about the powerful but pathetic disciples has given me pause whenever I speak of fellow believers, particularly those who come from other branches of God's church. Sometimes we're so eager to differentiate ourselves from certain denominations or spokespeople that we lose all sense of proportion and become outright critics. Let's honor what God has done, is doing, and will do through his imperfect church, even while trying to reform it. Not one disciple of Jesus lacked some serious faults — and yet Jesus still loved, called, and used each one.

God loves his church, and he loves the individuals who comprise it. If we become critics instead of encouragers, we risk offending God. I know, I know — there are a million things the contemporary church could be doing better, and we could spend our entire lives doing nothing but pointing out each other's shortcomings, theological prejudices, and stylistic embarrassments. But ask yourself this: If the current church is so bad, so ineffective, and so irrelevant, how did you come to faith while being a part of it?

Our sisters and brothers may have different hairstyles, speaking styles, and worship styles and even different emphases in their preaching, but they are still God's people. Sometimes our pride makes us ashamed to be a part of others who embarrass us, but from the perspective of spiritual formation, anything that assaults our pride is a good thing — even if it means being categorized with someone with whom we may have legitimate disagreements.

An Excellent Fire

Why is community worth the bother? Why is such love necessary, as painful as it is? Apart from being commanded by God,[2] the type of immediate, incarnational Christian experience I'm talking about must become corporate if it is ever to be sustained. The message of the early church is that "simple people could be amazingly powerful when they were members one of another."[3] Elton Trueblood creates a helpful analogy to explain the spiritual reality of the old cliché that there is strength in numbers:

> As everyone knows, it is almost impossible to create a fire with one log, even if it is a sound one, while several poor logs may make an excellent fire if they stay together as they burn. The miracle of the early church was that of poor sticks making a grand conflagration. A good fire glories even its poorest fuel.[4]

Our calling is so high that none of us will ever amount to much more on our own than the "poorest fuel." But when we come together, inspire each other, and collectively raise our expectations for normal Christian experience, something wonderfully inspiring and motivating happens. In the words of William Temple, "It is by the faith of others that our faith is kindled."[5]

My son experienced this joy of community one summer at a camp in a wonderful place in British Columbia called "Barnabas Family Camp." When Graham was there, the camp had fewer than a hundred adults and maybe two or three dozen high school students in attendance, but he says he's never experienced better fellowship. All of the students encouraged one another. When one high schooler started acting up, obviously trying to get attention, the others didn't gossip about him or take the bait to ridicule him; instead, they prayed for him and reached out to him. It was a helpful picture to Graham of what life could be like in his youth group at home.

When I see the love with which my friend Matt serves his wife, Nina, I'm inspired to love my wife in the same way. When I see the forthrightness of speech in my friends Steve and Rob, I'm inspired to courageously speak the truth. When I hear the encouraging words of my friend Shirley, I'm motivated to use my tongue to encourage others. When I receive the generous prayers and pastoral concern of my friend Dave — who lives over two thousand miles away — I'm challenged to pray for others too.

In short, when I see what is in them, I'm challenged by what might be in me. When I hear C. J. Mahaney preach with such passion, I want that passion. When my mentor J. I. Packer writes with such precision, I want that precision. When my wife, Lisa, diligently studies her Bible, I want that discipline. When my friend Mike Dittman talks to me, I want that spirit of authentic relationship.

I am so thankful for the body of Christ. Anything I do is built on the foundation of what former pastors and mentors have laid. And any battle I continue to fight is fought in the fellowship of strong, inspiring men and women. We simply need each other — to learn from each other, to be inspired by each other, to share Christ together.

Recently I met with a fellow church member over a serious and substantive theological disagreement. We were virtual strangers when we first met, but out of our discussion, a friendship was born. Though we continue to disagree on the issue that brought us together, we both sense Christ in each other. My new friend said to me, "After we met, I was shaking for three hours." His spiritual journey and love for Christ, his passion for Scripture and truth and God's power, inspire me. Being with me seems to do the same for him. In middle age, discovering a friendship like this is one of life's truest gifts. God made us and designed us for community.

I swim in a stream of inspiring witness, infectious faith, and shared power. I am humbled by ordinary women and men who have devoted themselves to God and whose lives bear the mark of his reflected glory. Having seen what is possible in them, I will never be content to settle for less in me.

The best gift you can give to God's church is to become your best and by your best to inspire others to fully embrace the experiential, realized life of the ascended Christ living through you. Elton Trueblood writes, "The renewal of the church will be in progress when it is seen as a fellowship of consciously inadequate persons who gather because they are weak, and scatter to serve because their unity with one another and with Christ has made them bold."[6]

Your life is part of God's overall tapestry. Don't settle for anything less. A single thread is just a thread, but take that single thread out of a beautiful tapestry and the first thing you notice is the flaw of that missing thread. Look at that single thread by itself, and it's just a piece of string. Weave it back into that tapestry, and both the greater work and the single thread complement each other's glory.

The red thread needs the yellow thread. The "contemporary" church needs the "traditional" church, and vice versa. The evangelical church needs the mainline church, and vice versa. We can and should challenge each other, occasionally rebuke each other, and even try to persuade each other, but we can never, *ever* stop loving each other.

We are but poor logs, bound together, called to carry God's mighty flame.

◌ **Looking Back** ◌

- We need each other. Quite simply, the Bible pictures community as weak individuals being supported and uplifted by a stronger corporate experience.

- Paul's words to the Ephesians, "In him you too are being built together to become a dwelling in which God lives by his Spirit," are spoken to a community, not to an individual. We are being built *together*.

- Jesus entrusted great authority and power to his followers. As individuals, we will occasionally look pathetic and weak. The mission, however, is corporate; as we go out together, Jesus builds his church and defeats the enemy.

- Being called to a community means sharing a mission with those with whom we may have legitimate disagreements. While it's proper to debate and occasionally even confront, we'll leave little time to complete our mission in the world if we focus on getting all those who call themselves "Christians" to agree with us on every point.

- We need to cultivate a sense of community in which we inspire each other to grow in Christ and to be transformed together by his presence.

Chapter 16

The God-Empowered Life

*Sin is a ceaseless, undying power in our life. A ceaseless, undying
power must come against it. And there is only one such power in the
universe — only one, which has a chance against sin: the power of the
living Christ.*

Henry Drummond

*The incorporation of man into Christ and his union with God require
the cooperation of two unequal, but equally necessary forces: divine
grace and human will. Will — and not intellect or feeling — is the chief
human instrument of the union with God. There can be no intimate
union with God if our own will is not surrendered and conformed to
the divine will.... But our weak human will remains powerless if it
is not anticipated and upheld by the grace of God.... It is grace that
achieves in us both the willing and the doing.*

A Monk of the Eastern Church

*"Now then," said Joshua, "throw away the foreign gods that are among
you and yield your hearts to the LORD, the God of Israel."*

Joshua 24:23

*Continue to work out your salvation with fear and trembling, for it is
God who works in you to will and to act according to his good purpose.*

Paul, in Philippians 2:12 – 13

I failed my wife big-time.

Normally, I try to be a thoughtful, loving husband. I want to come
through for Lisa whenever she needs me, but this time, I just caved.

Our oldest daughter stood in the lunch line at Trinity Western University, the first day at her new home as a college freshman.

We had helped set up her dorm room, but I had to drive back earlier to take our other daughter to — of all things — an *American Idol* concert.

So it came time to say good-bye.

Lisa saw me turn toward Allison, noticed the cloud covering my eyes, and then said, "Don't you *dare* cry. Don't you dare. If you lose it, I'm going to lose it too, and I have to stay here."

But I couldn't help it. I couldn't get the image of a two-year-old Allison out of my mind. It seemed just yesterday she was sitting in that pink dress, holding on to her Cabbage Patch doll. I couldn't get over the fact that she wouldn't be living under my roof anymore, and I couldn't, try as I might, keep the tears from coming.

My baby was leaving home.

After letting down my wife, I put on some dark sunglasses and barely made it back to the car before the dam burst.

The next day, after the concert, my youngest daughter, Kelsey, asked me, "Did you have a headache last night?"

"No. Why do you ask?"

"Because whenever I looked over at you, you were holding your head."

"Oh, *that*. I was mourning."

"Dad, her school is forty-five minutes away."

"It's in another *country*!"

"You're going to see her in a week."

"Yeah. A whole week."

During the concert I had indeed sat there and mourned. While the young singers whipped up the crowd with their music, I was mourning the loss of our oldest daughter.

But then God came through in a wonderfully reassuring way. My goal, with all my children, has been to raise sons and daughters of Levi. Malachi gives us a picture of what a godly child is: "[Levi] revered me and stood in awe of my name. True instruction was in his mouth and nothing false was found on his lips. He walked with me in peace and uprightness, and turned many from sin" (Malachi 2:5–6).

According to this passage, God wants us to maintain families that teach our daughters and sons to

- live in awe of God,
- revere his Word,
- walk with him in fellowship,
- live peacefully with others, and
- turn others from their sin.

God met me with an overwhelming sense that I had done what I could; now Allison needed to leave our home in order for God to complete his work in her. I regretted all of the lost opportunities, but God reminded me of opportunities caught. I thought of all that was left undone, but God encouraged me with visions of all he still is doing.

God is working in our children's lives. We have a role — a very important role — but we never parent alone. I had this strange sense of togetherness; I was like the assistant coach talking with the head coach about how we'll get this player ready — not for a game, but for life. I could rest, realizing that God has plans and a purpose and that he is taking the initiative. I had planted a tiny seed; God would make it blossom.

Living *with* God instead of just *for* God may sound like an abstract doctrine, but the fact is, we'll never come across a more practical help in life. I think of the words of the prophet Jeremiah, which are as true in our obedience as in our parenting:

This is what the LORD says,

"Cursed is the one who trusts in man,
who depends on flesh for his strength
and whose heart turns away from the LORD....

But blessed is the man who trusts in the LORD,
whose confidence is in him.
He will be like a tree planted by the water
that sends out its roots by the stream.
It does not fear when heat comes;
its leaves are always green.

It has no worries in a year of drought
and never fails to bear fruit."

Jeremiah 17:5, 7–8

Baking a Cake

The debate over divine sovereignty and human free will has rocked the church for almost two thousand years. This discussion is normally set in the context of salvation, but when we talk about "sanctification," growing in holiness, the Bible is clear that there is a sense in which human effort and divine provision complement each other rather than go to war with each other. This is the clear teaching of Philippians 2:12–13: "Continue to work out your salvation with fear and trembling, for it is God who works in you to will and to act according to his good purpose."

In the brilliant words of Dallas Willard, grace is opposed to earning, not effort. Indeed, Peter tells us to "make every effort" (2 Peter 1:5). Some people mistake "letting go and letting God" as a call to simply stop trying. But grace doesn't remove human effort; it focuses and empowers it.

This is a crucial point, because everywhere around us, we are reminded of what happens when we stop "tending." A garden can be overcome by weeds in a shockingly short period of time. If I don't change the oil in my car, the engine will break down. If I don't take a shower, I'll start to stink. In the same way, a soul that isn't taken care of, a heart that isn't tended, won't support a healthy life. If we are not intentional about our spiritual growth, not only will we stop growing; we'll regress. The apostle Paul urges, "Watch your life and doctrine closely. Persevere in them" (1 Timothy 4:16).

Teresa of Avila, John of the Cross, Dietrich Bonhoeffer, and R. Somerset Ward — all of whom preached against complacency — did not believe that we can do anything apart from God's grace. We are children of grace who are dependent on grace and desperately in need of God's empowering Holy Spirit. But when my faith can't keep my marriage and other relationships together; when my belief doesn't affect the way I speak, the way I care, the way I love — then, brothers and sisters, it's not God's fault; it's mine. It's because I have not been willing to pay the cost of Christlikeness, the daily dying to myself and rising in him so that I can truly live.

Henry Drummond uses a helpful analogy here. He begins where he should — by acknowledging the providence of God: "Nothing that happens in the world happens by chance. God is a God of order.... Realize it thoroughly: it is a methodical not an accidental world."[1] But even in a God-ordered world, we can make a difference and have an impact. Drummond uses the example of baking a cake. When someone puts the ingredients together and pops them in the oven, "it is not she who has made the cake; it is nature. She brings related things together; sets causes at work; these causes bring about the result."[2]

These causes were established by God. The fact that ingredients mix, that temperature changes their character, that the result nourishes us — all this is true because God designed it to be so. Having said that, it's obvious that God doesn't normally make cakes appear out of thin air. If we want to eat a cake, somebody — some human — has to make it happen.

If we only talk about God's sovereignty, we can leave Christians in the dark about bringing "related things together" for their own personal growth. For example, is Christian joy an accident, whereby all we can do is wait and see if God gives it? And if we want more of it, is there nothing we can do but ask? Is Christian rest merely the result of divine fiat, whereby some believers enjoy it and other Christians must do without it? More to our point, is obedience something like making a cake, whereby we can put certain things together that God has provided for and enjoy the product of his design?

Remember, I'm not talking about initial salvation here or about how God supplies the grace that prepares our hearts to be saved. After conversion — after God's Spirit rules in our hearts — what is our responsibility as we surrender to a God-empowered life? As an example of how God's empowering presence and our responsibility work together, let's consider a popular topic of spiritual growth, namely, Christian rest.[3]

The Journey into Rest

Those who speak only of God's sovereignty can point to Matthew 11:28, where Jesus says, "I will give you rest." There it is, some may say: God says he will *give* us rest. End of argument. It is solely a matter of God's will. We must wait and see what God decides concerning our rest — except that "I will give you rest" is the end, not the beginning, of Jesus' sentence. "Come to me," he says, and *then* "I will give you rest." "Take my yoke upon you and learn from me," he continues, and *then* "you will find rest for your souls."

God has set up the world so that spiritual rest is found in him alone. He gives it; it has no other source but him. But he invites us, he urges us, he calls us, to *come to him*, to take his yoke upon us and to learn from him. In other words, spiritually as well as physically, he asks us to actually bake the cake.

But then, lest those eager to champion human effort get too arrogant, Jesus reminds us that to learn from him is to model his humility: "Learn from me, for I am gentle and humble in heart." Ah — we need to acknowledge our helplessness and need.

So the structure of the passage is this: "Come to me" (human responsibility), and then "I will give" (God's provision). "Learn from me" (human responsibility), but do so in humility (i.e., in a spirit of receiving God's provision). And at the end comes the sure promise: "You will find rest for your souls."

I see no war here, do you? I see a practical passage addressing a vital spiritual need. Jesus isn't trying to win an argument or support a stand-alone doctrine; he's giving us vital spiritual food and the truth about how to find true rest. As my friend Dr. Randy Roberts suggests, "Even though we can't do this without Jesus, it doesn't mean that, with him, we do nothing. Every biblical imperative suggests an expected human response, albeit a divinely empowered one."[4]

Here's the upshot: we can do very practical things to enter into the rest that God gives.

It's worth pointing out that when Jesus says, "Come to me," "Learn from me," and "Take my yoke upon you," he's not speaking of a single choice. Spiritual rest is the result of a process, not a onetime human decision. Rest is found when I persistently come to Jesus, learn from him, and take up his yoke; when I don't just receive his commands but open up my heart to his character — his gentleness and his humility in particular. As that process takes place, he gives me rest.

So if I want rest, what do I do? I recognize first that rest is possible only in Christ and because of Christ. Therefore, I go to him, surrender to him (take up his yoke), and practice obedience (learn from him), but I seek his character ("Learn from me, for I am gentle and humble in heart") as much as anything else, for there is no spiritual rest for the harsh and arrogant person. I must be transformed to know rest — and transformation is a process of coming to Jesus, learning from him, modeling his character, and surrendering to his will.

There is no rest for those who initially come to Jesus but then refuse to become like him. Arrogant people — those who need to be noticed, appreciated, and praised — can't possibly find rest in a world full of slights. Harsh people — those who want their own way, resent the failings of others, and expect everyone but them to act perfectly and never make a mistake — can't possibly find rest in a fallen and broken world. There is no rest for lawbreakers — such people must constantly look over their shoulders, wondering when they will finally be exposed or caught. Just as withholding a very small ingredient in a recipe — baking powder or salt, for example — can doom the entire cake, so resisting Jesus on any front will undercut the deliciousness of our rest.

God gives us the grace at every step to move forward. Never are we left alone to find our own strength and our own power. But we must still receive this grace and come to Jesus, learn from him, and take up his yoke. We must surrender. As we follow Jesus and learn from him and actually live with him, receiving his presence, turning our hearts his way, over time, we find rest. Like any fruit of the Spirit, it must be grown. Henry Drummond writes, "No man can make things grow. He can get them to grow by arranging all the circumstances and fulfilling all the conditions. But the growing is done by God."[5]

Being engaged in this process requires humility and patience. We do not plant an apple tree expecting to pick apples the next day or even the next year. We know it takes time and that if things work in the way God has set up for this world and in the way he continues to rule this world, eventually we'll have apples. Eventually we will receive rest.

That's the brilliance of Jesus' symbol — "Take my yoke upon you." While a superficial look at yokes makes one think of work, deeper reflection reveals that a yoke is an offer of help. We aren't asked to bear the burden alone, which would be intolerable and impossible. But together with Christ, what is intolerable and impossible becomes easy and certain. In Drummond's words, "A yoke is not an instrument of torture; it is an instrument of mercy. It is not a malicious contrivance for making work hard; it is a gentle device to make hard labor light. It is not meant to give pain, but to save pain."[6]

This is a glorious picture of the God-empowered life. We are yoked with Christ. Yes, our heads are attached to his, but he is doing the pulling.

The Compelling Case of Changed Lives

The God-empowered life is one of tremendous hope and mercy. The old view of obedience, focusing primarily on morality, tended to pit God against us — as if he had set a standard, commanded us to live up to it, and then was eager to punish us as soon as we (inevitably) fell short. Most readers understand that's the old covenant talking, not the way of Christ.

In Christ, God is for us, so who can be against us? Even in our sin, God is for us. This comforting truth doesn't imply that we should rest complacently in our sin; to do so is to reject God's presence. It reminds us that God is our advocate who will forgive our sin and lift us out of that sin. We must keep these two emphases in balance to avoid falling into error: if we focus only on God's forgiveness and speak of grace only as "pardon," we will diminish Scripture's call for actual transformation; on the other hand, if we teach transformation apart from forgiveness, we'll inevitably lead our hearers into frustration and desperation. Once again, God-empowered living is "both-and," not "either-or."

Some people talk about grace in such a way that they appear to view God's commands as our enemy, as if Jesus came to save us from *them* rather than from judgment and disobedience. God didn't stop commanding us when he sent Jesus*; instead, he now gives us the power to obey those commands, as well as the will to surrender to them. Not only are we set free from the guilt and shame of not living up to God's laws; we are given the power to finally walk in love and as transformed people to walk in obedience.

"Old" commands such as honoring our parents, not stealing, taking care of the poor, keeping our families together, maintaining a sober life, giving God his due from our time and money — these still pertain, because they describe a spiritually healthy, God-honoring life. What is changed is that these commands are now possible to obey in a way they weren't before, because God lives in us, empowers us by his indwelling Holy Spirit, and grants us the grace to obey — and there are things we can do to "work out" this salvation, to more properly align ourselves with obedience.

Jesus didn't come to say, "Don't worry about being transformed; I'll love you anyway." That's how some mischaracterize his teaching, conveniently forgetting his words, "If you love me, you will obey what I command" (John 14:15), and "Be perfect, therefore, as your heavenly Father is perfect" (Matthew 5:48). Instead, Jesus came to say, "I have paid the price for your past and future disobedience, and I have released the power for you to be transformed from the inside out. What was once impossible has become possible. What was once burdensome now becomes a delight. You are no longer a slave to your sins. I have set you free, and in my freedom you are free indeed."

The reason I like the word *God-empowered* is that it reminds me that we need power. Christianity is not just about being forgiven; it

---

*Though, admittedly, some Old Testament commands, such as circumcision and food restrictions, are no longer binding on Christians. See Galatians 6:12 – 15 for one such example.

is about being given the power to change: "The kingdom of God is not a matter of talk but of power" (1 Corinthians 4:20).

In the early decades of the twentieth century, a powerful movement of God, variously described as the "Oxford Group" or "Moral Re-armament," swept through England and then through the world. This movement was not based on new thoughts, for the brand of Christianity Frank Buchman and his adherents taught was pretty basic stuff. Its influence sprang in part from their focus on the reality of changed lives — people discovering God's power to amend their ways.

This movement became so widespread that students at Oxford began taking bets over who would be the next to be "changed" (the word choice of these non-Christians is significant). What a wonderful assumption that to become a Christian was synonymous with transformation! What resulted was an electric atmosphere that paved the way for more effective evangelism — and it had its foundation in the verifiable evidence of radically transformed lives.

The evidence of the fall is everywhere present, even to the least discerning. It is up to God's people, however, to adequately display the evidence of Christ's resurrection, seen in supernaturally transformed ("God-empowered") lives.

The challenge, of course, is how this transformation can happen. Merely being convicted of the need to be transformed doesn't get me there, does it? Resolving to "try my best" will soon devolve into a joke. I can "try my best" to run a three-minute mile, but it's not going to happen. I can "try my best" to long-jump over the Grand Canyon, but I'll never make it. This is where God-empowerment comes in — understanding the conditions of coming to Christ, learning from Christ, and taking on his yoke so that transformation becomes a normal part of our daily experience.

A Greater Life

One of my early "life verses," chosen when I was just a boy, is Galatians 2:20: "I have been crucified with Christ, and I no longer live, but Christ lives in me." Here is essentially the thesis of this book: "I no longer live, but Christ lives in me."

When it comes to true transformation, there is no other way. Henry Drummond put it powerfully when he wrote, "Sin is a cease-less, undying power in our life. A ceaseless, undying power must come against it. And there is only one such power in the universe — only one, which has a chance against sin: the power of the living Christ."[7]

It is as we are joined to Christ, united in him, and then live in such a way that we are yoked to him that God transforms us. As I've already said, this is a process. The offering up of the members of our bodies — our eyes, ears, minds, and so forth — provides a helpful model to keep this process moving, but it would be overstating the case to suggest that "embodied spirituality" is sufficient in itself to fully understand the grace of holiness.*

Counselor and seminary professor David Powlison does a mar-velous job of capturing the ebb and flow of realized holiness:

> The rate of sanctification is completely variable. We cannot predict how it will go. Some people, during some seasons of life, leap and bound like gazelles.... For other people (and the same people, at another season of life) sanctification is a steady, measured walk. You learn truth. You learn to serve others con-structively. You build new disciplines. You learn basic life wis-dom. You learn who God is, who you are, how life works. You learn to worship, to pray, to give time, money, and caring. And you grow steadily — wonder of wonders! Other people (and the same people, at another season) trudge. It's hard going. You limp. You don't seem to get very far very fast. But if you're trudging in the right direction, someday you will see him face to face, and you will be like him. Some people crawl on their

---

*This book does not provide a systematic look at holiness. For that, I recommend any of several books by J. I. Packer or J. C. Ryle's *Holiness* (Moscow, Ida.: Charles Nolan, 2000). If you want to read outside the evangelical tradition, consider Jon Braun's *Divine Energy: The Orthodox Path to Christian Victory* (Ben Lomond, Calif.: Conciliar, 1995). An important issue that space has forced me to all but ignore is spiritual warfare, including the way Satan actively tempts us to fall. For this, I recommend Charles Stanley's *When the Enemy Strikes: The Keys to Winning Your Spiritual Battles* (Nashville: Nelson, 2006).

hands and knees. Progress is painful.... And then there are the times you aren't even moving, stuck in gridlock, broken down — but you're still facing in the right direction.... There are times you might fall asleep in the blizzard and lie down co-matose and forgetful — but grace wakes you up, reminds you, and gets you moving again. There are times you slowly wander off in the wrong direction, beguiled by some false promise, or disappointed by a true promise that you falsely understood. But he who began a good work in you awakens you from your sleepwalk, sooner or later, and puts you back on the path. And then there are times you revolt, and do a face-plant in the muck, a swan dive into the abyss — but grace picks you up and washes you off again, and turns you back. Slowly you get the point. Perhaps then you leap and bound, or walk steadily, or trudge, or crawl, or face with greater hope in the right direction.[8]

Bono, the lead singer for U2, talks about how God has worked in his life:

Your nature is a hard thing to change; it takes time.... I have heard of people having life-changing, miraculous turnarounds, people set free from addiction after a single prayer, relation-ships saved where both parties "let go, and let God." But it was not like that for me. For all that "I was lost, I am found," it is probably more accurate to say, "I was really lost. I'm a little less so at the moment." And then a little less and a little less again. That to me is the spiritual life. The slow reworking and rebooting of a computer at regular intervals, reading the small print of the service manual. It has slowly rebuilt me in a better image. It has taken years, though, and it is not over yet.[9]

Sin sets the mere moralist back to square one. If your faith is defined by what you don't do, once you start doing it again, you're right back where you started. God-empowered transformation is a process that takes a little different approach. While not accepting sin as a legitimate act, it understands that sometimes sin is something we have to grow out of. When I sin, rather than have my entire spiritual life crash down on my head, I know that God will unleash the full forces of heaven to bring me to conviction, repentance, and ultimately redemption. Instead of hiding my sin, I want to confess it and even learn from it — why I fell, where I'm lacking — not to indulge myself, but so that I can leave it. Eventually, as I cooperate with God, I enter a season when I don't sin in that particular way because I don't *want* to; former temptations no longer appeal to me, and my response becomes, "Why would I want to do *that*?"

The reason I can be so up-front and honest about my present sin is that, like Paul, I know that "if God is for us, who can be against us?" (Romans 8:31) — providing such essential comfort that I can't possibly overstate its importance. Grace means we have the amazing, overwhelming joy of living life with God as our loving ally. He is *for* us. In our obedience, in our service, in our sin, in our humanity, in every sense, God is for us, redeeming us, loving us, forgiving us, empowering us, drawing us to himself. Once adopted by him, we will never, ever — not even for a second — be forced to live as orphans. Transformation is never about winning his favor but rather about revealing his presence.

Transformation will wear us out if it becomes our duty in order to be accepted by God; but transformation is a life-giving force when it becomes God's gift ("Now a righteousness from God, apart from law, has been made known" [Romans 3:21]) that calls us to respond accordingly ("Just as you used to offer the parts of your body in slavery to impurity and to ever-increasing wickedness, so now offer them in slavery to righteousness leading to holiness" [Romans 6:19]). There is no hope without God's gift; on the other hand, there will be no transformation without our response and cooperation.

Great leaders of the church consistently adopted a long-term, lifelong view of growing differently through the seasons of life — but consistently committing to face forward. Peter Howard, a world-influencing Christian and member of the early-twentieth-century Oxford Group, said in a speech, "I hope that before I die I shall have changed out of all recognition and be wholly different tomorrow from what I am today — just as indeed I am different today from what I was yesterday."[10]

Are you experiencing God's empowerment? Are you different today from what you were yesterday? Does the road you're traveling on give you any hope that you will be even more changed five years from now than you are today?

You can cooperate with God to help make this happen. And in the final "Looking Back" feature, we'll use the structure of this book as the framework.

⊙ Looking Back to Finish the Fight ⊘

- First, we must gain a new vision for how compelling Christianity can be (chapter 1). We need a larger understanding of what it means to be strong "oaks of righteousness" (Isaiah 61:3) for the display of God's splendor. Until we are captured by this vision, we won't let go of our old way of life.

- Second, we must grow in our understanding of what it means to experience God and to be empowered by his Holy Spirit (chapter 2). We must not accept or attempt a Christian faith that sets a high standard and then tells us to get there on our own strength. Instead of just knowing about God, daily experiencing God's power and presence must become an essential element of our faith.

- Third, we need to recapture the theological importance of the ascension (chapter 3). The ascension gives us hope that we can become more like Jesus is now and leads us to look at our bodies in a new way (chapter 4). Unlike other religions that talk about "good minds" or "good souls" but "bad bodies," Christianity embraces the sanctity of our flesh and even seeks to reveal God's presence through the body's transformation.

- This sets us on a journey of offering up our eyes to see as God sees (chapter 5), closing our eyes to what is against God, and opening our eyes to God's goodness and power. We also begin cultivating mouths that speak God's words (chapter 6) and embark on a life of active listening (chapter 7). We train our minds to think God's thoughts (chapter 8) and our hearts to feel what

234

he feels (chapter 10). This leads us to offer up our hands and feet to be God's servants and to go to the needy and lost (chapter 9).

- With transformed bodies, we start living a life of intentional and conscious availability (chapter 11), motivated by gratitude and a desire to give God his due glory (chapter 12). Lest we grow weary in the Beautiful Fight, we remember the need to pursue perfection (chapter 13). Even though we'll never achieve perfection, the journey toward it keeps us from the snare of complacency.

- We'll face many obstacles along the way. The Beautiful Fight is certainly not an easy struggle (chapter 14). But when we submit and surrender to God, we accept the lessons we can learn from our disappointments, illnesses, and failures, trusting that God will use them to conform us to the image of Christ.

- On top of all this, we recognize the importance of being an active member of a Christian community (chapter 15). The Beautiful Fight is not a solo pursuit; we need to cultivate healthy, inspiring relationships — in person primarily, but also receiving inspiration through books and study to keep us from becoming too ingrained by our local culture and age.

- Finally, we recognize that while God is the force, power, and inspiration behind all of this, we have a responsibility to cooperate with his work and make decisions accordingly (chapter 16). We can put ourselves in places that encourage growth.

Transformation is not a quick fix. Rather, it's a lifelong journey — but I agree with the apostle Paul: in the end, it's the only race worth running (see 2 Timothy 4:7). On our own, we cannot grow very far or very fast; but empowered by God, filled with his Spirit, and guided by his Word, we can become radically different people available to him for his glory. We can, over time, actively cooperate with God's transforming power and offer up each part of our bodies to him, asking God to help us see as he sees, to hear as he hears, to think as he thinks, and to feel as he feels.

A Tale of Two Ananiases

I once failed a man greatly and so bear some responsibility for his shame. A mutual acquaintance brought us together to play a round of golf. The man was an influential pastor with a widespread ministry, and my brother in Christ thought the meeting would be mutually beneficial. I thought it presented a good opportunity, and so the pastor and I spent the round sharing a cart as we talked about ministry and about my books and speaking engagements.

I left the course that day praying that God would use our meeting to open a few doors for my "ministry influence" to spread (it pains me now to be honest about so ugly a motivation, but it's the truth).

Months later, I found out that at the very time we were playing golf, this pastor was involved in an extramarital affair — among other spiritual sicknesses. He needed spiritual care, but I was enamored by his position. My spiritual radar wasn't fired up. I didn't pray about this man's needs before we got together; I wasn't listening to God about this man's welfare. I didn't see his spiritual sickness, and during our time together, my heart was set on selfish pursuits — I wanted him to know about my ministry. Here was a brother in great need, and I failed him.

It is so easy to become blinded by our ambition and self-interest.

Later, God provided a contrast in Scripture that can keep me from falling into this sin again. It's the tale of two Ananiases, and it's the most appropriate and perhaps most memorable way to bring our time together to an end.

Ananias #1 is a poster boy for symbolism over substance, religiosity over true faith (see Acts 5:1–11). Ananias and his wife, Sapphira, were active members of the early Christian community, but they didn't take the reality of God in the midst of that community as seriously as they should have. In fact, they openly lied to the early apostles about a community gift, suggesting they had made a sacrifice they really hadn't made. Keep in mind that Ananias didn't have to sell his property; and even after selling it, he wasn't required to give 100 percent of the proceeds to the early church. But because he wanted to please the others and build up his reputation, he lied about the extent of his generosity.

And God killed him for it.

Commentators are likely to soften this outcome a bit. They might speculate that it was the shock of being found out that proved fatal. Or perhaps it was the natural fright that follows any breaking of a religious taboo that led to a heart attack. But I want to ask, are we supposed to believe that *two* people were this frightened — to the point of death — and that Peter was able to predict it in the case of Sapphira?

One conclusion is inescapable. According to renowned Bible commentator F. F. Bruce, "What this narrative does emphasize is the reality of the Holy Spirit's indwelling presence in the church, and the solemn implications of that fact."[1]

How my heart — and I suspect it's true for your heart too — yearns to recapture "the reality of the Holy Spirit's indwelling presence in the church"!

F. F. Bruce concludes that Peter responded so solemnly when he predicted Sapphira's death (Acts 5:9) because "so real was the apostles' appreciation of the presence and authority of the Spirit in their midst."[2] Tremendous good came out of this troublesome episode: "Great fear seized the whole church and all who heard about these events" (verse 11). The early believers realized the Holy Spirit was not to be trifled with; God became real to them.

Perhaps it was this renewed reality that set up Ananias #2 to be the poster boy for incarnational spirituality. This is the Ananias whom God sent to speak to Saul, the early church's most fervent, even frenzied, foe (see Acts 9:1–19). Think about what it must have felt like for Ananias to hear God tell him to visit the man who was "breathing out murderous threats against the Lord's disciples" (verse 1). I know what I'd say: "You know, Lord, I can't find this instruction in the Bible, and I know I'm not supposed to follow mere impressions, so if you really want me to do this, let the Seattle Mariners finally win the World Series, and that'll be my sign that you want me to risk my neck by talking to such a hate-filled man."

Thankfully for us, Ananias was far nobler. He courageously approached Saul and then led him to a saving knowledge of the truth.

Have you ever asked yourself why God chose Ananias?

In part it was because Ananias was *available*. He lived in such a way that he had a real relationship with God and possessed a willing heart to receive marching orders — even hazardous marching orders — from God.

Second, he clearly had gone through real, vibrant *experiences* with God. God was able to speak to him in a way that Ananias could hear. It's unlikely that this was the first time Ananias had heard God speak. The text in Acts 9 points to a dialoguing intimacy that demonstrates a clear familiarity between two friends.

In short, Ananias was "holy available."

As this book comes to an end, ask yourself a few questions:

- Are you the type of person ready to be called and used?
- If God needs to reach out to someone with a word, a gift, a hug, a listening ear, are you available?
- Are your eyes open?
- Are your hands and feet willing servants?
- Does your heart feel what God feels?

The spiritually blind can't lead others to the light. The spiritually deaf can't pass along insights they never hear. The heartsick can't demonstrate Christ's compassion. Interestingly, Ananias #2 says to Paul, "The Lord ... has sent me *so that you may see again* and be filled with the Holy Spirit" (Acts 9:17, emphasis added). Yes, Ananias was talking about Paul's physical eyes, but as we've seen in many places throughout this book, this image is so ingrained in Scripture that we would do it injustice not to look beyond it to Paul's spiritual eyesight as well.

Ananias's ministry was so compelling (not just relevant, but *compelling*) that Paul later remembered this episode as an encounter between him and God, not between him and another man. In his letter to the Galatians, Paul forcefully denies that his apostolic commission came from any man (see Galatians 1:15–16). F. F. Bruce writes the following:

> Ananias for this special purpose occupied such an exalted status that his words to Saul were the very words of Christ. Having been sent by the Lord to lay his hands on Saul, he was on this particular occasion a duly commissioned apostle. But he was more: he was a duly authorized prophet. It was as the spokesman of Christ — as his very mouthpiece — that he went to Saul; he had nothing to say beyond the words that the Lord put in his mouth. Ananias uttered the words, but as he did so it was Christ himself who commissioned Saul to be his ambassador. Ananias laid his hands on Saul, but it was the power of Christ that in the same moment enlightened his eyes and filled him with the Holy Spirit.... Ananias enters and leaves the narrative thus, and we know nothing more of him. But as Saul's first friend after his conversion, the first Christian to greet him as a brother, as well as the one who faithfully bore the Lord's commission to him, he has an honored placed in sacred history, and a special claim upon the gratitude of all who in one way or another have entered into the blessing that stems from the life and work of the great apostle.[3]

The ascended and reigning Christ has not gone to sleep. He will give us, as he gave Ananias and Paul, eyes to see, ears to hear, minds to think, hearts to feel, and hands and feet to move in his service.

Which Ananias will we be — the religious Ananias, focused on pleasing others; or the holy available Ananias, a willing servant in a true, dynamic, and living relationship with God?

We have to remember that the Beautiful Fight is not eternal; one glorious moment, it will all come to an end. And in that instant, we will be fully like Jesus, our hearts' delight. The moment of that rest is different for each one of us, but it is as certain as anything can be.

When that moment comes, will we have truly fought? Will we have vigorously run the race? Or will we be merely sauntering and slinking toward the finish line?

A fellow writer, British author and artist Rob Lacey, succumbed to cancer in May 2006. Though not particularly well known in the United States, Rob has been justly described as a pioneer for communicating the story of Jesus in creative ways. At the end of his memorial service, as Rob's casket was carried out, the members of the overflow crowd at Glenwood Church spontaneously rose to their feet, giving Rob a standing ovation. They clapped and cheered for a man who had fought the fight, who had run the race, and who, by God's grace, mercy, and power, had won.

Will you?

Notes

Chapter 1: Kissing the Leper

1. Cited in Omer Englebert, *St. Francis of Assisi: A Biography*, trans. Eve Marie Cooper (Cincinnati: Servant Ministries, 1979), 32.
2. Told in "The Martyrdom of Perpetua," in *A Lost Tradition: Women Writers of the Early Church*, ed. Patricia Wilson-Kastner et al. (New York: University Press of America, 1981), 20.
3. "The Passion of Saints Perpetua and Felicity," *Internet Medieval Sourcebook*: *www.fordham.edu/halsall/source/perpetua.html* (April 9, 2007).

Chapter 2: Aching for Experience

1. I don't call this book a "pastoral masterpiece" lightly; I wish every pastoral staff member would read it (Nelson, 2001).
2. Gerrit Scott Dawson, *Jesus Ascended: The Meaning of Christ's Continuing Incarnation* (Phillipsburg, N.J.: P & R, 2004), 168.
3. J. I. Packer, *Knowing God* (Downers Grove, Ill.: InterVarsity, 1973), 19. In context, Dr. Packer is talking specifically about meditation; I hope I'm not distorting his thought by applying it to all of the spiritual disciplines.
4. Cited in James Gilchrist Lawson, *Deeper Experiences of Famous Christians* (1911; reprint, Anderson, Ind.: Warner Press, 1970), 224.
5. Ibid.
6. Ibid., 226.
7. A Monk of the Eastern Church, *Orthodox Spirituality* (Crestwood, N.Y.: St. Vladimir's Seminary Press, 1978), 23.
8. Austin Farrer, *Saving Belief* (1964; reprint, Harrisburg, Pa.: Morehouse, 1994), 124.
9. Cited in Monk, *Orthodox Spirituality*, 74.
10. See Philippians 2:12–13; 2 Peter 1:5–9; 1 John 3:3.
11. Cited in Alan Jacobs, *The Narnian: The Life and Imagination of C. S. Lewis* (New York: HarperCollins, 2005), 229, emphasis added.
12. Cited in Omer Englebert, *St. Francis of Assisi: A Biography*, trans. Eve Marie Cooper (Cincinnati: Servant Ministries, 1979), 190.

13. Charles Spurgeon, *Spiritual Parenting* (New Kensington, Pa.: Whitaker House, 1995), 127, emphasis added.

14. Rodney Stark, *The Rise of Christianity* (Princeton, N.J.: Princeton Univ. Press, 1996), 56.

15. Aaron Milavec, *The Didache: Text, Translation, Analysis, and Commentary* (Collegeville, Minn.: Liturgical, 2003), 40.

16. Stark, *Rise of Christianity*, 82.

17. Ibid., 83.

18. Ibid., 211, emphasis added.

19. Lawson, *Deeper Experiences*, 227.

20. Ibid., 228.

Chapter 3: Still in Flesh

1. Gerrit Scott Dawson, *Jesus Ascended: The Meaning of Christ's Continuing Incarnation* (Phillipsburg, N.J.: P & R, 2004), 53.

2. Ibid.

3. Elton Trueblood, *The Incendiary Fellowship* (New York: Harper & Row, 1967), 115.

4. Cited in Jim Corbett, "Palmer, Donor Family Bond," *USA Today*, December 6, 2006, 9C.

5. Dawson, *Jesus Ascended*, 54.

6. Ibid.

7. Cited in Dawson, *Jesus Ascended*, 181–82.

8. Dawson, *Jesus Ascended*, 182.

Chapter 4: Full-Bodied Faith

1. J. N. D. Kelly, *A Commentary on the Epistles of Peter and Jude* (Grand Rapids: Baker, 1969), 302.

2. C. E. B. Cranfield, *The Epistle to the Romans* (Edinburgh: T&T Clark, 1979), 600.

Chapter 6: Mouths That Speak

1. R. Somerset Ward, *To Jerusalem: Devotional Studies in Mystical Religion* (1931; reprint, Harrisburg, Pa.: Morehouse, 1994), 193.

2. Ibid., 193–94.

3. For the record, *Sacred Marriage* (Grand Rapids: Zondervan, 2000); *Devotions for a Sacred Marriage* (Zondervan, 2005); *Sacred Influence* (Zondervan, 2006).

4. Ward, *To Jerusalem*, 131.

5. Ibid.

6. Ibid.

Chapter 7: Ears That Hear

1. Augustine, *The Confessions* (Philadelphia: Westminster, 1955), 10.26.37.
2. Ibid., 12.16.23.
3. Cited in Klaus Bockmuehl, *Listening to the God Who Speaks* (Colorado Springs: Helmers & Howard, 1990), 8.
4. Bockmuehl, *Listening to the God Who Speaks*, 49.
5. Ibid., 52.
6. Ibid., 64.
7. John R. W. Stott, *The Epistles of John* (1960; reprint, Grand Rapids: Eerdmans, 1983), 115.
8. Marilyn Hontz, *Listening to God* (Wheaton, Ill.: Tyndale House, 2004), 157.
9. Ibid., 172.
10. John Wesley, *John Wesley's Journal* (London: Isbister & Co., 1902), 265.
11. Cited in Bockmuehl, *Listening to the God Who Speaks*, 8.
12. Cited in ibid., 106.
13. Bockmuehl, *Listening to the God Who Speaks*, 78.
14. Ibid., 140.

Chapter 8: Minds That Think

1. J. P. Moreland, *Love Your God with All Your Mind: The Role of Reason in the Life of the Soul* (Colorado Springs: NavPress, 1997), 39.
2. C. E. B. Cranfield, *The Epistle to the Romans* (Edinburgh: T&T Clark, 1979), 606.
3. Cited in Wayne Grudem, "Keep Your Heart with All Vigilance" (speech, Sovereign Grace Leadership Conference, April 2004; available through www.sovereigngraceministries.org).
4. Gregory of Nyssa, "Life of Saint Macrina," in *Women in Early Christianity*, ed. Patricia Cox Miller (Washington, D.C.: Catholic University of America Press, 2005), 200.
5. See his "On the Soul and the Resurrection" and "Teachers."
6. Cited and paraphrased in Elton Trueblood, *The Incendiary Fellowship* (New York: Harper & Row, 1967), 49.
7. Cited in Gary Hook, "Everest Is Crowning Glory of Woman's Seven-Peak Dream," *USA Today*, December 19, 2006, 8C, emphasis added.
8. Cranfield, *Epistle to the Romans*, 607.
9. C. S. Lewis, *God in the Dock* (Grand Rapids: Eerdmans, 1970), 201.
10. R. Somerset Ward, *To Jerusalem: Devotional Studies in Mystical Religion* (1931; reprint, Harrisburg, Pa.: Morehouse, 1994), 162.
11. Cited in *The Paris Review Interviews, 1* (New York: Picador, 2006). From a Hemingway interview with George Plimpton in *The Paris Review* 18 (Spring 1958).

Chapter 9: Hands and Feet Used by God

1. Henry Drummond, *The Greatest Thing in the World: and 21 Other Addresses* (London: Collins, 1953), 236.
2. Ibid., 237–38.
3. A Monk of the Eastern Church, *Orthodox Spirituality* (Crestwood, N.Y.: St. Vladimir's Seminary Press, 1978), 80–81.
4. Klaus Bockmuehl, *Listening to the God Who Speaks* (Colorado Springs: Helmers & Howard, 1990), 81.
5. Ibid.
6. Elton Trueblood, *The Life We Prize* (New York: Harper & Brothers, 1951), 49.
7. Ibid., 48–49.
8. Ibid., 49.
9. Ibid., 50.
10. Ibid., 51.
11. Gene Easley, "Why Doesn't Somebody Do Something?" *Life in the Spirit* (March–April 2003), 12.
12. Ibid., 13.
13. Ibid.
14. Ibid., 15.
15. Cited in Omer Englebert, *St. Francis of Assisi: A Biography*, trans. Eve Marie Cooper (Cincinnati: Servant Ministries, 1979), 40.
16. N. T. Wright, *Jesus and the Victory of God* (Minneapolis: Fortress, 1996), 170.
17. Drummond, *Greatest Thing*, 91.
18. Ibid., 94.
19. Ibid., 268.

Chapter 10: Hearts That Feel What God Feels

1. Andrew Murray, *The Holiest of All* (New Kensington, Pa.: Whitaker House, 1996), 39.
2. John Piper, *The Pleasures of God* (Portland, Ore: Multnomah, 1991), 205–6.
3. Augustine, *The Confessions* (Philadelphia: Westminster, 1955), 8.7.17.
4. If you want biblical support, consider the scene in Acts 14, where Paul and Barnabas tell idol-worshiping people that "[God] has not left himself without testimony: He has shown kindness by giving you rain from heaven and crops in their seasons; he provides you with plenty of food and fills your hearts with joy" (verse 17) — clearly showing the common blessings of earthly life to be heavenly gifts we should receive as coming from the hand of God. God cares for us now — spiritually, physically, and emotionally — as a foreshadowing of how he will also meet our needs in heaven.
5. Cited in Richard Willing, "Custody Case Colors Pledge Battle," *USA Today*, March 16, 2004, 3A.

6. Brian Jones, *Second Guessing God* (Cincinnati: Standard, 2006), 68.
7. Gerrit Scott Dawson, *Jesus Ascended: The Meaning of Christ's Continuing Incarnation* (Phillipsburg, N.J.: P & R, 2004), 137.

Chapter 11: Holy Available

1. George Saunders, "The Incredible Buddha Boy," *GQ* (June 2006), 175.
2. Ibid., 227.
3. "The Concept of Holiness Baffles Most Americans," February 20, 2006, *The Barna Group*: *www.barna.org/FlexPage.aspx?Page=BarnaUpdate&BarnaUpdateID=219* (April 16, 2007).
4. Cited in A Monk of the Eastern Church, *Orthodox Spirituality* (Crestwood, N.Y.: St. Vladimir's Seminary Press, 1978), 6.
5. My thanks to Dr. Randy Roberts of Western Seminary for making this point.
6. Monk, *Orthodox Spirituality*, 55.

Chapter 12: Holy for God

1. Quotes are from a personal interview with Joe Belzer.

Chapter 13: Pursuing Perfection

1. John Wesley, *John Wesley's Journal* (London: Isbister & Co., 1902), 347.
2. John Piper, *Future Grace* (Sisters, Ore: Multnomah, 1995), 148, second emphasis added.
3. Wesley, *John Wesley's Journal*, 386.
4. Notice how Matthew 5:48 provides the concluding thought to verse 20, which reads, "Unless your righteousness surpasses that of the Pharisees and the teachers of the law, you will certainly not enter the kingdom of heaven." Jesus then mentions six challenges in which righteousness in his kingdom surpasses that of the Pharisees: not just refraining from murder but being reconciled; not just avoiding physical adultery but guarding your thoughts; holding your marriage together instead of taking the easy way out; cultivating speech and truthfulness that honor God; learning to forgive in a way that mirrors God's grace; and loving not just our neighbors but also our enemies. How anyone could read this passage and suggest that Jesus isn't establishing a higher form of righteousness is beyond me. Some people take one comment, "Do not judge, or you too will be judged" (Matthew 7:1), and act as though that's all Jesus ever said.
5. Cited in *The Little Flowers of Saint Francis*, trans. Raphael Brown, (New York: Doubleday, 1958), 285.
6. In fact, the apostle Paul championed his efforts: "Not that I have already obtained all this, or have already been made perfect, but I press on to take hold of that for which Christ Jesus took hold of me" (Philippians 3:12).

Chapter 14: What If It's Not Easy?

1. R. Somerset Ward, *To Jerusalem: Devotional Studies in Mystical Religion* (1931; reprint, Harrisburg, Pa.: Morehouse, 1994), 177–78.
2. John Piper, "Sex and the Supremacy of Christ: Part One," in *Sex and the Supremacy of Christ*, ed. John Piper and Justin Taylor (Wheaton, Ill.: Crossway, 2005), 33.
3. Charles Spurgeon, *Come Ye Children* (Pasadena, Tex.: Pilgrim, 1976), chapter 18.
4. John Chrysostom, "Instruction and Refutation Directed against Those Men Cohabiting with Virgins," in *Women in Early Christianity*, ed. Patricia Cox Miller (Washington, D.C.: Catholic University of America Press, 2005), 129.
5. John Chrysostom, "On Virginity," in *Women in Early Christianity*, 112–13. Again, in context, Chrysostom is talking specifically about living a life of celibacy, not a life of holiness; I place his warning in its broader context.
6. Ward, *To Jerusalem*, 178.
7. Ibid., 186.
8. Ibid., 194.
9. Cited in James Gilchrist Lawson, *Deeper Experiences of Famous Christians* (1911; reprint, Anderson, Ind.: Warner Press, 1970), 73.
10. Ibid., 77–78.
11. Ibid., 78.
12. Ibid.
13. Julian of Norwich, *Revelations of Divine Love*, trans. Elizabeth Spearing (London: Penguin, 1998), 32.
14. If you still have doubts, consider Paul's teaching in 1 Corinthians 15:19, 30–32, and in 2 Corinthians 11:23–28.
15. John Piper, *Future Grace* (Sisters, Ore.: Multnomah, 1995), 406n1.

Chapter 15: Poor Logs, Bound Together

1. See N. T. Wright, *Jesus and the Victory of God* (Minneapolis: Fortress, 1996), 300.
2. See 1 John 4:20–21, for starters, but I could list many others.
3. Elton Trueblood, *Incendiary Fellowship* (New York: Harper & Row, 1967), 107.
4. Ibid., 108.
5. Cited in ibid., 108.
6. Ibid., 31.

Chapter 16: The God-Empowered Life

1. Henry Drummond, *The Greatest Thing in the World: and 21 Other Addresses* (London: Collins, 1953), 118–19.
2. Ibid., 119.
3. For the record, I'm restating Drummond's discussion of this reality; see *Greatest Thing*, 120 and following.
4. This was a comment that Dr. Roberts made while reviewing an earlier draft.
5. Drummond, *Greatest Thing*, 130.
6. Ibid., 126.
7. Ibid., 209.
8. David Powlison, "Making All Things New," in *Sex and the Supremacy of Christ*, ed. John Piper and Justin Taylor (Wheaton, Ill.: Crossway, 2005), 81–82.
9. Cited in U2 (with Neil McCormick), *U2 by U2* (New York: HarperCollins, 2006), 7.
10. Cited in Klaus Bockmuehl, *Listening to the God Who Speaks* (Colorado Springs: Helmers & Howard, 1990), 7.

Epilogue: A Tale of Two Ananiases

1. F. F. Bruce, *The Book of Acts* (Grand Rapids: Eerdmans, 1981), 112.
2. Ibid., 113.
3. Ibid., 200–201.

Questions for Discussion and Reflection

Chapter 1: Kissing the Leper

1. In the rush of God's presence, Francis of Assisi kissed a leper, whom he had formerly found repugnant. What's the most dramatic act that God has called you to perform in response to your faith in him?

2. Perpetua's faith required heroic sacrifice — first, she suffered her father's displeasure; next, she was willing to part from her daughter; finally, she offered up her body to martyrdom. What's the greatest sacrifice God has asked you to make? Do you believe you've ever withheld something God was asking you to offer up? Were there consequences to this refusal?

3. Perpetua's comment "I cannot be called anything else than what I am, which is a Christian" seems so straightforward, but why do you think so few Christians really live by this principle? We make compromises all the time. Why do you think this is? Moral weakness? A watered-down understanding of the faith? Or something else? What needs to happen for the church to regain integrity, especially with young people?

4. Gary writes, "Today's believers often lose touch with this sense of the glory of being a Christian. We settle for so little — a tame religion, a few rituals, maybe even an occasional miraculous answer to prayer — and so pass our lives without understanding our

true identity in Christ, embracing our calling as God's children, or fulfilling our divine purpose." Do you think people believe that Christianity is a "glorious" calling? If not, why not? Do you agree with Gary that we "settle for so little"? In what ways do contemporary Christians settle for less than what could be?

5. Have you ever been in a church setting that taught the "religion of prohibition," whereby holiness is defined by what you don't do? If so, how did being in that setting affect your faith? How can believers recognize the importance of avoiding immorality while not making avoidance the goal or definition of their faith?

6. Gary suggests that teaching "mere moralism" will tire people out and eventually leave them discouraged and perhaps even disillusioned. Do you agree? Have you seen this happen to anyone you know? What was it like?

Chapter 2: Aching for Experience

1. Think back to a time when you've been seriously convicted by a book or sermon. Did you eventually act on it, or did you gradually forget about it? Discuss how believers can bridge the application gap more effectively.

2. Do you think Gary overstates the case when he suggests that it is possible to lead "ungodly" family devotions or preach an "ungodly" sermon if we do either without relying on God? Do you find it difficult to depend on God's real empowerment, or is relying on him something you've learned to do? Do you believe it's possible to grow in this area?

3. Which of these three statements do you most agree with?

   • Christians don't rely on God's empowering presence primarily because they are prideful and rebellious and want to live life on their own terms in their own way.

- The main reason most Christians don't rely on God is that they don't believe he's intimately involved in our lives today. He gave us his Bible, and he might step in for something really big, but for the most part he lets us find our own way.

- Most Christians want to rely on God's empowering presence, but they've never been taught how. They are simply uninformed about how to get there.

  Did the teaching here challenge you to grow in experiencing God's presence, or did you become convinced that a real experience probably isn't possible for today's believers?

4. Is Frances Ridley Havergal's desire for a "deeper, richer, fuller Christian experience" ill advised, likely to lead to discontentment for most believers, or is it an appropriate yearning that honors God? Have you ever been in a season when you've cried out to experience more of God's empowering presence? Was that prayer ever answered to your satisfaction? What did you learn through the whole process?

5. Do you agree with the ancients that there are ascending stages in the spiritual life? If so, why aren't they commonly known and taught? Do you think there's a better way to describe spiritual growth? If so, what is it?

6. Have you ever been tempted to compensate for a lack of spiritual weight with cleverness or something else? Describe the experience. How did you come out of it?

7. What are some ways in which contemporary believers can "put out the Spirit's fire" (1 Thessalonians 5:19)?

8. In which area do you think you need to grow more — understanding the Scriptures, or understanding how to walk in God's power? Which of these does the church emphasize more, or do you think there's an appropriate balance being taught and modeled today?

Chapter 3: Still in Flesh

1. How do you think focusing on Christ's death and resurrection, almost to the exclusion of teaching on the ascension, has influenced our understanding of spiritual formation and the Christian life?

2. How does the fact that Christ is reigning now affect the way you view your own struggles in this world?

3. Discuss the difference between seeing your life as fulfilling your own ministry and viewing it as an extension of Christ's ongoing ministry.

4. Have you ever consciously experienced the ascended Christ ministering through you? How was this experience different from other times when you relied on your own natural strengths and gifts?

5. Gary writes, "God isn't glorified through weak, indecisive, and defeated subjects; he is glorified through weak but *victorious* subjects." How might this perspective affect the importance we place on spiritual growth and transformed living?

6. How does the reality of the historical ascension give us hope for today and tomorrow?

Chapter 4: Full-Bodied Faith

1. Buddhism seeks to escape the "illusion" of bodily suffering. Neoplatonism teaches that the mind is good, while the body is bad. Gnosticism teaches that the soul is good, while the body is evil. Christianity is distinct in its acceptance and celebration of the body. God's creation and Christ's incarnation, resurrection, ascension, and promised return all affirm the bodily state. What are some implications for the Christian life? In other words, how

should Christianity's acceptance of the body as a good creation of God affect the way we think and live?

2. In what ways have you experienced and witnessed the "disintegrating power of evil"?

3. Have sinful choices ever made you "spiritually blind" or "spiritually deaf"? Describe what it was like. How was it different from being able to see and hear clearly?

4. Do you know people who fit Isaiah's prophecy: "Each man will be like a shelter from the wind and a refuge from the storm, like streams of water in the desert and the shadow of a great rock in a thirsty land" (Isaiah 32:2)? What distinguishes such people from other Christians? Why do you think there are so few of them?

5. Have you ever thought of offering your body to God as "a spiritual act of worship" (Romans 12:1)? What do you think it means to do so?

Chapter 5: Eyes That See

1. Has God ever opened your eyes to a truth or insight you've never thought of before? What did it feel like? How did it change you?

2. How might viewing this world through God's eyes affect what we value most in this life? Where do you think God-sight and human-sight differ most radically in this day and age?

3. Gary notes, "Sometimes, in answer to prayer, God does change our situation.... But just as often, instead of changing the situation, he chooses to change our perception." Is it possible you're in such a situation right now, praying that God will change your situation when all the while he wants to change your perception? Why don't you take a few moments to consider this?

4. Which people in your life tend to become most invisible to you? How can God-sight help to change this?

5. How might viewing your spouse, children, roommate, or parents through God's eyes make a difference in your home?

6. Is there someone for whom you've given up hope? How can viewing their situation through God's eyes restore your hope?

7. How might viewing others through God's eyes affect most moral temptations?

8. Have you ever offered your eyes to God as his servants? If so, what change occurred? If not, will you consider making such an offering right now?

Chapter 6: Mouths That Speak

1. Describe a personal experience in which somebody's spoken words changed the entire climate of the room or relationship: What was said? How was it said? Was the experience positive or mostly negative? What did this experience teach you about the power of words?

2. Has there ever been a time when God inspired you to speak a word of encouragement or perhaps confrontation, and the end result was one of blessing? Imagine if you had remained silent. What do you think might have happened? How can this encourage you to use your tongue more actively in the future?

3. How might Moses' transformation encourage those of us who feel we have untrained or "slow" tongues and are therefore afraid to speak up?

4. According to 1 Thessalonians 5:14, we need to temper our mode of speech to fit the situation. Have you ever spoken "true" words but in the wrong place or at the wrong time? Have you ever com-

forted someone who needed to be rebuked, or rebuked someone who needed to be comforted? How can we learn to apply the right words in the right way with the right tone?

5. How many times have you remained silent when you knew that God was asking you to speak up? Was it with a spouse, a child, a friend, a coworker? Is there sinful silence in your life right now?

6. How will the notion of cooperating with God in your public and private ministry give you motivation, encouragement, and boldness to use your tongue on God's behalf?

7. Gary writes, "Armed with this power, this potential, this force, we are invited by God to submit our tongues to speak the purifying, encouraging, convicting, challenging, soothing, and sometimes confrontational words of Christ." Have you ever offered up your tongue in this way? What can you do in the near future to surrender your tongue as an instrument of God?

Chapter 7: Ears That Hear

1. Do you agree with Frank Buchman that "divine guidance must become the normal experience" and that "definite, accurate, adequate information can come from the mind of God to the minds of men"? Why or why not? How does this square with what you were taught as you were growing up?

2. What are some of the dangers involved in seeking specific guidance from God? What are some benefits?

3. How can Christians maintain a healthy balance between what John Stott calls the Word as an objective safeguard and the anointing of the Spirit as a subjective experience?

4. How faithful have you been to hold firmly to what you've heard and to be a good steward of what you've been taught (see 2 Timothy 1:13; Titus 1:9)? What can you do to avoid future carelessness?

5. What spiritual threat is the most likely culprit to steal away God's revealed and convicting truth? Is it worry? The love of money? A lack of faith? The love of sinful pleasure? What can you do to overcome this hearing "block"?

6. What are some appropriate safeguards as we listen to God on behalf of others? How can we communicate such truth in a redemptive rather than a destructive way, and how do we evaluate whether we should even share what we've "heard"?

7. What are some practical things believers can do to become "turned" Christians? Name at least two or three things you can begin applying this week.

8. Has anyone given you a "word from God" that you doubted really was from God? What are some tests we can use when receiving such advice?

9. Gary writes, "The listening life must therefore be a devout life." Is there a point of persistent disobedience in your life that may be affecting your spiritual hearing? Does the idea of hearing God more clearly give you increased motivation to repent?

Chapter 8: Minds That Think

1. Do you believe Gary overstates the case when he writes, "I believe that my self-absorbed attitude offended God every bit as much as if I had picked up a *Playboy* magazine at the airport, cussed out the attendant who kept telling me that the shuttle would be there 'soon,' drained my frustration with a pint of whiskey, or took the paycheck I had earned on the trip and stopped at a casino on the

way home, putting all my family's money on red"? Have you ever considered how your mental state reflects God's presence?

2. Do you agree with J. P. Moreland, who wrote, "The spiritually mature person is a wise person"? Do you think it's possible to be spiritually mature but theologically uninformed?

3. Have you ever watched someone become "increasingly stupid"? Did you try to speak into his or her life? If so, what was the response? Have you ever experienced this same reality in your own life, where you compounded poor moral choices with increasingly misguided ones? What brought you out of it?

4. Gary observes that we can develop or lose our ability to discriminate. Are you moving toward becoming more discerning, or are your life choices and mental processes causing you to become less discerning? In what way?

5. In your own life and ministry, have you been able to keep a balance between the need to be transformed and the possibility of receiving God's pardon, or do you tend to place one in opposition to the other? Which one are you most likely to emphasize? Have you emphasized it to an improper degree, or are your life, thinking, and message in relative balance?

6. Have you ever met someone like Macrina, whose mind has been filled with God's wisdom and insight through a lifetime of study and devotion? What was it like being with him or her?

7. In your own church home, do you believe there's a temptation to compensate for a lack of spiritual insight with clever presentations? If so, what have been some of the consequences of that kind of compromise?

8. Have you ever taken control of your mind, or have you acted like a helpless victim of your own thought processes? What can you do to grow in this area?

9. Do you think people who aren't academically inclined can still become diligent students of God's Word and wisdom? How so?

10. What things in your life most often crowd out the cultivation of a godly mind?

Chapter 9: Hands and Feet Used by God

1. What do you most often bring into your home, your office, or your church — your sin, or the presence of Christ? In what way?

2. Have you ever experienced God's equipping you and then using you, almost as if he had been waiting years for that day to come? What was it like?

3. Do you have any sense of a call on your life through which you can glorify God by completing the work he has given you to do? Are you being faithful to this call?

4. How can we make God's will for our lives more important to us than our own plans and dreams? How often do you think the two intersect?

5. Gary argues that "we evangelicals experience a huge gap between the mystical force of God promised in the New Testament and our actual experience of it." Do you agree? Have you experienced this gap in your own life? If so, what can you do to start working *with* God instead of just *for* him?

6. In what way has serving God spiced up your life? Do you tend to see ministry as a burden, or as a blessing?

7. Have you ever encountered someone clearly in need, as Gene Easley did when he tracked down the malnourished girl? Did you do anything to help? Do you find yourself asking why God allows such suffering, or do you ask how God can use you to help

alleviate the suffering? Discuss the difference between these two perspectives.

8. In what ways do your personal ministry struggles compare with Christ's? Have you found that service enhances your friendship and intimacy with God? If so, how can you build on this benefit in the future?

9. Do you live your life with the mind-set of a "self-employed" person or one who is on commission and must give account of his or her time? Is this an area you need to grow in? How so?

Chapter 10: Hearts That Feel What God Feels

1. Has there ever been a time when you knew you had lost your heart for a ministry or life situation God wanted you to be a part of? What did you do? Was your heart ever renewed? If so, how? What can this experience teach you about keeping your heart in the future?

2. What are the main temptations against which you need to guard your heart? What are you doing to consciously protect your heart from them?

3. Describe a time when your heart became intoxicated with sin. What led up to your spiritual inebriation? How did you eventually sober up?

4. Is there any area in your life in which your heart may be growing calloused?

5. Do you find it difficult to find the balance between loving God and fearing God? How can Christians simultaneously do both?

6. What are some practical things churches can do to help members see sin as it really is?

7. Are you feeding your heart with appropriate and holy pleasure? If not, what can you do in the next few weeks to grow in this area?

8. How can you begin to cultivate God's heart for your family and those around you?

Chapter 11: Holy Available

1. In your own words, how would you define what it means to be "holy"? How do you think most Christians define "holy"? What about those outside the Christian church?

2. Have you previously lived with a strong sense of being available to God? If so, how has that commitment changed your life? If not, what has held you back — a lack of passion, distractions, preoccupation with sin, or perhaps never even thinking about faith as requiring availability? Do you agree that being available to God is an important part of what it means to live a holy life?

3. How would you advise those Christians who are less available to God because they feel stuck in their sin? How would you advise those Christians who are less available to God because they have reduced their faith almost entirely to *not* sinning?

4. What differences do you see between the gospel of transformation and a religion of prohibition?

5. Has there ever been a time in your life when you were unexpectedly called into a ministry situation? Were you ready? How can we order our lives in such a way that we will always be ready, in season and out?

6. Write a worshipful prayer of availability. In your own words, offer yourself up to God to be his ambassador and representative everywhere you go.

Chapter 12: Holy for God

1. What has been your primary motivation to pursue a life of holiness up to this point?

2. Compare a Pharisee's motivation to be holy with a mature Christian's motivation. How might they differ?

3. How can you help younger believers move from viewing sin only as it affects them to how it reflects on God and his work on this earth?

4. Discuss how gratitude toward God helps us grow in Christlikeness.

5. Consider how your current weaknesses and sinful tendencies are affecting your family, your witness, your testimony, and God's church. How might this kind of regular searching of your heart energize your desire to be transformed?

Chapter 13: Pursuing Perfection

1. Have you ever been in a period of complacency, when you figured you were "close enough" to godliness and really didn't need to "make every effort to add to your faith" (2 Peter 1:5)? Is it possible you're in a period like that now? Why do you think it's so easy to slip into these seasons of complacency?

2. What are the primary dangers of a legalistic faith — for both individuals and churches? What are the dangers of complacency — for both individuals and churches? What are the warning signs that a church or individual is leaning toward one or the other?

3. How are your spiritual devotions actually changing the way you live — and doing so in a way that others can witness?

4. What are the dangers to others of a mother or father who stops making spiritual growth and progress a priority? What about a pastor? What kind of message does this lack of commitment send?

5. What does it mean to use grace as an excuse instead of as motivation?

6. Have you ever witnessed how your sin or lack of spiritual maturity has hurt someone else? What happened? Has this been a pattern in your life?

7. Have you ever gone through a series of events in which God seemed to be trying to point out a spiritual or moral weakness in your life? What happened? How did you receive his message?

8. Do you agree with Gary that when Christians stop growing, they usually regress?

9. How can we encourage one another to pursue perfection, even though on this side of heaven we'll never get there?

Chapter 14: What If It's Not Easy?

1. Gary writes that "character transformation, though dependent on grace and God's empowerment, requires a lot of hard work, vigilant oversight, rigorous thought, self-discipline, and a life marked by repentance." Do you agree? Do you think most Christians look at the Christian life as a difficult life? Why or why not?

2. Describe a time when you faced the misery of your immaturity. What was it like? Did the experience motivate you to put in the hard work necessary for spiritual growth?

3. How can being honest about self-destructive pain lead you to embrace redemptive pain?

4. How does presenting the Christian life as an easy life, free from toil and struggle, ill prepare and even mislead young Christians? How do you think it affects mature Christians, who may be struggling in some areas? In light of all this, why do you think the contemporary church still tends to teach a "soft" Christianity?

5. What ordinary events of your current family or work life might God be using to polish your rough edges and refine your character? Think of something or someone who is really frustrating you. What can you learn from this person or situation?

6. What makes it so difficult to persevere in the Christian life? How can Christians remain faithful when they feel they are being pushed too hard and too long and simply want their struggles and pain to end? How can the church comfort and encourage such believers without getting in the way of God's transforming touch?

7. Gary notes that the process of growing through difficulties requires several qualities — the fear of God, humility, surrender, perseverance, and gratitude. Which one is most difficult for you? How can you grow in this area?

8. As you were growing up, were you taught an unbalanced, "easy" faith without a cross? How can you proclaim the glorious promise of Christianity and the reality that it's the "only race worth running" (2 Timothy 4:7 MSG) while still being honest about the difficulties involved?

Chapter 15: Poor Logs, Bound Together

1. Why do so many people view the church as nonessential when it comes to fully experiencing God?

2. Do you think modern worship experiences cultivate God's real presence, or do you sense that churches talk more *about* God?

What are some things modern churches can do to invite God's real presence?

3. What are the implications of Jesus' giving his authority to a *group* of believers? How does Jesus' example help us understand Paul's communal sense of church growth, namely, that we grow *as a body*?

4. What branch of the Christian church is most likely to embarrass or frustrate you? What can you learn from that expression of the faith?

5. What are appropriate ways to express disagreement with fellow believers?

6. Elton Trueblood wrote, "A good fire glories even its poorest fuel." Have you seen this principle in practice — how a group of people coming together can raise the level of glory among even the weakest members? How do you think this can happen in a family? In a church?

7. Pick one or two people who inspire you and challenge you to grow in Christ. What is it about them that makes you want to grow? Is your life such that you are an inspiration to others? If not, what can you begin doing to get to that point?

8. Describe two branches of the Christian church that have serious disagreements with each other. What can they learn from each other? What are the fundamental truths on which they should not compromise?

9. What can you begin doing to become a more active participant in God's family?

Chapter 16: The God-Empowered Life

1. How are you affected by the reminder that God is still working in the lives of your children, your parents, your coworkers, your spouse — that it's not all on our shoulders, that God cares even more about their welfare than you do, and that he is persistently working to bring them closer to him? How should this affect the way we talk with our loved ones and the way we pray for them?

2. Have you previously believed that there's something wrong with trying harder or giving an all-out effort? How might this be a misunderstanding of grace?

3. Is there any situation in your life to which you can apply Henry Drummond's analogy of baking a cake? Do you believe you've been too passive? If so, what can you begin doing differently?

4. What are the dangers of stressing human effort undertaken apart from God's empowering presence? What are the dangers of talking only about God's activity in the soul while ignoring our need to cooperate and surrender?

5. Gary writes, "Christianity is not just about being forgiven; it is about being given the power to change." Where do you need this power most in your life? Have you given up hope? Has this book provided any encouragement in terms of the possibility of long-term growth for you? How so?

6. How does Scripture's truth — that "if God is for us, who can be against us?" (Romans 8:31) — help you be honest in your struggle against sin and keep you from being discouraged? Have you ever felt that God was your opponent, just waiting for you to fall so that he could hold you accountable? What would you say to another believer who is experiencing that feeling right now?

7. Discuss the difference it makes to view transformation as a gift instead of as an obligation.

Gary Thomas

Feel free to contact Gary. Though he cannot respond personally to all correspondence, he would love to get your feedback. (Please understand, however, that he is neither qualified nor able to provide counsel via email):

Gary Thomas
P.O. Box 29417
Bellingham, WA 98228-1417
GLT3@aol.com

For information about Gary's speaking schedule, visit his website (www.garythomas.com). To inquire about inviting Gary to your church, please write or call the Center for Evangelical Spirituality at 360-676-7773, or email his assistant: Laura@garythomas.com.

The Center for Evangelical Spirituality (CFES) is a ministry dedicated to fostering spiritual growth within the Christian community through an integrated study of Scripture, church history, and the Christian classics. We believe evangelical Christians can learn a great deal from historic Christian traditions without compromising the essential tenets of what it means to be an evangelical Christian. Accepting Scripture as our final and absolute authority, we seek to promote Christian growth and the refinement of an authentic Christian spirituality.

Sacred Marriage

What If God Designed Marriage to Make Us Holy More Than to Make Us Happy?

Gary Thomas

Your marriage is more than a sacred covenant with another person. It is a spiritual discipline designed to help you know God better, trust him more fully, and love him more deeply.

Scores of books have been written that offer guidance for building the marriage of your dreams. But what if God's primary intent for your marriage isn't to make you happy — but holy? And what if your relationship isn't as much about you and your spouse as it is about you and God?

Everything about your marriage is filled with prophetic potential, with the capacity for discovering and revealing Christ's character. The respect you accord your partner; the forgiveness you humbly seek and graciously extend; the ecstasy, awe, and sheer fun of lovemaking; the history you and your spouse build with each other — in these and other facets of your marriage, *Sacred Marriage* uncovers the mystery of God's overarching purpose.

This book may well alter profoundly the contours of your marriage. It will most certainly change you. Because whether it is delightful or difficult, your marriage can become a doorway to a closer walk with God and to a spiritual integrity that, like salt, seasons the world around you with the savor of Christ.

Softcover 0-310-24282-7

Pick up a copy today at your favorite bookstore!

ZONDERVAN®
.com

Authentic Faith

What If Life Isn't Meant to Be Perfect, but We Are Meant to Trust the One Who Is?

Gary Thomas, Bestselling Author of Sacred Marriage

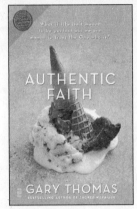

What if the spiritual disciplines that bring us closer to God are not the ones we control? Bestselling author Gary Thomas reveals the rich benefits that derive from embracing the harder truths of Scripture. With penetrating insight from Scripture and the Christian classics, along with colorful and engaging stories, Thomas's eye-opening look into what it means to be a true disciple of Jesus will encourage you, bolster your faith, and help you rise above shallow attachments to fix your heart on things of eternal worth.

Thomas shows us that authentic faith penetrates the most unlikely places. It is found when we die to ourselves and put others first. It is nurtured when we cultivate contentment instead of spending our energy trying to improve our lot in life. It is strengthened in suffering, persecution, waiting, and even mourning. Instead of holding on to grudges, authentic faith chooses forgiveness. And it lives with another world in mind, recognizing that what we do in this broken world will be judged.

Softcover 0-310-25419-1

Pick up a copy today at your favorite bookstore!

Sacred Pathways

Discover Your Soul's Path to God

Gary Thomas, Bestselling Author of Sacred Marriage

"Thou shalt not covet thy neighbor's spiritual walk." After all, it's his, not yours. Better to discover the path God designed *you* to take—a path marked by growth and fulfillment, based on your own unique temperament.

In *Sacred Pathways*, Gary Thomas strips away the frustration of a one-size-fits-all spirituality and guides you toward a path of worship that frees you to be you. If your devotional times have hit a snag, perhaps it's because you're trying to follow someone else's path.

This book unpacks nine distinct spiritual temperaments—their traits, strengths, and pitfalls. In one or more of them, you will see yourself and the ways you most naturally express your relationship with Jesus Christ. Whatever temperament or blend of temperaments best describes you, rest assured it's not by accident. It's by the design of a Creator who knew what he was doing when he made you according to his own unique specifications. *Sacred Pathways* will reveal the route you were made to travel, marked by growth and filled with the riches of a close walk with God.

Softcover 0-310-24284-3

Pick up a copy today at your favorite bookstore!

We want to hear from you. Please send your comments about this
book to us in care of zreview@zondervan.com. Thank you.

ZONDERVAN.com/
AUTHORTRACKER
follow your favorite authors